From Library of
Mike Mc Coy

$1 \frac{00}{}$

D1065047

THE PROMISE

You can do more than just recover from the past. The full joy of living is waiting for you when you experience ... ...

THE PROMISE

"Honor your father and mother...that it may go well with you and that you may enjoy long life on the earth."

PHILIP ROSENBAUM

BROADMAN & HOLMAN PUBLISHERS

Nashville, Tennessee

© 1994
Philip Rosenbaum

4261-41
0-8054-6141-8

Dewey Decimal Classification: 230
Subject Heading: THEOLOGY
Library of Congress Card Catalog Number: 93-44778
Printed in the United States of America

Unless otherwise stated, Scripture quotations are from the *King James Version* of the Bible. Scripture quotations marked (NASB) are from the *New American Standard Bible*, © The Lockman Foundation, 1960, 1962, 1963, 1968, 1971, 1972, 1973, 1975, 1977; and (MKJV) from the *Holy Bible, Modern King James Version*, © 1962, 1990, 1993, used by permission of the copyright holder, Jay P. Green, Sr. Quotations from *The Interlinear Bible* are from *The Interlinear Hebrew-Greek-English Bible*, © 1976, 1977, 1978, 1979, 1980, 1981, 1984, second edition © 1985 by Jay P. Green, Sr., and are used by his permission.

Library of Congress Cataloging-in-Publication Data
Rosenbaum, Philip.
    The promise / Philip Rosenbaum.
       p. cm.
    ISBN 0-8054-6141-8
    1. Ten commandments—Parents.   I. Title.
BV4675.R67   1994   93-44778
241'.63—dc20   CIP

**To my parents,
who always loved me.**

Mike McCoy · Smith

2/21/22

Not even genius can repeal the Decalogue.

Augustine Birrell, "John Milton,"
Obiter Dicta, 1887

Contents

Acknowledgments

And what hast thou that thou didst not receive?
(1 Cor. 4:7)

Without the example and Christian obedience of my wife, Jeanne Chrissos Rosenbaum, this book would not have been possible.

The counsel and wisdom of Rev. Harold Lee Hendricks were also essential to my undertaking this work.

Pastor Hendricks, Rev. James B. Jordan, and Pastor Jack Lash all read this book in manuscript and made numerous helpful suggestions.

I am greatly indebted to those who came to me for counseling and tried to follow my advice. From them I learned many things, including the need for a book on this subject.

Dr. Peter Dally gave generously of his time and his knowledge of Miss Elizabeth Barrett and her father.

I am grateful to my aunt, Mimi Jenkins, for her interest and hospitality while I was working on this project.

I do not take for granted the discernment, persistence, tact, and sense of humor of my editor, Vicki Crumpton.

Honor thy father and mother;
which is the first commandment with promise;
that it may be well with thee,
and thou mayest live long on the earth.
(Eph. 6:2–3)

Introduction

Is It Well with You?

Do you have the security that comes from knowing God as a loving, just, and benevolent Father? Are you sure that He made you, cares for you, and allows only what is best for you?

Are you certain of your parents' love for you? Do you think of their love as something real, meaningful, helpful, and unconditional?

If you are married, do you trust your spouse? Are you sure that your spouse wants only the best for you?

If you have children, young or old, do they respect you? Do they trust you enough to open their hearts to you?

Are you engaged in some kind of meaningful work, work that accords well with the abilities and/or handicaps that God has given you? Do you relate well to those in authority over you? Is your work prospering?

Are you free from bondage to habitual sins?

Are you edifying the church with your spiritual gifts? Are you bringing forth fruit to the glory of God?

Has God given you blessings in this world—family, friends, health, talent, or wealth? Have you been a good steward of those blessings?

If you know or suspect that it is not well with you, this book will guide you in taking an essential and often overlooked first step toward enjoying the full blessing of God. After all, what have you got to lose?

Proclaiming Liberty to Captives

As a parent hopes never to see his or her child mistreated or abused, a concerned author hopes his work will be used well in the world. I had rather see the pages of this book recycled into newsprint than employed in compelling people to mind their elders. Why? Bludgeoning your grown children with this book, like calling down fire from heaven on poor Samaritans, would be an inappropriate use of a good thing. Jesus Himself said, "Ye know not what manner of spirit ye are of" (Luke 9:55). The spirit behind "Honor your father and mother" is one of love, not compulsion. Actually, the compulsion should come from within, from the child's reverence for God and desire to please Him.

Here's how you can use this book to get your kid to respect you. Read it yourself. Learn how to honor *your* parents. Then this book will help your child to honor you, even if he never reads a word of it, even if he never knows that *you* read a word of it. The sins of the fathers are visited on their children (Ex. 20:5); so, I trust, are their virtues. It's hard for your kid to honor you if you despise your parents; it's easier for him if you honor and esteem them. French moralist Joseph Joubert observed, "Children are more in need of models than of critics."

When you can present some mildly convincing evidence of your having read this book and profited from it, then I fully support you in asking your child to read it. I am less enthusiastic about your compelling him, but I will support you in that also—if, that is, you have truly "earned your stripes."

A Word to Younger Readers

Most readers of this book, I expect, will be adults. Why? Not because it's too hard for teens to understand, and not because it cannot be helpful to them; but because most of us have to be humbled by life before we are willing to examine our ways. If you have been humbled early, or if you are mature beyond your years, you are most welcome here. Nothing could please me more than to help young people avoid a sin that so easily ensnares them.

When you find me suggesting what my readers ought to have done when they lived at home, simply apply the words to your current situation. The principles involved are the same for you or your parents; only the application changes. As you remember your Creator in the days of your youth, He will surely bless you for it.

Orthodox, Catholic, and Protestant

I refer to "Honor thy father and mother" as "the first commandment with promise" because Christians are not agreed on how to number the Ten Commandments. We all agree that there are ten, and we agree on the words God spoke with His own voice, but we differ in dividing them into ten distinct commandments. The Almighty, you see, did not number them for us.

The Orthodox churches and most Protestant churches begin thus:

1. Thou shalt have no other gods before me.

2. Thou shalt not make unto thee any graven image. . . .

3. Thou shalt not take the name of the Lord thy God in vain. . . .

4. Remember the Sabbath day, to keep it holy.

5. Honor thy father and thy mother . . . .

6. Thou shalt not kill.

Catholics and Lutherans number them this way:

1. Thou shalt have no other gods before me. Thou shalt not make unto thee any graven image . . . .

2. Thou shalt not take the name of the Lord thy God in vain . . . .

3. Remember the Sabbath day, to keep it holy.

4. Honor thy father and thy mother . . . .

5. Thou shalt not kill.

They end with two commandments on coveting (while the Orthodox and most Protestants have only one):

9. Thou shalt not covet thy neighbour's house

10. Thou shalt not covet thy neighbor's wife . . . .[1]

Thus we all have ten commandments, but for some of us "Honor thy father and thy mother" is number four, while for others it is number five.

One of my priorities is to write for all kinds of Christians. This is not always easy to do. First one has to understand the differences between the churches. Next, one must find a way to deal with them. Therefore, I have decided not to refer to "Honor your father and your mother" as "the fourth commandment" or "the fifth command-ment," but as "the first commandment with promise." Does this make me a compromiser? In this case, I hope so.

Part One:
Getting Started

CHAPTER 1

God Knows
More Than We Do

Long after I had made a mess of my life and started to recover from it, God began to show me where I had gone wrong. Here's how He opened my eyes to the first commandment with promise.

A Secret and an Argument

Not long after we were married, I discovered there was something my wife wouldn't tell me. I got the strong impression that she thought, once I knew her secret, I wouldn't love her any more. That bothered me. I wanted to prove to her that "love conquers all."[1] So about once a year I would bring the subject up. I would remind her that I knew she had a secret, and that it troubled me to think she wouldn't trust me with it.

Like the persistent widow in Luke, I finally got what I wanted. Jeanne told me her secret. But then I was puzzled. Her iniquity, which she considered so scandalous, was mediocre in my book. To me it seemed neither better nor worse than other things she had freely told me. Why had it troubled her so? Then it dawned on me: this was something that would have offended her father. Perhaps she was projecting his reaction onto me.

It seemed to me that I had stumbled onto something significant. We went to our pastor for counseling, and little by little things got

7

clearer. While outwardly Jeanne had a polite but distant relationship with her father, there were some serious problems under the surface. In fact, there were sins. She had not really trusted her father with her deepest feelings since she was a little girl. She had withdrawn from him emotionally, yet she had never told him why or given him an opportunity to explain himself to her. Suffice it to say, we all agreed that Jeanne needed to talk to her dad. However, she was not yet prepared to do so. A couple of weeks later, after much prayer and many tears, she was ready. She called her father, confessed how she had wronged him, and asked his forgiveness. He graciously forgave her. They had a long, heart-to-heart talk on the phone. Afterwards she felt wonderfully healed—and certain that her relationship with her father had improved.

I thought that was the end of the story, but it was just the beginning. That precious phone call, which seemed good for Jeanne but not relevant to me personally, was the start of profound changes in both our lives. Those changes, in due time, would stimulate me to write this book. But I was still unaware of them: God hadn't caught my attention yet. It wasn't until Jeanne and I got into an argument that I began to catch on.

I don't remember what we argued about, but I do remember the eerie feeling that something was different. Something all-too-familiar was missing in the way she reacted to me. To describe the change, as I perceived it, I have to tell you a little about Too-Tall Jones.

The Commandment and Too-Tall Jones

The Dallas Cowboys football team used to have a 6' 9" defensive end named Ed "Too-Tall" Jones. It was his job to make trouble for opposing quarterbacks, and he was very good at it. When Jeanne and I used to argue, there was something in her tone, a subtle but almost tangible quality that I can only describe in Too-Tall imagery. I would feel like a quarterback going back to pass, just getting ready to release the ball, when—wham!—out of nowhere Too-Tall would clobber me from behind. I could never sense him coming, so I could never do anything to avoid him. After Jeanne was reconciled with her dad, however, I felt as if Too-Tall had retired. When we would have an argument, I could see all the linemen coming, so I could do something with the ball before they could get to me. I wish I could tell you how strange, how pleasant, how notable the difference was.

What I *can* tell you now is that trust was the key. Looking back, I can see that Too-Tall was really an insidious distrust. Jeanne didn't trust me, but neither of us was fully aware of it. Since we didn't know who the adversary was or where he was coming from, we couldn't deal with him effectively.

At first I was bewildered. I couldn't figure out what was different or why. But the change was so conspicuous, the timing so remarkable, that there was only one conclusion to draw. Jeanne's changed view of her dad had changed her relationship with me. For the next few months we enjoyed a honeymoon-like period, which more than convinced us that our theory was correct. It was sweeter than our honeymoon, really, because we knew each other better and could communicate more freely. It was a blessed time of trust. Sure, we got back to reality after a while, but rarely to that ragged turf where Too-Tall used to roam.

Attending to the Word

Simply by calling it "the first commandment with promise," God has highly exalted the duty of honoring our parents (Eph. 6:1–3). We do well to search the Scriptures to understand what He means by this unusual phrase. However, there is often a serious obstacle to our doing so—complacency. Our attitude is this: "I get along with my parents. I don't curse them or insult them, as some people do. Why should I search the Scriptures about a duty I understand and fulfill, when there are others I know much less about?" Thinking like this can short-circuit the design of the Scriptures.

We must all be wary of a know-it-all attitude, especially where the Word of God is concerned. It is a form of pride to finish God's sentences for Him, to assume that we already know what He's saying. I ask you: How do you read these three verses?

> Children, obey your parents in the Lord: for this is right.
>
> Honor thy father and mother; (which is the first commandment with promise;)
>
> That it may be well with thee, and thou mayest live long on the earth. (Eph. 6:1–3)

Do you tune out verse one because it says "Children"? Do you say, "I'm not a child any more, so this doesn't apply to me"? Do you read the beginning of verse 2 and neglect what follows? Do you react defensively, "I honor my parents—well, at least I don't dishonor them. That's not my problem. Let's get on to verse 10. The 'whole armor of God'—that's the stuff for me"?

I'm all for putting on the whole armor of God. But he is a fool who skims over the first half of Ephesians 6 to dwell upon the second. Jesus taught us that a wise man builds upon a sure foundation. If you want to be strong in spiritual warfare, take time to consider the beginning of the chapter.

A Very Simple Test

Remember when you got your first driver's license? Did you waltz into the department of motor vehicles, tell them, "I know how to drive," and walk out with a license? I didn't. I had to take a test. In fact I had to *pass* the test before I got my license. Well, God has put a very simple test in the first commandment with promise. We may use it to measure how we're doing, to determine our success in complying with His will. Before you venture out into spiritual warfare, consider how well you have mastered the basics. If you save yourself from even one avoidable collision, won't your time have been well spent?

Here's the test: *Is it well with you?* "What kind of a question is that?" you may ask. A scriptural one—(you'll find it in 2 Kings 4:26). Moreover, it's a sensible one for our purposes. There is only one major commandment in the Bible linked to the words, "that it may be well with you," and that is our "first commandment with promise."[2] Ephesians 6:1–3 is the *only* New Testament passage which uses the words "that it may be well with you." If we don't care about our welfare, we may safely neglect these verses. But if we want it to be "well with us," we had better pay attention.

Here's what I suggest. Don't ask yourself, "Do I honor my parents?" Ask yourself instead, "Is it well with me?" The two questions are not the same, I know. But I've learned by experience that most of us have a marvelous capacity for self-deception on the first question. We tend to answer the second more realistically. Shouldn't we begin where we are likely to be real? If, after you have read the first section of this book's introduction, you can honestly say, "Yes, it is well with me"—I joyfully release you from further study.

But if you know or suspect that it is not well with you, I implore you to slow down and pay close attention. Consider that God knows more than you do. Perhaps He has something to teach you about the first commandment with promise.

Getting Started

After a few years of marriage, I began to see that Jeanne and I were not alone. Other couples had troubles like ours, and I had an itch to see if we could do something about them.

I told a few friends about what had happened to us, and I asked some of them about their relationships with their parents. I remember the conversation that bothered me most at the time. One of our friends seemed to be in a situation very much like Jeanne's. Her relationship with her father was similar, only more extreme. She neither trusted him nor communicated with him in any meaningful way. When our families got together, I told her what we had learned from Jeanne's experience—and felt very disappointed with her lack of response. Two years later, however, in the Lord's time, she was ready. Like Mary, she had "kept all these things and pondered them in her heart" (Luke 2:19). She called me up for a brief refresher course; then she invited her dad out to lunch. It was a great day in my life when she told me about it.

"I found out he was a real human being," she said. "I opened up to him; then he opened up to me. Instead of the cold, unfeeling person I thought was my father, there was a warm flesh-and-blood human being. He had gone through so much that I knew nothing about." Clearly she was now able to have compassion for him.

This young woman did not rest on her laurels. She rebuilt her relationship with her father and stepmother. Though they had been virtual strangers for years, they began to visit each other at holidays and other times. They were a family again.

When I spoke to her recently, however, she was less enthusiastic than she had been after first talking with her dad. Their relationship was once again more distant than she wanted. And, she noted, the improvements in her marriage, while real, were less than I had advertised. Then she added, "But, you know, the anger is gone. I'm not angry with my father any more, not with *that* kind of anger."

Attempting to honor her father didn't put an end to her problems, to be sure; but it did produce change. In my book, at least, it's a change worth pursuing.

Here a Little and There a Little

Over the years since Too-Tall retired from our relationship, and as people have told me the history of their feelings toward their parents, I have learned many things. I have learned that this principle has many applications. It isn't just our domestic life that suffers when we fail to honor our fathers and mothers. We may have troubles at church, at school, or at work, with our finances or even our health, that are directly related to dishonoring our parents. (If you don't believe it, that's okay—neither did I at first. I had spent too many years breaking the commandment. Looking back, I can see that that time includes the least productive, the most wasteful, and the loneliest years of my life.)

When I stumbled on Jeanne's secret, I found a major stumbling stone for the pilgrims of our time. But since most of the boulder is hidden—buried under ignorance, delusion, or fear—we have trouble getting at it. What can Satan do to us, but scare us or deceive us?[3] Ah, but the old devil has learned how to get maximum mileage from the vehicles most commonly allowed him. You would not believe how successfully he has fooled or frightened us out of keeping the first commandment with promise—until you see how successfully he has done it to *you*. Believe me, it's an eye-opener.

Little by little I have learned that broken relationships are the norm in our culture, even in Christian families. It's a rare thing today to find a young adult who knows his parents love him and who trusts them with the secrets of his heart. For some people this "generation gap" is common knowledge. What is little known to most of us, I believe, is the incalculable damage these broken relationships have caused in our lives. It is not only the delinquent, the criminal, and the emotionally disturbed who have suffered from disregarding the first commandment with promise. The mature and productive members of God's kingdom are often troubled by the same sin. Yet few of us have a clear vision of this iniquity in our lives, much less of its remedy.

Whether we are young or old, whether our parents are living or dead, good or bad, Christians or nonbelievers, we must come to grips with the first commandment with promise. How do we begin? I beg you, I implore you: Do not ask yourself, "Have I honored my parents?" Although it's a good question, it is too soon to ask it. Ask yourself instead, "Is it well with me?" Really and truly, in the presence of God, ask yourself that question.

CHAPTER 2

We Are Saved by Hope

I once counseled a man in jail who was charming, intelligent, and successful at his highly specialized work. He was also convinced that his mother didn't care about him.

Divorce and drug-addiction were the current problems in his life, but we were seeking the roots of those difficulties. The key event seemed to have happened before he was ten years old. His parents had gone out one evening and told him to take care of a younger sibling. For reasons I no longer remember, he and the little one became very fearful, and they agonized for hours until the adults returned. He tried to tell his mother what a horrible experience it had been for him, but she seemed not to take him seriously. After one or two attempts, he gave up on her, deciding that he could no longer trust her to take good care of him. Things might still have been all right if he had told her what he was thinking, but he never did. They were never close after that. His subsequent relationships with women were all clouded because he gave up on the first woman in his life.

He and I both could see the links between giving up on his mom and his later addiction and divorce. It was a revelation to him, and a relief, to realize that his mother might have cared for him much more than he had thought. And when he visited my church the Sunday after his release, I knew how much our meeting had meant to him.

This man's situation was not much different from my wife's in chapter 1. Both of them had given up on the parent of the opposite sex. Yet they saw things very differently. Jeanne was unconcerned, thinking that things were okay when they weren't. The man in jail was despairing, thinking his situation hopeless when it wasn't. Sometimes people with the same sin in their lives need to be approached very differently. This chapter is for those who know that something's wrong but are sure it can never be fixed.

The Second Impediment

Complacency is the primary impediment to keeping the first commandment with promise. The second most common is despair: "Sure, I dishonor my parents. You would too, if they were yours. It's taken me years to get over living with them (or being rejected by them), so that I can function a little in the world. I survive by *not* communicating with my parents, at least not about anything that really matters. You're asking me to open up to them, to reopen all those wounds? Forget it."

If that sounds like you, I assure you of my sympathy. I have no desire to criticize you; and it would be foolish to say that I could have done better than you did. But I do have a reply I would like you to consider:

> Now unto him that is able to do exceeding abundantly above all that we ask or think, according to the power that worketh in us, Unto him be glory in the church by Christ Jesus throughout all ages, world without end. Amen. (Eph. 3:20–21)

Is anything too hard for the Lord? If you have seen Him do the impossible before, trust Him now to heal your relationship with (or your memory of) your parents. And if you've never experienced His healing power in your inmost soul, what are you waiting for?

Don't wait for Peter to walk on the water before you step out also. The first disciple out of the boat was the only one—and the only one the Lord took hold of. If you always wait to see if it's safe, you'll never go far as a Christian. Peter really did walk on the water, however briefly, and the Lord delivered him from all his fears. All you have to do is to say, "Lord, if it be thou, bid me come unto thee on the water" (Matt. 14:28). Oh, there's one more thing. When He says, "Come"—keep your eyes on Him.

How shall I convince you that this journey might be worth the risk? By asking our standard question: Is it well with you? Have you received your full inheritance from the Lord? Whether you are complacent or despairing, the desire for God's blessing and His glory should be your motivation. As I will show in the following chapters, the first commandment with promise is indispensable for those who truly serve their Maker. It is not one of many good options. It is an essential first step for everyone obeying the great command to love the Lord.

Expecting to Find a Way

I have spent years working with what are now called "dysfunctional families," although to me there is no clear line between sick and healthy families. Every family is a sacred institution, liable to the attacks of Satan, and much in need of grace. In any event I am familiar with the sicknesses of soul and spirit that often attend the victims of obvious abuse and neglect. I do not claim to have professional expertise, but I write with considerable knowledge of wounded or broken families and the difficulties involved in helping them. Such knowledge as I have attained does not deter me from insisting that this duty is required of us all.

Shall the victims of incest, abandonment, or abuse be required to honor their parents? What does the Lord say? He placed no exclusion clauses in the Ten Commandments. He does not permit some of us to take His name in vain. He does not let others steal with impunity. In His own voice He pronounced our duties from Mount Sinai, and the New Testament writers were careful to confirm them—especially the first commandment with promise. Since it applies to us all, regardless of our circumstances, let us search the Scriptures hopefully, expecting to find a way to honor sinful parents.

People who despair of better relations with their parents may take comfort from some of the biblical stories. The sons of Noah had a wonderful father, yet a curse was pronounced on one of their families (Gen. 9:18–29). Noah's goodness could not countervail Ham's breaking the first commandment with promise. Now imagine the converse of that lamentable situation—imagine a parent as bad as Noah was good. If the child of that parent honored and esteemed him, wouldn't the Lord's blessing rest upon him?

The lesson of Genesis 9 is that it is not the parent, but *the child's reaction to the parent*, that determines whether or not it is well with the child (see chap. 5). If you honor your parent, you will be blessed. He or she doesn't need to change at all for wonderful things to happen in your life. All that needs to change is you.

The rest of this book will help you to see what modifications you may need to make. The emphasis is on the "inner man," on the changes of heart and soul that alter our lives for good. (See chaps. 14 and 15 for specific suggestions on how to exhibit those changes in practical ways.)

We can derive further encouragement from the example of David when he was fleeing from King Saul. Toward the end of his life, Saul was nearly as bad as Noah was good. Yet David risked his life more than once to honor Saul (and to vindicate himself). The Lord preserved David through the perils of honoring his father-in-law, and the Lord will preserve you too, if you act as David did. Though your parent should be a most ungodly person and come to a most ungodly end, you should say with David:

> The Lord judge between me and thee, and the Lord avenge me of thee: but mine hand shall not be upon thee. As saith the proverb of the ancients, Wickedness proceedeth from the wicked: but mine hand shall not be upon thee. (1 Sam. 24:12–13)

If your tongue, as well as your hand, is not employed against your parent, you shall be blessed indeed. (See chap. 6 for more on Saul and David.)

I am not encouraging you to compare your parent to King Saul in his derangement. Far from it. For every person who really has a father or a mother in that kind of condition, there are hundreds who dishonor sane and reachable parents by thinking them little better than monsters. Consequently, my emphasis is on helping a person see the good side of his father or mother, on changing his focus from negative to positive.

In changing our focus, there are some basic things we need to understand:

• *Our parents are people too*. They are neither gods nor demons, but fallen creatures like ourselves. They have their own likes and dislikes, their own strengths and weaknesses, their own sins and virtues. If, as often happens, they found it hard to express their love for us in ways and words that really touched our hearts, we must be careful not to react wrongly to that weakness. Remember, "Blessed are the merciful: for they shall obtain mercy" (Matt. 5:7).

• *Our parents loved us better than we knew*. This one can be very hard to hear, yet it is almost universally true. The best way to understand it is to become a parent and to watch your own kids fail to comprehend your love for them or take your love for granted. Short of that, I trust, reading this book will bring most open-minded readers to the same realization.

• *We sometimes failed our parents by not being open to them.* Either we gave up on them because they disappointed us, or we failed to communicate our deepest hopes and fears and needs. Sometimes of course we hardly knew what these were ourselves. But if we didn't understand ourselves, should we blame our parents for not knowing us well enough to meet our deepest needs?

If you find one or more of these basic ideas hard to accept, all I ask of you is to keep reading with an open mind. If my exposition of God's Word is not faulty, you may learn something from it, something that could bring a blessing to you and your loved ones.

I must concede, however, that some parents *are* as unreachable as Saul. What hope can I offer their children? It is this: The blessing of God for your life depends only on you; it does not depend on your parent. Honor God by keeping His commandment, and He will bless you for it. Whether your parent loves you or hates you, knows you or neglects you, wins the Nobel prize or moulders in a lunatic asylum, you are in this respect the master of your fate; you are the captain of your soul. You shall be blessed or cursed, you shall be rewarded or punished, according to the way that *you* respond to this awesome responsibility.

Part Two:
Searching the Scriptures

CHAPTER 3

Commandments and Case Laws

The oldest person I ever counseled about getting along with a parent was a woman in her sixties. The key event for her occurred not in early childhood, but just before her second marriage. Her fiancé was not yet legally released from his first marriage, so they were unable to wed as soon as she had hoped. Since she couldn't bear to tell her parents that she was "living in sin," she lied to them, saying that she was married when she wasn't.

Many years after everything had become legal, and after she had become a Christian, she came to me for counseling. I told her that honoring her father meant telling him the truth. (Her mother had since passed away.) After a time of prayer and reflection, she decided to come clean. She confessed the lie and asked her dad to forgive her. Evidently he did, because she often told me how much better things were between them. In fact, he even thanked her for telling him the truth. Now that the cloud of her deceit no longer overshadowed their relationship, they were able to enjoy each other's company.

I was amazed to see that age has so little to do with our commandment. Though she was in her sixties and he was nearing ninety, the effects of honoring her father were as marked as if she had been a teenager. It was wonderful to see her begin her own retirement excited about her friendship with her dad. The blessing of long life is much enhanced by good relations with—or good memories of—one's parents.

The first commandment with promise is exceedingly simple: "Honor thy father and mother . . . that it may be well with thee." (Eph. 6:2–3). Yet its effects are as profound and pervasive as its words are clear. Might there not be more to it than you have understood? There is little to be lost, and much to be gained, by searching out its full significance in your life.

In the psalms we are told about God's laws:

> More to be desired are they than gold, yea, than much fine gold: sweeter also than honey and the honeycomb. Moreover by them is thy servant warned: and in keeping of them there is great reward. (Ps. 19:10–11)

Have you really desired to understand and keep this commandment more than you have desired the finest and sweetest things of the world? "How many times shall I make you swear that you tell me nothing but the truth in the name of the Lord?" (1 Kings 22:16).

If you have fully kept this law, you should be able to point out the "great reward" you have received from keeping it. If you cannot do so, you may be missing something important. And if you think the reward for keeping the Ten Commandments is to be found only in heaven (and the punishment for spurning them only in hell), you must have little practical experience with the first commandment with promise.

The Commandments

While the commandment to honor one's father and mother reaches its fullest form in Ephesians 6, it is first introduced as one of the Ten Commandments:

> Honor thy father and thy mother: that thy days may be long upon the land which the Lord thy God giveth thee. (Ex. 20:12)

Notice that this is the first commandment of the second group,[1] which is all devoted to charity or love of others; the first group is devoted to piety, or love of God. Why would God mention it first, even before "Thou shalt not kill," unless it had some special and far-reaching significance? This preeminence is the first of many distinctions the Bible gives to our commandment.

In the repetition of the Ten Commandments in Deuteronomy 5, the first commandment with promise appears in expanded form:

> Honor thy father and thy mother, as the Lord thy God hath
> commanded thee; that thy days may be prolonged, and that it
> may go well with thee, in the land which the Lord thy God
> giveth thee. (Deut. 5:16)

This verse adds the emphasis of "as the Lord thy God hath commanded thee." It also amplifies the promise by introducing the memorable clause, "that it may go well with thee."

That this should be the only major addition to the commandments of the second tablet is a fact worthy of our attention. In the common version of the Scriptures in Jesus' time (the Greek translation known as the Septuagint), the new clause is inserted before the old part of the promise, so that it reads "that it may be well with you, and that you may live long in the land."[2] This change in order is all the more significant because the apostle Paul adopted it in his chief passage dealing with the commandment:

> Children, obey your parents in the Lord: for this is right.
> Honor thy father and mother; (which is the first commandment with promise;) That it may be well with thee, and thou
> mayest live long on the earth. (Eph. 6:1–3)

Here Paul strengthens the commandment by adding the specific duty of obedience, and he further distinguishes it as "the first commandment with promise." In other words, it is the first of God's commandments to which a specific promise is attached. In Exodus the promise is long life and possession of the land of Canaan; in Ephesians the promise expands to include a general state of blessing and long life upon the earth. The promise in Paul's letter is no longer limited to one geographical region or one particular blessing; instead it has the widest possible implications for good.[3]

"That You May Live Long"

It is rarely possible to say that life-threatening health problems are the clear result of dishonoring parents. The chief exceptions, in my experience, are illnesses stemming from alcohol or drug addiction or from sexual promiscuity. Many of these can be traced back to serious, but often unrecognized, violations of our commandment. A person who has mistakenly and sinfully rejected a parent's love is likely to fall into substance abuse or sexual bondage.

As for other diseases, I would simply suggest that we avoid the sin of King Asa, who "was diseased in his feet, until his disease was exceeding great: yet in his disease he sought not to the Lord, but to the physicians" (2 Chron. 16:12). We may and should find physicians to help us, but we should not trust in their help alone. God may be dealing with us through our illness. If we ignore Him as Asa did, our doctors, like his, will prove ineffective. If we diligently seek the Lord, sooner or later we will encounter the first commandment with promise.

If you are troubled by suicidal thoughts, habits, or actions, you need to pay special attention to the phrasing of this commandment. We can safely say that all is not well with a suicidal person. Yet "that it may be well with thee" is the promise attached to our commandment. The promise of long life is directly linked over and over again in Scripture to the honoring of father and mother.[4] How shall we overcome suicidal tendencies if we ignore the law that God has joined to the blessing of longevity?

Sometimes Scripture is too simple for us to understand. "The testimony of the Lord is sure, making wise the simple" (Ps. 19:7). Though suicide is a complex subject, little enough understood by experts in the field, and though there is no single formula for dealing with all its varied manifestations, even a simple-minded believer may benefit from the Bible's teaching.

Taking one's life is a direct violation of God's Word: "Thou shalt not kill" (Ex. 20:13). The best foundation for keeping that directive is to lay hold of the previous commandment, "Honor your father and mother." We who have come round to honoring our parents have almost always discovered that their love for us was greater than we knew. And the unconditional love of parents, rightly received, is a great help in dealing with suicidal tendencies. It is a great comfort amidst the slings and arrows of this fallen world to know that someone really loves you.

We do not all have spouses or children or pastors or therapists who love us without reserve. Yet I do not hesitate to assert that most of us have (or had) parents who fit that description. Their sins notwithstanding, they have loved us with a deep and lasting love which God often compares with His own. That's why Satan is busy working overtime to convince so many of us that we are not truly loved. Let us not be ignorant of his devices.

Blessings and Curses

What are the blessings that come to us from keeping the commandment—and the curses that follow its violation? Can we really discover in our own lives the effects and consequences of how we observe this law? Paul wrote:

> For whatsoever things were written aforetime were written for our learning, that we through patience and comfort of the scriptures might have hope. (Rom. 15:4)

And of the trials of the Old Testament saints he said:

> Now all these things happened unto them for ensamples: and they are written for our admonition, upon whom the ends of the world are come. Wherefore let him that thinketh he standeth take heed lest he fall. (1 Cor. 10:11–12)

In chapters 5 and 6 we shall examine some of the stories of the Old Testament, that we may better understand how the blessings and curses associated with this commandment still operate in our lives.

The Case Laws

The command to honor our father and mother is expressed in several different forms in Scripture and repeated with surprising frequency. Did you know that the Book of Proverbs alone has a dozen passages on the subject? (See chap. 4.) In this section we shall look at two laws in Exodus which add to our understanding of the initial commandment.

After the Ten Commandments were spoken by the Lord in His own voice, the terrified people requested that they might receive their instructions through Moses. Then Moses gave them a number of laws, as the Lord instructed him. Theologians call these the "case laws" of the Old Testament, because they interpret the Ten Commandments, applying them to particular situations.

Prominent among the first of these are two about honoring and obeying parents:

> And he that smiteth his father, or his mother, shall be surely put to death. . . . And he that curseth his father, or his mother, shall surely be put to death. (Ex. 21:15, 17)

It is difficult for modern Christians to make a right use of these verses and others like them. Most of us have been raised in a culture where murderers become eligible for parole after a few years in prison. If the laws of Moses seem harsh to us, we need to make an extra effort to understand the mind of the Lord in giving these commandments.

Remember that God's law is designed for our benefit. He promises that if we honor our parents it shall be well with us, and we will live long on the earth. God's purpose in forbidding the striking or cursing of parents is not to oppress children. Rather, it is to make possible a culture in which He can pour out His blessings. The severe sanctions given in these case laws are like strong walls erected to protect a tropical village from wild beasts. If the walls are weakened, all who live inside them will soon be in danger. Therefore, the gravest penalties are required for those who would break down even a small part of the lifesaving barrier.

Let us consider the state of modern American culture; although I fear many other countries are like us in this respect, I am not informed enough to be sure. Reverence for parents is hardly what it was a century—or even a generation—ago. As it has diminished, we have had massive promiscuity, divorce, drug addiction, abortion, and crime. Both our standard of living and our standard of education have declined.

It remains to be seen what further judgments may be coming on us for our sins. The generation (or the remnant) which survives those judgments will be better equipped than we are to comment intelligently on the case laws in question. I believe that where we saw only severity, that generation, or we ourselves when chastened and wiser, will see a profound benevolence which we foolishly cast aside.

Equivalent to Treason

Now, perhaps, we can consider the case laws themselves. The Hebrew word for "strikes" in Exodus 21:15 is often used in Scripture. It usually means either to kill or to wound severely. The Jewish commentators tell us that the law applied to incidents where noticeable physical damage was done to the parent. In other words, God did not require the death of an adolescent who slapped his mother. But He did intend to protect the person of the parent from serious harm. In His eyes wounding a parent was an act which caused a grave danger to society as a whole. In this respect it was equivalent to treason, for which even we still permit the death penalty. Think about why selling a few technological secrets to a foreign power should be punishable by death. Then remember that in Moses' time wounding a parent was considered a subversive act, which revealed one's allegiance to the enemy of Israel.

It is remarkable that while Exodus 21:17 ("cursing") has many parallel passages in Scripture,[5] Exodus 21:15 ("striking") has none.[6] Why is this? Possibly the Jews agreed that striking parents was one of those things "you just don't do."[7] There is little need to repeat the prohibition of an action that is generally abhorred.

But as Christ has taught us, many a man harbors sin in his heart that, for one reason or another, he has not yet fulfilled in his actions. In any event, the biblical emphasis is against cursing one's father and mother—against hating them and wishing the worst for them. The stress is not on sins of the arm and fist, but on sins of the mouth and heart. If you wonder why, consider which set of sins is more common in our day. To which type of iniquity are you more likely to succumb?

In his affliction Job "cursed the day of his birth" (Job 3:1). Jeremiah took the same thought a step further:

> Cursed be the day wherein I was born: let not the day wherein my mother bare me be blessed. Cursed be the man who brought tidings to my father, saying, A man child is born unto thee; making him very glad. (Jer. 20:14–15)

Yet notice how patriarch and prophet both refrained from dishonoring their parents. No matter how great their distress was, they refused to curse either father or mother. We would do well to remember their example.

Why is it such a serious sin to curse one's parents? Why is that worse than cursing the messenger who told of one's birth?[8] I believe the person who curses his parents is ultimately in rebellion against God. Allow me to get personal here. However little your parents may have loved each other, however little they may have expected or desired your birth, God knew all about you before the beginning of the world. Even if the circumstances were bizarre or disgraceful, God chose to bring you into the world through the union of your parents. He made them the source of life to you. When you curse them, you are cursing the source of your own life. You are committing verbal suicide; you are a stride closer to actual suicide than you were before you opened your mouth—or before you cursed your parents in your heart. You are in effect taking the Lord's name in vain, and "the Lord will not hold him guiltless that taketh his name in vain" (Ex. 20:7).

Two Parallels

Of the many parallel passages to Exodus 21:17, I shall consider two. The first is Deuteronomy 27:16. When the children of Israel entered the promised land, they were to stand on two mountains, pronouncing the Lord's curses from one and His blessings from the other. The twelve curses are found in Deuteronomy 27:14–26; notice which two come first:

> And the Levites shall speak, and say unto all the men of Israel with a loud voice, Cursed be the man that maketh any graven or molten image, an abomination unto the Lord, the work of the hands of the craftsman, and putteth it in a secret place. And all the people shall answer and say, Amen. Cursed be he that setteth light by his father or his mother. And all the people shall say, Amen. Cursed be he that removeth his neighbor's landmark. And all the people shall say, Amen. Cursed be he that maketh the blind to wander out of the way. And all the people shall say, Amen. . . . Cursed be he that lieth with his father's wife; because he uncovereth his father's skirt. And all the people shall say, Amen.

The order here resembles the order of the Ten Commandments. The primary curse sums up our duty to God; all the others have to do with our duty to others. And the first of these has to do with our father and mother. Right after the curse against idolatry comes the curse against dishonoring parents. This order is not accidental, but part of the divine wisdom, which we have neglected at our peril.

The emphasis is strong: *Before you worry about stealing, cruelty, or sexual sins, you should worry about dishonoring your parents.* Failure to keep the first commandment with promise makes it harder to keep the commandments that follow it. The performance of this duty is a foundation stone on which you may build a solid Christian life. Yet I often meet sincere and otherwise mature Christians struggling with a sin like anger or lust while ignoring their sin against their parents. I tell you with sorrow: It is not well with them. For your own sake and the sake of your loved ones, please think about this.

"There Is a Generation"

The second parallel passage is Proverbs 30:11–17:

> There is a generation that curseth their father, and doth not bless their mother. There is a generation that are pure in their

own eyes, and yet is not washed from their filthiness. There is a generation, O how lofty are their eyes! and their eyelids are lifted up. There is a generation, whose teeth are as swords, and their jaw teeth as knives, to devour the poor from off the earth, and the needy from among men. The horseleech hath two daughters, crying, Give, give. There are three things that are never satisfied, yea, four things say not, It is enough: The grave; and the barren womb; the earth that is not filled with water; and the fire that saith not, It is enough. The eye that mocketh at his father, and despiseth to obey his mother, the ravens of the valley shall pick it out, and the young eagles shall eat it.

Those who curse their parents are likely to be self-deceived. Imagining that they are pure, their filthiness remains. They are characterized by pride (v. 13) and predatory greed (vv. 14–16), and they come to a dreadful end (v. 17). Moreover, there is a *generation* (or a class of men) corrupted by this sin. These sinners come in droves. A politician once remarked that he found it cheaper to buy legislatures wholesale. The devil has a similar strategy regarding the first commandment with promise. Why ruin just one life, when with a single lie you can ruin millions?

"Come now, and let us reason together" (Isa. 1:18). Let us take heed to our ways. Have we honored and obeyed our parents? Are we known for our humility? Are we content with a small portion in this life? Considering the whole passage, I wonder: What shall the end of all our striving be?

CHAPTER 4

Listen . . . and Do Not Despise:
The Proverbs of Solomon

I know a woman with several children whose husband long ago deserted them. She never received financial or emotional support from him. She made the best of that bad situation, but life has been hard for her—and consequently for her children and her parents.

When years ago we talked about how she was getting along with her father (for her mother had died), she complained that he seemed distant and less supportive than he might be. She loved her dad, but she was hurt by his apparent lack of interest in her and her children. I asked, among other things, if her parents had approved of her husband. "Oh, no," she said, "they were certain he was carrying around some kind of garbage. There were too many unanswered questions about him." But, of course, she married him anyway.

Was there anyone else they had thought she should marry? "Oh, Daddy would never approve of anyone . . . ." Fortunately, I challenged this assumption, and on closer examination it turned out that there *had* been a suitor who had her parents' approval. She gave this excuse, "But he was still in the army, and my boyfriend was on the scene." In other words, rather than accept her parents' warning— rather than wait for their blessing—she did what seemed best to her. The result was a personal disaster.

I asked if she knew what had happened to the former suitor. Lo and behold!—he is married with children and is a good provider for his family. As we looked over her life, she began to see how her own impatience and willfulness had contributed to her misfortunes. She had been blaming her parents for things that were mostly her own fault. Her attitude toward her dad began to soften as a result.

She told her dad what she had learned and expressed her sorrow about it. Then he got more involved with her and her children. In fact, he became a big help to them all. Though she had been forsaken by the second man in her life, she went back to the first man and made things right with him.

A Common Theme—and Our Misconception

There is a common theme in Proverbs about parents:

> My son, hear the instruction of thy father, and forsake not the law of thy mother: For they shall be an ornament of grace unto thy head, and chains about thy neck. (Prov. 1:8–9)

> A fool despiseth his father's instruction: but he that regardeth reproof is prudent. (15:5)

> Hearken unto thy father that begat thee, and despise not thy mother when she is old. (23:22)

Let me see if I can make this plain to you. In the biblical view of the world:

Your parent is someone who knows more than you do.

Your parent is someone who knows more than you do.

Your parent is someone who knows more than you do.

Now of course this needs clarification. You may well know more about plumbing or computers or theology than your parents. But they have lived longer than you have, which means they have learned more from their mistakes than you have; and they have been gifted by God with special insight into the real needs of their children. God knows better than you do that they can be wrong or pigheaded or less spiritual than their children. Yet He continually advises us to pay close attention to their instruction. If we think we know more than our parents, we still must admit that we know less than God. When we take His proverbs seriously, we offer living testimony to His wisdom and His glory.

It's one thing to say that our parents know more than we do; it's another to "read, mark, learn, and inwardly digest"[1] the biblical doc-

trine on the subject. We don't so much contradict Scripture in this
area of our lives as we discount it. We assent to the teaching, but we
treat it like a bargain on the clearance rack at Macy's: "This was a
fine dress when it came out, but it's out of fashion now. Why else
would they have marked it down three times? The material *is* beauti-
ful, but it couldn't fit me. No, you won't catch me in this old thing."
So we move on down the clearance rack of philosophy, imagining
that we have paid proper respect to a lovely but obsolete notion. We
have praised the idea, but it's not our fault that times change. Why
shouldn't it be well with us?

Before we can absorb this oft-repeated biblical teaching, we must
deal with the multiple discounts we have attached to it. Let's look at
a few of the ways we diminish the concept of parental wisdom.

1. "If it hasn't sold, there must be a reason why."[2] The concept
that parents know more than their children is not selling well these
days. Imagine telling your friends that you won't marry someone you
love because your parents disapprove. "What are you," the jury of
your peers might rejoin, "a latter-day Victorian?" But our biblical
heroes often appeared in dress that seemed ludicrous to their con-
temporaries. Keeping God's dietary laws was hardly the rage in
Babylon (Dan. 1), and *Paul's Letters on Chastity* probably never got
much window space in the bookshops of Corinth. In this world the
cross is never in fashion.

2. "It's not my size." Our internal monologue goes something like
this: "This might fit most people, but it couldn't fit me. Just look at
my parents. They're too [choose one from each pair]:

- insensitive/impractical,

- uneducated/intellectual,

- selfish/hypocritical,

- materialistic/irresponsible,

- self-indulgent/puritanical,

- pagan/legalistic,

- overbearing/indifferent to the things that matter most to me,

- abusive/neglectful,

- unable to understand/unwilling to understand.

"And besides, I can get better advice from my [choose several]:
friend, lover, pastor, guru, professor, boss, therapist, lunatic neigh-

bor, aunt, uncle, garbage collector, or broker. I just happen to be the exception that proves the rule. Why can't you understand that? Why can't you stop bugging me about my parents?"

In clothes or commandments, it's hard to believe that "one size fits all." But is anything too hard for the Lord? Is it only Dupont that makes miracle fabrics? God has not excepted you from keeping the Ten Commandments. Trust Him. Yes, it is difficult to trust God when you don't trust your own parents. But if you are unwilling to take the risk of trusting either Him or them, how shall it ever be well with you?

Allow Him to show you how to do your duty. Then you shall discover the great reward He has promised you in His Word.

3. "You can't return items in this sale. If I don't like it, I'll be stuck with it." This is true. There is no satisfaction-guaranteed-or-your-money-back offer attached to the proverbs about parental wisdom. It takes a lot more than thirty days for most of us to feel satisfied with this purchase. In fact, there's likely to be some discomfort at first. Confined and constricted, we long for our freedom. "If only I hadn't got carried away at that sale! I should have known better. I hate this dress now, and I can't afford another one."

This is really a very hopeful condition, however. With a little trust and patience, it can blossom into blessing. God's miracle fabric only begins to work when we've gotten ourselves in a hopeless condition. When there seems to be no way out of our predicament—and when we refuse to extricate ourselves by sinful means—then the miracle begins. Little by little our new dress becomes us. Is it we that have changed, or is it the garment? Sometimes it's hard to tell. But it's a wonderful experience to wear a tailor-made dress from the Greatest Designer going. It's wonderful to look your best—and find your best is better than you dreamed.

Some Practical Questions

When we stop discounting the proverbs about listening to parents, some practical questions naturally arise: "Aren't there any limits on this thing? Are parents never wrong, and their children never right? When will you consider me a grown-up, when I'm a hundred and seven?" These questions, and others like them, need to be answered. Yet I believe their hour has not yet come. I shall deal with them later, in chapters 12 and 13.

Why don't I answer the questions now? The first step in dealing with God-given authority is to learn to accept it. Until we can take the first step, we should not attempt to function at more advanced stages of development. Of course this requires patience and humility, which cut against the grain of our pride. If you are not sure that God cares for you, or if you do not trust the man who is explaining His Word, you may feel oppressed and anxious to close the book. Let me ask you, if you have such feelings, neither to suppress them nor to heed them fully. I know it's hard to do, but live with them for a while—and hear me out. Your feelings could be a healthy warning against false teaching; or they could be the flesh's fear of the truth that sets you free.[3] If you hear me out, you may be better able to discern what your feelings really are.

Notice also that the proverbs don't tell us to follow our parents' example. They tell us instead to follow their "law," their "instruction," or their "commandment." Solomon was the wisest of men, but he wasn't the best example of godly living. And Jesus told His disciples, "The scribes and the Pharisees sit in Moses' seat: all therefore whatsoever they bid you observe, that observe and do; but do not ye after their works: for they say, and do not" (Matt. 23:2–3). As our children know only too well, this is also true of parents.

I think we may safely say that parents do better at giving advice to their children than at setting them a godly example. The best parent will sometimes be a bad model, and many a wicked parent has given godly instruction to his own sons and daughters. If we, being evil, know how to give good gifts to our children (see Matt. 7:11), may we not also give them good advice?

Children must discern the difference between their parents' example and their instruction. If the former is bad, the latter may still be good. Solomon is telling us, in effect, not to throw the baby of good advice out with the bath water of bad living. If we reject our parents' instruction because their walk doesn't match their talk, we have not understood the wisdom of David and Bathsheba's son.

Proverbial Wisdom

So you are thinking, "All right, already! My parent is someone who knows more than I do. Now what?" Let's look at some of the proverbs, so that we may deepen our understanding of this essential truth.

The Beginning of Knowledge

Notice the context of the first proverb on our subject:

> The fear of the Lord is the beginning of knowledge: but fools despise wisdom and instruction. My son, hear the instruction of thy father, and forsake not the law of thy mother: For they shall be an ornament of grace unto thy head, and chains about thy neck. (Prov. 1:7–9)

Matthew Henry groups these three verses together and begins his commentary on them this way:

> Solomon, having undertaken to *teach a young man knowledge and discretion,* here lays down two general rules to be observed in order thereunto, and those are, to fear God and honour his parents, which two fundamental laws of morality Pythagoras begins his golden verses with . . . *First worship the immortal gods, and honour your parents.*[4]

The Word of God, godly commentators, and pagan philosophers all agree: The first step after learning to fear God is learning to honor one's parents. Here again we see the order we noticed in the Ten Commandments: our duty to God first, then our duty to our parents, then our duties to other men.

Since "the fear of the Lord is the beginning of wisdom,"[5] may we not say that honoring our parents is the second step toward knowledge? What profit or pleasure, then, can a parent expect from a child who learns reading and writing in school, or French and calculus for that matter, without learning obedience at home? Let us not pay lip service to God's priorities, but rather count our children's instruction in obedience as more important than math or English.[6] They'll learn more from our example than from anything we say.

I will consider the valid exceptions in a later chapter, but for now let me give you a useful rule of thumb: *You should have done what your parent told you to do, unless it violated the Ten Commandments.* We must not steal, lie, or commit adultery. But not many of us have parents who ordered us to do such things. The truth is, most of us have despised at least some of our parents' good instruction, and few of us have accomplished a full repentance for it.[7]

Have you routinely heard your father's instruction and remembered the law of your mother? If you haven't, I wonder if repentance or excuses come first into your mind. If it's repentance, you are blessed more than you know. May God perfect the good work He has begun in you.

If excuses come first to mind, how do you know that God accepts your excuses? Need some examples of excuses? "Yes, I should have listened to my parents, but . . .

- my parent (is/was) not a Christian."

- my parent (is/was) an alcoholic."

- my parent (is/was) too selfish to think about what I need."

- my parent (has/had) no parenting skills."

- as the king of Siam was fond of saying, 'Etcetera, etcetera, etcetera.'"

The burden of proof is on you. You must prove that you are guiltless in God's eyes, for this opening passage in Proverbs gives no endorsement to your excuses.

The Credentials of Solomon

At the start of Proverbs 4, Solomon encourages us with his own experience:

> Hear, ye children, the instruction of a father, and attend to know understanding. For I give you good doctrine, forsake ye not my law. For I was my father's son, tender and only beloved in the sight of my mother. He taught me also, and said unto me, Let thine heart retain my words: keep my commandments, and live. (Prov. 4:1–4)

"[My father] also taught me," says the wisest of men. Let us take time to consider this statement. The man to whom God said, "Lo, I have given thee a wise and an understanding heart; so that there was none like thee before thee, neither after thee shall any arise like unto thee" (1 Kings 3:12)—this is the man who tells us his father taught him wisdom. Though Solomon had a diploma more impressive than any on earth, he retained his father's instruction from his youth. Moreover, he makes listening to his father one of his chief credentials as a teacher.

Let's put this in contemporary terms. Imagine a man receiving an emeritus professorship from one of our great seminaries. He has degrees from Harvard, Oxford, and the University of Berlin. He has published scholarly monographs which have been well received by experts in the field. Christian leaders acknowledge him as the wisest man of his generation. Sitting before a board of distinguished interviewers, who are happy just to be in his presence on this august occasion, he presents as a mere formality his credentials as a Christian teacher. Hear what he says to them: "My parents feared God. My father taught me, my mother loved me, and I have listened to their words." Does this seem possible today? Hardly. But it is just what Solomon is saying: "Don't take me on my own authority. I was taught by my godly parents, and I retained their teaching. Listen to me, as I listened to them: Hear, and your soul shall live."

According to the Bible, even if you are King Solomon himself, *your parent is someone who knows more than you do.*

The Way of Life

Proverbs 6:20–23 is a fascinating passage.

> My son, keep thy father's commandment, and forsake not the law of thy mother: Bind them continually upon thine heart, and tie them about thy neck. When thou goest, it shall lead thee; when thou sleepest, it shall keep thee; and when thou awakest, it shall talk with thee. For the commandment is a lamp; and the law is light; and reproofs of instruction are the way of life.

While there is much to learn from these verses, I am specially attracted by two points. The simpler of the two, "Reproofs of instruction are the way of life," should be often in our thoughts. Those finest of the fine arts, the giving and receiving of such reproofs, are too little practiced among us. It's easy to criticize or take offense at criticism, but much harder to give or receive the correction that leads to life. Our duty is to receive such reproofs from our parents *and to assume that their reproofs are the way of life for us.*

Even when their instruction falls short of Dr. John Gill's definition—"kind reproofs given by parents agreeable to the word of God"[8]—we should assume that parents have our best interests in mind. We should remember that they know, if not more than we do, at least many things that we do not. Unless their instruction clearly contradicts the Word of God, we should be quick to receive it and slow to reject it. Our parents are the way of life to us, the means by which God brought us into the world. Whatever their sins and hypocrisies may be or may have been—and we are not the best judges of those things—we should be quick to receive their correction.

More mysterious is the passage, "When you awake, it shall talk with you." I love the two translations of *The Interlinear Bible:* "When you awaken, it shall muse with you," and "When you awaken, it will meditate with you." Charles Spurgeon preached an entire sermon on this passage, applying it to the wondrous Word of God. In it he emphasized the communion we have with the Word, which deigns to speak *with* us and not merely to us. But the context here concerns "your father's command" and "the law of your mother," commands designed to save us from unchastity and destruction. Even when parental dictates were not formed directly from Scripture, they may well have been compatible with it. Few of us, I hope, have parents who urged us to visit prostitutes or to commit adultery,[9] while many of us were cautioned by our parents against those very sins. May their words not return to us later in life and speak with us upon our beds, either to confirm us in purity or to convict us of transgression?

The Despising Fool

Several of the proverbs deal with the man who despises his parents.

> A fool despiseth his father's instruction: but he that regardeth reproof is prudent. (15:5)

> A wise son maketh a glad father: but a foolish man despiseth his mother. (15:20)

> Hearken unto thy father that begat thee, and despise not thy mother when she is old. (23:22)

Though these passages employ different Hebrew words for "fool" and "despise," their general meaning is clear. As it is the mark of wisdom to honor and esteem one's parents, so it is the mark of folly to despise them. This kind of folly is commonly a hidden sin of the heart. Many people today outwardly honor their parents but inwardly despise them. Sometimes we conceal this contempt even from ourselves, but it can be detected in our fleeting thoughts or during times of stress. It's easy to honor our parents in the summer of their consent; the winter of their disapproval reveals what's in our hearts.

Do you despise your mother? This is a great sin. Honoring her does not mean pretending that she's perfect, but no accumulation of her faults allows you to despise her. In later chapters, I will do my best to teach you the art of honoring a very fallible parent. But for now, if in fact you have despised your mother—or your father, the main thing is to acknowledge the sin and to prepare your heart for repentance.

The End of the Matter

Some of the proverbs focus on the consequences of dishonoring our parents.

> Whoso curseth his father or his mother, his lamp shall be put out in obscure darkness. (20:20)

> An inheritance may be gotten hastily at the beginning; but the end thereof shall not be blessed. (20:21)

> Whoso robbeth his father or his mother, and saith, It is no transgression: the same is the companion of a destroyer. (28:24)

> The eye that mocketh at his father, and despiseth to obey his mother, the ravens of the valley shall pick it out, and the young eagles shall eat it. (30:17)

God is very serious about this business of honoring our parents. He promises a variety of dire fates to those who spurn His commands on the subject. They shall reap what they have sown, and it will be bitter fruit indeed. Though the ravens be drug dealers, swindlers, or unfaithful spouses—the devourer, in one form or another, will search out and destroy the happiness of ungrateful children.

Shakespeare tells us in *King Lear* what many a parent has found to be true:

> How sharper than a serpent's tooth it is
> To have a thankless child.[10]

Yet the Scriptures emphasize that the thankless child is no better off than his parent. He is a marked man, and he shall not escape the fangs of divine justice. The pain he has inflicted on his parents shall be visited on him, unless, of course, the ingrate come to his senses and repents. Then, though he may still suffer the consequences of his actions, the blessing of God may rest upon him.

I once heard a family story which sounded like a perfect illustration of Proverbs 20:21. A middle-aged son threatened his father, forcing him to sign over the family business against his will. For a time nothing unusual happened. But very soon after the old man died of natural causes, the extorter himself came down with a dreadful disease. He wasted away painfully in the hospital, then went to meet his Maker. The inheritance he gained hastily at the beginning was never a blessing to him.

Before we proclaim our shock at such criminal behavior, let's examine our hearts. Are we in a position to throw stones? Perhaps we have desired the death of a parent or grandparent. Whether our motivation was to gain an inheritance, to escape restricting authority, or to be rid of a nagging crone, we may have been the "companion of a destroyer" (28:24) without knowing it. We may have robbed our parents of the respect and gratitude that were due them—due not because of their merits, but because of the first commandment with promise.

Notice that mocking and scorning parental authority (30:17) lead to a dreadful fate. This should give pause to those who honor their parents in public but despise them in their hearts. Jesus warned, "Fools! Did not He who made the outside also make the inside?" (Luke 11:40, MKJV). God save us from such ruinous hypocrisy!

CHAPTER 5

Old Testament Illustrations

When God took human form, He taught us much through stories. The Messiah was a story-telling Man. He loved parables because they make the truth plain and because they keep the truth hidden, because they are shallow and because they are deep. He knew how to make His point with a story—and how to tell it so that some people would miss the point.

The stories of the Old Testament may be entertaining, but that's not all they are. They teach us how to live—and how not to live. They operate on different levels: young children and old theologians fall under their spell. Many of them deal with the ramifications of "Honor your father and mother." As you see the commandment working itself out in the lives of men and nations, you'll find there's more to these stories than first meets the eye.

The Sons of Noah (Genesis 9:18–27)

The student of the Bible learns, sooner or later, to pay special attention to how Scripture introduces a given subject. For example, how strange and significant it is that prayer is first mentioned in the context of Abraham's sin, that the first intercessor of the Bible should be so clearly a sinner![1] Just after Abraham pretended to Abimelech that he was not Sarah's husband, God accepted the patriarch's prayer for the pagan king and his family. In an equally remarkable way, the subject of this book is introduced at the end of the ninth chapter of Genesis.

If ever children had cause to be grateful to a parent, Noah's three sons had reason to be grateful to him. Their preservation from the Flood was due solely to their relationship with him; no mention is made of their righteousness, only of his (see Gen. 6:7–10; 7:1). But Noah was not perfect, and his imperfection provided his sons an opportunity to dishonor him.

> And Noah began to be an husbandman, and he planted a vineyard: And he drank of the wine, and was drunken; and he was uncovered within his tent. And Ham, the father of Canaan, saw the nakedness of his father, and told his two brethren without. And Shem and Japheth took a garment, and laid it upon both their shoulders, and went backward, and covered the nakedness of their father; and their faces were backward, and they saw not their father's nakedness. (Gen. 9:20–23)

There is a wealth of information and instruction in this short passage. First, concerning parents, there is no parent so good that the child cannot find some reason, real or imagined, to belittle or dishonor him. The opposite, I believe, is also true: there is no parent so evil that the child cannot find some way to honor and esteem him. As this story clearly points out, *it is not the parent's goodness or wickedness that determines whether the child shall be blessed or cursed; it is the child's reaction to the parent that is crucial.*[2] This concept needs to be emphasized, because it runs counter to so much that is taken for granted in our society.

Why would the same incident produce a blessing for two sons and a curse for the third? Did Noah play favorites among his sons, as Isaac did with his? I think not. Apart from their actions in this incident, we know of no other difference among the sons of Noah. Nor is there any reason to suspect their father of prejudice. The outcome for each child was determined by his own reaction to his parent's moment of weakness. The first commandment with promise knows no favorites.

Today we tend to excuse the behavior of people from troubled families. Their critics, or their prosecuting attorneys, are told that "they couldn't help themselves," because of the bad examples or the deprivations they encountered in their youth. Since the sins of the fathers are visited on the children (Ex. 20:5), we need to bear in mind the great temptations to sin that some children are exposed to.

However, we need to balance that teaching with the lesson of Genesis 9, that the child has a choice about how he responds to parental sin. Some children from troubled families become model citizens. And some children with all the advantages end up unproductive or criminal or insane. I believe that, generally speaking, these outcomes accord well with the individuals' observance of the first commandment with promise. That's one reason why biblical justice demands greater responsibility for one's actions than do our present courts of law.

As Proverbs 10:12 states: "Love covereth all sins." (See also Prov. 17:9 and 1 Pet. 4:8.) It is a great sin to make our parents' failures known; it is a great virtue to cover them. Whether or not Ham sinned in seeing his father's nakedness (why was he in Noah's tent?), it was surely sin for him to tell others about it. Shem and Japheth not only refused to gossip about their father's drunkenness and nakedness, but they took pains to cover him up without looking at him. They kept themselves pure, while their brother defiled himself. The contrast could hardly be clearer.

> And Noah awoke from his wine, and knew what his younger son had done unto him. And he said, Cursed be Canaan; a servant of servants shall he be unto his brethren. And he said, Blessed be the Lord God of Shem; and Canaan shall be his servant. God shall enlarge Japheth, and he shall dwell in the tents of Shem; and Canaan shall be his servant. (Gen. 9:24–27)

That this was not a vengeful, drunken speech on Noah's part is made clear by events. Over the course of centuries his prophecy was fulfilled. Surely, in spite of his previous intoxication, this was an oration of the Holy Spirit. Ham's descendants through Canaan were cursed. They became such wicked sinners that they had to be destroyed. Some eight or nine hundred years later, the Jews under Joshua killed most of the Canaanites, and those who survived became slaves to the children of Shem. Meanwhile God blessed Shem, bringing forth the chosen people and the Messiah from his offspring. Thousands of years after Noah gave this prophecy, the children of Japheth came to "dwell in the tents of Shem" when they, the Gentiles, embraced the Semitic Messiah and put their trust in the God of Shem. How's that for far-reaching consequences?

We do not know for sure why Canaan was singled out among Ham's four sons to be the object of Noah's curse.[3] What should be stressed—and often is not—is the Lord's mercy in exempting the other three sons from the curse.[4] In any event, the outcome indicates that Noah's prophecy came from God; therefore, within it there can be nothing unjust.

This cursing of Canaan, like the deaths of Ananias and Sapphira in the New Testament (see Acts 5:1–11), has been set up as a warning to God's people through the ages. Not every person who lies to the church is struck dead on the spot, and not every soul who dishonors his parent will have his descendants slaughtered wholesale. But he is a fool who will not pay close attention to such a warning from the Lord.

Jacob the Deceiver, Jacob the Deceived (Genesis 27—29)

I can safely say that better commentators than I have failed to do justice to this strange and controversial story. Moreover, we must limit ourselves to considering only one aspect of it, the honor and dishonor Jacob paid to his parents, and the consequences that came upon him for it.

We shall start with what often seems to be glossed over in this story—the sin of Isaac, namely his disregard of God's word and his bias toward Esau. Though he must have known what God told Rebekah about the older serving the younger,[5] we find it clearly stated that Isaac loved Esau "because he did eat of his venison" (Gen. 25:28). In other words, Isaac preferred Esau because of the gratification he received from him. His love appears to have been conditional, based on performance. We should not assume that Isaac did not love Jacob, but it seems clear that Esau was preferred and Jacob had a secondary status in his father's eyes. Rebekah also was guilty of preferring one son to the other, but at least her love was not so performance oriented.

What incalculable woe this sin of favoritism brought into the chosen family! Yet we are never told that Jacob or his mother ever approached Isaac about his sin. Presumably, if they did object at first, they soon became weary of well-doing. Ultimately they responded in kind, and the family became a house divided. When Isaac sought to bless Esau in defiance of the word of God, Jacob and Rebekah took the fulfillment of the prophecy into their own hands.

Did Jacob sin by obeying his mother and deceiving his father? The commentators are nearly unanimous in affirming that he did.[6] My own answer to the question is heavily influenced by what God allowed to happen to Jacob and his family over the next five decades. It seems to me that Jacob sinned and paid an enormous price for his sin. He deceived his father, and in turn he was deceived by Laban. The question is this: If Jacob was innocent, why did God allow him to fall into Laban's snare? Consider all that Jacob endured as the result of Laban's treachery. He never enjoyed a single day of monogamous marriage to his beloved Rachel; their whole relationship was tainted by the tension, jealousy, and manipulation that resulted from his having slept with Leah first. His children were brought up in an atmosphere of competition and distrust; they were all pawns in the power struggle between his wives. Jacob's favoritism for Joseph, Rachel's son, caused Joseph's brothers to hate him. That hatred caused an agony for Jacob that can scarcely be imagined by those who have not felt it.

To me it seems clear that God gave Jacob a very bitter taste of his own medicine. When Laban substituted his elder daughter for his younger one, he reenacted in reverse the deception Jacob played upon his father. I cannot account for Laban's successful deception of Jacob, and the terrible results of that deception in Jacob's family life, except by assuming that God was displeased with what Jacob had done to Isaac—and made the punishment fit the crime. It is written: "He who digs a pit will fall into it" (Eccles. 10:8). (See also Prov. 26:27 and Ps. 7:15.)

Jacob's lies and deception may not have been his only sins against his father. It seems likely that he failed to honor Isaac by communicating the true condition of his heart. Of course we cannot be sure, for Scripture is silent on the subject. A breakdown in communication usually precedes the advent of lying and rebellion in a family. As Jacob was unwilling to confront Laban with his true feelings before he fled from Syria, so he may have failed to tell Isaac how he felt about his favoring Esau. Apparently Jacob did not believe that a prayerful appeal in the moment of crisis would do any good. If, as seems likely to me, the roots of Jacob's sin lay in his unbelief, or even in his cowardice—remember that these things were written for our learning.

Miriam and Aaron (Numbers 12)

This is not a story about the first commandment with promise. However, in it the Lord makes a passing remark that is relevant to our theme. When Miriam and Aaron spoke against Moses, the Lord showed His displeasure by striking Miriam with leprosy.

> And Moses cried unto the Lord, saying, Heal her now, O God,
> I beseech thee. And the Lord said unto Moses, If her father
> had but spit in her face, should she not be ashamed seven
> days? let her be shut out from the camp seven days, and after
> that let her be received in again. And Miriam was shut out
> from the camp seven days. (Num. 12:13–15)

The way the Lord refers here to the customs of the time has considerable implications for our study. Would He have reasoned thus, if He abhorred the Jews' practice in honoring their parents? How our Maker views a father's spitting in his child's face is not apparent here. But He does indirectly approve the child's banishment, compulsory or self-imposed, for the interval following such discipline.

God's statement to Moses, it seems to me, means something like this: "Now, just a minute, Moses. Not so fast. I'm willing to grant your prayer, but you must consider the gravity of what I have done. Your sister has committed a serious offense, and she has received a signal sign of My displeasure. How much more disgraceful this is to her, than if her earthly father had spit in her face! Yet if that were to happen, wouldn't she hide herself for shame? Should Miriam then reenter My holy camp? Am I not worthy of the honor commonly afforded to a father? Let her wait outside the camp—and remember My disfavor."

God would not desire to be treated like the earthly fathers of Moses' day, if their common practice were wicked or oppressive. His insistence on this sign of respect shows us that, in addition to trembling at any sign of God's dissatisfaction, we should tremble at the displeasure of our parents. We should have a holy fear of displeasing them, rather than a fleshly fear of their wrath.[7] Today, I know, many of us resent, rather than fear, the correction of a parent. He who has the mind of the Lord will beware of such resentment.

Ruth and Naomi (Ruth 1—4)

We can learn many good things from Ruth the Moabitess, the great-grandmother of King David. First, she shows us that the honor we owe our parents must not take precedence over the honor we owe to God. By marrying into a Hebrew family she had come to know the true and living God; notice her use of the Hebrew oath, "The Lord do so to me, and more also" (1:17). After a series of tragedies in which Ruth's husband and father-in-law died, her mother-in-law, Naomi, suggested that Ruth return to the *gods* of her people.

This suggestion provoked Ruth's famous statement of loyalty (1:15–17). In other words, the primary factor in Ruth's decision to accompany Naomi on her return to Bethlehem was Ruth's choosing the God of Israel to be her God. Much as she loved Naomi, she did not leave family and country just for her sake.

We must be careful in applying the example of Ruth to our own lives. Some might use it to justify themselves in forsaking their unbelieving parents. They should consider, first, that Ruth was a widow, not an unmarried woman living under her parents' authority. She had been a member of Naomi's household for some ten years (1:4). Second, it is reasonable to assume that Ruth had her parents' blessing when she became the wife of Mahlon. If so, they had encouraged or at least permitted her to begin a relationship with the God of Israel. Third, in Ruth's time there was only one nation that knew the Lord. There would be no way for her to continue worshiping Him if she were left alone in an entirely pagan culture.[8] There was no godly remnant in Moab; but there is one in most nations today. Fourth, we do not know if Ruth had any further contact with her parents. Her following the Lord would not necessarily mean that she never told them about her new husband and son. So we see that Ruth's situation in leaving her parents was quite different from that of a young single person in a Christian or post-Christian culture. Need I say more?

Ruth's example teaches us that the honor we owe our parents also belongs to our in-laws.[9] When Ruth was a poor widow from an alien culture, and later when she was a wealthy member of Bethlehem's inner circle, she constantly cared for Naomi's physical and emotional needs. Naomi mentions Ruth's kindness to her (1:8); Boaz tells Ruth that he has full knowledge of her care for her mother-in-law (2:11); and the women of Bethlehem refer to Ruth as "thy daughter-in-law, which loveth thee, which is better to thee than seven sons" (4:15). We see Ruth carefully providing for Naomi's welfare (2:18) and following her instructions to the letter (3:5).[10] If only we would treat our natural parents as well as Ruth treated her mother-in-law!

Ruth shows us how a great blessing may come *as a direct result* of keeping the first commandment with promise. As soon as Boaz meets her, he gives her preferential treatment.[11] When she asks him why he does so, he replies, "It hath fully been showed me, all that thou hast done unto thy mother-in-law since the death of thine husband" (2:11). Clearly the first thing that attracted Boaz to Ruth was her faithfulness in keeping our commandment. Their marriage and the blessings that came from it were the direct result of Ruth's honoring Naomi with loyalty, obedience, and hard work.

"Oh," you say, "my parents are so different from Naomi." I could point out that you aren't exactly Ruth yourself, but I prefer a different response. "Jesus Christ the same yesterday, and today, and forever" (Heb. 13:8). The God who watched over Ruth is watching over you. Won't you give Him the same reason to bless you?

David, the Son of Jesse (1 Samuel 16 and 17)

God's blessing and His perfect timing can operate through a parent who seems oblivious to his child's special gifts. David and Jesse show us this principle at work.

When Samuel called Jesse and his sons to the sacrifice, David was not even among them. He was out in the fields keeping sheep. Surely, if his father had thought it important for David to be present, he could have found a sheep-sitter for a few hours. Evidently Jesse had no idea that his youngest son had a special calling from God.

Yet even after Samuel had anointed him in the presence of his brothers, David received no special treatment from his father. When the Philistines invaded Israel, the three oldest brothers went off to war. David returned from his position at Saul's court—to feed his father's sheep again! (Picture, if you will, a modern young man, who has somehow become a personal aide to the leader of his country. A great crisis arises, all the leader's aides and advisers are rushing to perform their crucial duties—and our hero is called home to flip hamburgers in his father's restaurant. Would that be easy for him to endure?) It may be that David still went back and forth to Saul's camp, but even so the transition from a courtier to a shepherd is a sharp one, requiring a strong dose of humility to enable one to grin and bear it.

We do not know if Jesse was wisely giving David a course in self-denial or if he was motivated merely by the need for an extra farmhand. But through it all we never hear a word of complaint from David. He was ready to do his father's will, never mind how menial the task. He proved it on the fateful day in which he later met Goliath. After leaving the sheep with a keeper (1 Sam. 17:20), which shows us how fully he accepted his humble duties, he went to deliver some food to his brothers. Thus, as God would have it, David arrived at the time appointed for him to slay Goliath.

Remember, "Now all these things . . . are written for our admonition" (1 Cor. 10:11). These stories present relevant and valid guidelines for Christians today. A young man or woman may have great gifts and an important calling from God, but he or she is not thereby excused from obeying a parent, even one that seems oblivious to the child's spiritual potential (see chap. 12).[12] In fact God may be preparing His chosen servant for ministry though his or her obedience to that oblivious parent. The child who refuses to obey may miss some essential training from the Lord. Furthermore, God's perfect timing for His young servant to begin public ministry may be expressed through what seems merely a whim of the parent. Through humility and obedience God prepares us for great things. But when the world, the flesh, and the devil are urging us to do great things *now*, who among us is wise enough to stay home with the sheep?

Rehoboam, Son of Solomon (1 Kings 12)

"The father of a fool hath no joy," wrote Solomon (Prov. 17:21). How it would have grieved him to see his son in action!

> And king Rehoboam consulted with the old men, that stood before Solomon his father while he yet lived, and said, How do ye advise that I may answer this people? And they spake unto him, saying, If thou wilt be a servant unto this people this day, and wilt serve them, and answer them, and speak good words to them, then they will be thy servants forever. But he forsook the counsel of the old men, which they had given him, and consulted with the young men that were grown up with him, and which stood before him. And the king answered the people roughly, and forsook the old men's counsel that they gave him; And spake to them after the counsel of the young men. (1 Kings 12:6–8, 13–14)

The results of this counsel were the division of the kingdom of Israel and chronic civil war among the people of God.

God had already decreed that the kingdom must be divided (see 1 Kings 11:11–13). Rehoboam's foolishness was the means to this end, but it was not the only possible means. God had many ways to fulfill His Word. It is the particular shame of Rehoboam that he was the channel by which this offense came upon Israel. From his example we can learn something about the *spirit* of the first commandment with promise. He did nothing, as far as we know, to violate the letter of that law, but he broke the spirit of it. He forsook his father's counselors and listened to his own. Was it well with him?

It is good to remember the maxims and instructions of our ancestors, assuming that they do not violate the Ten Commandments. Though they have departed this life, we can honor them still by keeping their counsel. Does this recommendation seem foolish or excessive to you? If so, stop and consider our next illustration.

Jeremiah and the Rechabites (Jeremiah 35)

Jeremiah was called to his prophetic ministry in the darkest hour of the Jewish people. Consequently, his book speaks mostly about the sins of the people and God's impending judgment. The bright spots in the Book of Jeremiah are mainly promises of God's future mercies to Israel, such as the promise of the New Covenant, and praise for a few godly individuals, such as Baruch and Ebed-melech. However, there is one group of people in the book who shine like a light in a dark place. These are the Rechabites of Jeremiah 35, and we do well to understand how they were different from those around them.

God commanded Jeremiah to go to the Rechabites, to bring them into the house of the Lord, and to give them wine to drink (v. 2). He did as he was told. He set wine before them and said, "Drink ye wine!" (v. 5). Notice that he did *not* say to them, "Thus says the Lord, 'Drink wine!'"; that would have been a different matter altogether. The Rechabites replied:

> We will not drink wine, for Jonadab the son of Rechab, our father, commanded us, saying, "You shall not drink wine, you or your sons, forever. And you shall not build a house, and you shall not sow seed, and you shall not plant a vineyard or own one; but in tents you shall dwell all your days, that you may live many days in the land where you sojourn." And we have obeyed the voice of Jonadab the son of Rechab, our father, in all that he commanded us, not to drink wine all our days, we, our wives, our sons, or our daughters, nor to build ourselves houses to dwell in; and we do not have vineyard or field or seed. We have only dwelt in tents, and have obeyed, and have done according to all that Jonadab our father commanded us. (Jer. 35:6–10, NASB)

The remarkable thing about the obedience of the Rechabites is that this Jonadab the son of Rechab lived some three hundred years before the time of Jeremiah (see 2 Kings 10:15). For three centuries the Rechabites had kept *all* the commandments of their godly ancestor, even though their obedience required a lifestyle different from that of their neighbors. And even though the Babylonian invasion had caused them to take shelter temporarily in Jerusalem, they continued to keep Jonadab's commandments to the best of their ability.

Then the Lord spoke through Jeremiah. Three times He took notice of the obedience of the Rechabites, contrasting it with the Jews' disobedience to God (vv. 14, 16, 18). At the close of the chapter, Jeremiah pronounced God's blessing on the descendants of Jonadab: "Therefore thus saith the Lord of hosts, the God of Israel; Jonadab the son of Rechab shall not want a man to stand before me forever" (35:19). Commentators have different ideas about what exactly that blessing means, but they agree that the Lord conferred on the Rechabites some important and long-lasting distinction. (It seems likely that He protected them during the destruction of Jerusalem.)

Here we see the Lord's blessing on those who honor ancestral commands. Perhaps you have such a command in your family. Did one of your ancestors say, "Stay out of debt," "Don't flaunt your wealth or your looks or your talent," "Don't forget your ethnic heritage," "Take care of your siblings"—or some other such maxim? Have you had a respectful attitude toward this family wisdom? Or have you despised it? "Experience keeps a dear [expensive] school," said Ben Franklin, "but fools will learn in no other."

The example of the Rechabites encourages us to pay attention to the wishes of our parents, even if they require us to be different from our neighbors. The significance of this example for us can hardly be overestimated. Our culture encourages young people to reject their parents' advice and to listen to their peers. Jonadab possessed a special wisdom concerning the future welfare of his family, but in that he was not unique. Fathers and mothers often are given special insight about what will be best for their children. Many of the proverbs recognize this and urge us to heed parental instructions (see chap. 4). What was remarkable in Jonadab's case was that he had descendants wise enough to listen to him for centuries. The Lord was much impressed with their obedience. And wherever the gospel is preached in the whole world, their story will be told as their memorial.

CHAPTER 6

Dealing with Perverse Authority:
David and Jonathan and Saul

Before I began writing this book, I knew the stories of David and Jonathan well (1 Sam. 18—2 Sam. 1). I had read them many times with interest and admiration. Yet I've learned by experience that when I know enough to write on a topic, I will learn a lot more in the writing. That's how it is with the things of the Lord. The more you know, the more you see how much there is to learn.

These chapters are the Bible's chief lessons on handling a sinful or deranged parent. Yet I had never thought of them that way before; I had never looked at David and Jonathan as models for dealing with perverse authority. Now that my eyes are opened, and because the topic is essential to our theme, we shall examine the stories in some detail.

David is known to most of us as the slayer of Goliath and the "sweet psalmist of Israel" (2 Sam. 23:1). He is known too for his great sin with Bathsheba and his heartfelt repentance for it. Because of his other accomplishments, however, we hardly seem to have noticed that Jesse's son is also a model of our commandment in action. I trust you will agree with me, after we have studied these stories, that they add real luster to the name of David, and indirectly to the name of David's greater Son.

Saul was Jonathan's father and David's father-in-law. He was also their sovereign. Saul was to them what God is to us—both father and king. Their dealings with him cannot be distilled: We cannot separate the subject from the son. Yet his double authority over them only served to double his sin against them. It gave them twice the reason to resent Saul's abuse of his God-given power. Thus David and Jonathan have earned their credentials as teachers of our commandment.

Saul is the symbol of perverse authority. It is important to remember that he had a legitimate commission from God. God had made him king of Israel. Every parent has a similar commission. However pure or sinful the union was which resulted in your conception, God blessed that union with life. God used it—He selected it—to bring you into the world. Though you may have been the last thing your parents were thinking of at the time, you were very much in the mind of God. *He* chose your parents for you; *He* made you their child. As surely as He raised up Saul as His authority over Israel, He raised up your parents as His authority over you. "Shall what is formed say to him who formed it, 'He has no understanding'?" (Isa. 29:16, NASB).

Saul had a legitimate commission, but he abused it. He sinned against God, and he never sustained any meaningful repentance. To judge by the way God dealt with David, it was Saul's lack of repentance more than his sin that made him unfit to be king. Have your parents abused their commission? Have they fallen short of true repentance? Then behold the examples of David and Jonathan, and discover how you may be blessed by the Lord.

The Example of David

David had little time to savor either his conquest of Goliath or his newfound fame. Almost as soon as his leadership was established, he had to deal with Saul's jealousy. Saul tried to murder him with a javelin (see 1 Sam. 18:10–11). From that point on, Saul made a series of plots on David's life. How did the son of Jesse deal with them?

Providing for His Parents

Even while David was running for his life, he thought of his parents and tried to provide for them.

> And David went thence to Mizpeh of Moab: and he said unto
> the king of Moab, Let my father and my mother, I pray thee,

> come forth, and be with you, till I know what God will do
> for me. And he brought them before the king of Moab: and
> they dwelt with him all the while that David was in the hold.
> (1 Sam. 22:3–4)

If you are tempted to think that you have too much important work or too much stress in your life to care for your parents, please consider David's example. He was Israel's anointed king, but he had time to find shelter for his father and mother. His persecutors were seeking him everywhere, yet he thought of their safety as well as his own. He took care of his parents; he did what he could do. And the Lord took care of him, as only He knows how.

Avoiding Conflict

Does anyone doubt that David could have defeated Saul in battle? Yet David refused to fight with his master. The man who slew Goliath chose to run away from Saul.[1] Self-interest alone might have caused him to do so. David might have reasoned: "Since there's a God in heaven, and since I will soon be king, I should treat the current king as I want my subjects to treat me. If I don't, God will surely cause me to remember it. If I try to end Saul's reign, some day my subjects may try to end mine."[2] We can make the same application: "Since I may be a parent (or other authority figure) some day in the future I should treat my parents (and other authorities) with respect. If I honor my parents, very likely my children will honor me. If I dishonor my parents . . . ."

However, I'm convinced that David was motivated by more than self-interest. We have seen how David, even when anointed king, did just what Jesse told him. As a man after God's own heart, one who understood the first commandment with promise, he simply applied to Saul the attitude toward authority which he had learned at home. He could never have resisted Saul's many provocations, each one tempting him to take matters into his own hands, if he were not well-schooled in godly reverence for authority.

Notice that David did not run away for trivial reasons. He feared for his life. More than that, he had real evidence—a javelin in the wall—to show that his fears were well grounded. We should not leave home because a parent is angry with us. But we should leave when our lives are in danger. We must try to speak the truth in love, but when that becomes impossible, we must avoid violent conflict. It is God's job, not ours, to humble our parents, if indeed they need humbling. We may need to get out of the way for a time, while God tutors them in humility. But he who uses David's flight as a model for his own ought to consider that it was only one part of his program for dealing with Saul.

Appealing to Authority (1 Samuel 24 and 26)

David didn't just run away from Saul. He looked for ways to show him he still loved him. Unlike many of us, he didn't cut off communication. No, he looked for opportunities to appeal to Saul's better nature. Though Saul had tried to kill him, he still could think the best of his sovereign. And when he risked his life to make his appeal, God preserved him from all harm. More than that, he carried away a testimony from his persecutor that he was a righteous man. After the first encounter, Saul said to David: "Thou art more righteous than I: for thou hast rewarded me good, whereas I have rewarded thee evil" (1 Sam. 24:17). Thus we see: "When a man's ways please the Lord, he maketh even his enemies to be at peace with him" (Prov. 16:7)— at least for a while. . . .

Let's look at these incidents in detail. The Lord thought them worthy of two chapters in the Bible, and I'm beginning to understand why. Please realize, however, that I am treating these passages symbolically. To me they exemplify how one ought to act with a parent who makes you fear for your life *emotionally* or *spiritually*. I am not qualified to advise you on how to approach a parent whom you truly think might kill you. I do not have much experience with such matters, and I refer you to those who do. But I have a lot of experience dealing with children both young and old, who fear for their emotional well-being as they approach, or even think of approaching, their parents. And I do not hesitate to recommend these stories as God's advice to them.

> Then Saul took three thousand chosen men from all Israel, and went to seek David and his men in front of the Rocks of the Wild Goats. And he came to the sheepfolds on the way, where there was a cave; and Saul went in to relieve himself. Now David and his men were sitting in the inner recesses of the cave. And the men of David said to him, "Behold, this is the day of which the Lord said to you, 'Behold; I am about to give your enemy into your hand, and you shall do to him as it seems good to you.'" Then David arose and cut off the edge of Saul's robe secretly. And it came about afterward that David's conscience bothered him because he had cut off the edge of Saul's robe. So he said to his men, "Far be it from me because of the Lord that I should do this thing to my lord, the

Lord's anointed, to stretch out my hand against him, since he
is the Lord's anointed." And David persuaded his men with
these words and did not allow them to rise up against Saul.
And Saul arose, left the cave, and went on his way. Now
afterward David arose and went out of the cave and called
after Saul, saying, "My lord the king!" And when Saul looked
behind him, David bowed with his face to the ground and
prostrated himself. And David said to Saul, "Why do you listen to the words of men, saying, 'Behold, David seeks to
harm you'? Behold, this day your eyes have seen that the Lord
had given you today into my hand in the cave, and some said
to kill you, but my eye had pity on you; and I said, 'I will not
stretch out my hand against my lord, for he is the Lord's
anointed.' Now, my father, see! Indeed, see the edge of your
robe in my hand! For in that I cut off the edge of your robe
and did not kill you, know and perceive that there is no evil
or rebellion in my hands, and I have not sinned against you,
though you are lying in wait for my life to take it. May the
Lord judge between you and me, and may the Lord avenge
me on you; but my hand shall not be against you. As the
proverb of the ancients says, 'Out of the wicked comes forth
wickedness'; but my hand shall not be against you. After
whom has the king of Israel come out? Whom are you pursuing? A dead dog, a single flea? The Lord therefore be judge
and decide between you and me; and may He see and plead
my cause, and deliver me from your hand." Now it came
about when David had finished speaking these words to Saul,
that Saul said, "Is this your voice, my son David?" Then Saul
lifted up his voice and wept. And he said to David, "You are
more righteous than I; for you have dealt well with me, while
I have dealt wickedly with you. And you have declared today
that you have done good to me, that the Lord delivered me
into your hand and yet you did not kill me. For if a man finds
his enemy, will he let him go away safely? May the Lord therefore reward you with good in return for what you have done
to me this day. And now, behold, I know that you shall surely
be king, and that the kingdom of Israel shall be established in
your hand. So now swear to me by the Lord that you will not
cut off my descendants after me, and that you will not destroy
my name from my father's household." And David swore to
Saul. And Saul went to his home, but David and his men went
up to the stronghold. (1 Sam. 24:2–22, NASB)

The first thing I want to point out is the terms in which David
addressed Saul: "My lord the king! . . . My father." He spoke first with
respect, then with intimacy. Notice also his posture: "David stooped
with his face to the earth, and bowed down." In every way David

exemplified this teaching, which is attributed to Goethe, "Treat someone as if they were what they should be, and you help them become what they are capable of being." Saul was still able to have lucid moments, but it took a David to discover them.

Did you observe that David resisted the advice of his peers? They wanted to kill Saul, and they were happy to quote the words of God to justify their crime. Note that the prophecy they refer to did not mention Saul by name. David, thinking the best of Saul, refused to treat him as his enemy. In the same way, you may have Scripture-quoting friends who will justify you in dishonoring your parents. If you heed their advice, you will not be following David's example.

After addressing Saul with respect, and bowing down before him—presumably at a distance—David began with a question: "Why do you listen to the words of men, saying, 'Behold, David seeks to harm you'?" This is an excellent beginning.[3] To appreciate it, we must, I fear, contrast it with the kind of response that flesh is often heir to: "You dirty so-and-so, look what you've done to me!" See the difference? David asked; he did not accuse. He attributed any offense against him to "men," not to Saul himself. Then he followed up his question with *tangible evidence* that he meant Saul no harm.

David finished by speaking humbly of himself and referring the matter to the judgment of God. He did not deny Saul's sin against him: "You are lying in wait for my life to take it"—but he neither condemned Saul, nor cursed him. He left him to God. Read the end of the story again, and see how beautifully God answered David's prayer.

In the second story (1 Sam. 26) David acted just as he did in the first. The chief difference is that this time he deliberately risked his life to demonstrate his loyalty to Saul. The first time their meeting was providential; the second was David's doing. Once more he got advice to kill Saul and refused to accept it.[4] Once more he offered tangible evidence of his good intentions toward his master. And once more he obtained Saul's testimony that he was a righteous man.

Saul's confession after this second incident was more remarkable than his first one: "Then Saul said, 'I have sinned. Return, my son David, for I will not harm you again because my life was precious in your sight this day. Behold, I have played the fool and have committed a serious error'" (1 Sam. 26:2, NASB). It is behavior like David's that enables a sinful authority to see the truth of the matter. If you approach the Saul in your life in a hostile or aggressive manner, you do not know what manner of spirit you are of (Luke 9:55).

David did not accept Saul's invitation; he did not return to his place at court. There are times when we need to follow his example. If our Saul has abused his authority over a long period of time, we may wait to see if he will "Bring forth fruits worthy of repentance" (Matt. 3:8, MKJV). But we ought to be helping, not hindering, the process.

I would be doing you a disservice if I encouraged you to think that your parent is a hopeless case. Remember that David was Saul's son-in-law, not his son. He did not have the special bond with him that Jonathan did. In Saul's eyes David was a rival, not a relative. Remember that before you lump your parent with King Saul.

At this time of his life David sinned in a number of ways. He was ready to murder Nabal and his family over a mere insult, though a grievous one, when Abigail prevented him (1 Sam. 25:34). He lied brazenly to Achish, king of Gath (1 Sam. 27:10–12). Yet when it comes to dealing with Saul, David is a shining example for us, one the Lord thought worthy of several chapters in His Book.[5]

The real question here, I think, is this: Are we willing to accept these stories as relevant to our own lives? It's one thing to delight in Old Testament knowledge; it's another to live by such biblical wisdom. There are literally millions of Christians in this country who need to apply David's example to their relationship with, or their memory of, their parents. Could you be one of them?

The Example of Jonathan

Children's choice of friends often leads them into conflict with their parents. Divided loyalties! What a difficult subject! Yet Jonathan's credentials in this area are the very highest. His father was chosen by God to be the first king of Israel. His best friend was raised up to take his father's place. He loved and respected them both, but his father hated and feared his friend. It is the parent's duty to protect his children from unwholesome influences. What do we do when our parent is (or seems to be) the bad influence in our life and our friend is (or seems to be) the man after God's own heart?

At the time they became friends, Jonathan and David were the two bravest men in Israel. Jonathan with one man (1 Sam. 14), and David by himself (1 Sam. 17), had routed the entire army of the Philistines. They had defied all the forces of the enemy, and all the fears

of their countrymen, and won. Yet soon they had a common affliction to go with their common valor: On separate occasions Saul tried
to put each of them to death.[6] What a difficult situation for Jonathan!
How did he cope with it?

The Loyal Son

Jonathan was loyal to Saul. Make no mistake of that. He proved it
by dying with him in the battle on Mount Gilboa (1 Sam. 31:1–6).
Despite his father's sins against David, against the Lord, and even
against himself, Jonathan served his deluded parent to the bitter end.
Instead of evaluating his actions or speculating on what he should
have done, it is good first simply to discover what he did. Later, if
need be, we can express our opinions about it.

You couldn't have a more impossible and unjust situation with
your parent, than Jonathan's first trouble with Saul (1 Sam. 14).
Jonathan, with only one man's help, had put to flight an army of the
Philistines. Almost single-handedly, he had delivered his people
from their oppressors. The result? Saul swore that he must die,
because he had eaten a little honey and unknowingly violated the
king's command. See how Jonathan reacts, when, after eating the
honey, he is informed of his father's decree against taking any nour-
ishment:

> Then Jonathan said, "My father has troubled the land. See
> now, how my eyes have brightened because I tasted a little of
> this honey. How much more, if only the people had eaten
> freely today of the spoil of their enemies which they found!
> For now the slaughter among the Philistines has not been
> great." (1 Sam. 14:29–30, NASB)

This just criticism shows Jonathan's mental independence from his
father. Indeed, without such independence he would never have
attacked the Philistines, for they had intimidated Saul.[7] Expecting,
therefore, that Jonathan will resist—with words, if not deeds—the
unjust death sentence decreed by his father, we are astonished by his
response. "Then Saul said to Jonathan, 'Tell me what you have
done.' So Jonathan told him and said, 'I indeed tasted a little honey
with the end of the staff that was in my hand. Here I am, I must
die!'" (1 Sam. 14:43, NASB). This was all Jonathan had to say. He did
not mention Saul's cowardice, his own bravery, his ignorance of the
command, or the foolishness of it. He said nothing about Saul's terrible lack of compassion for his son. Instead he bleated sadly, like a
sheep being led to the slaughter, and prepared himself for death.

What shall we make of this? I consider myself a radical, by current standards at least, when it comes to honoring parents. I am full of unusual suggestions on ways to implement the first commandment with promise. But in my wildest dreams I couldn't imagine, much less require, a submission as extreme as Jonathan's. We mustn't submit to an undeserved death to honor the whim of a parent. Jonathan was nobody's fool, however. He knew the Lord well enough to risk his life in an impossible venture—and to come off a winner. What on earth was he doing in this situation?

First, let's look at the natural side of things. Jonathan was tired, in fact, exhausted. He had scaled a cliff early in the day, killed a dozen soldiers in single-handed combat, and then pursued the enemy until evening. Only God knows how much running and fighting Jonathan had done that day. But the Word of God tells us something about it: "And they struck among the Philistines that day from Michmash to Aijalon. And the people were very weary." (1 Sam. 14:31, NASB). We know the locations of Michmash and Aijalon. They are separated by some fifteen miles of hill country to the north of Jerusalem.[8]

Knowing Jonathan as we do, we can be sure that he was at the front of the battle all day long. Having eaten nothing but a mouthful of honey since the fighting began, he must have been exhausted. Perhaps Jonathan's state was not too different from Samson's after he had slain a thousand men:

> And he was sore athirst, and called on the Lord, and said,
> Thou hast given this great deliverance into the hand of thy
> servant: and now shall I die for thirst, and fall into the hand of
> the uncircumcised? (Judg. 15:18)

Weakness follows close upon heroism in the life of a Christian. Exhaustion was a factor in Jonathan's response to Saul.

But physical exhaustion was not the whole story. Jonathan, like David, had great respect for parental and regal authority. I think this, more than exhaustion, accounts for his accepting the sentence of death. In his *Antiquities of the Jews*, Josephus, the ancient Jewish historian, gives an interesting version of this exchange:

> [Jonathan's] answer was this, "O father, I have done nothing
> more than that yesterday,[9] without knowing of the curse and
> oath thou hadst denounced, while I was in pursuit of the
> enemy, I tasted of a honey-comb." But Saul sware that he
> would slay him, and prefer the observation of his oath before
> all the ties of birth and of nature. And Jonathan was not dis-
> mayed at this threatening of death, but, offering himself to it

> generously and undauntedly, he said, "Nor do I desire you,
> father, to spare me: death will be to me very acceptable, when
> it proceeds from thy piety, and after a glorious victory; for it is
> the greatest consolation to me that I leave the Hebrews victo-
> rious over the Philistines."[10]

Josephus shows us Jonathan protesting his ignorance of Saul's instructions, something the Scriptures do not mention. But he goes on to tell us in no uncertain terms that Jonathan was willing to die. Matthew Henry puts it this way:

> He might very fairly have pleaded his invincible ignorance of
> the law, or have insisted upon his merit, but he submitted to
> the necessity with a great and generous mind: "God's and my
> father's will be done:" thus he showed as much valour in
> receiving the messengers of death himself as in sending them
> among the Philistines.[11]

Neither Josephus nor Matthew Henry seems to fault Jonathan for this submission to his father's decree. They seem, if anything, to admire him for it. I, on the other hand, would have no problem with your mounting a vigorous legal defense, if you were in Jonathan's situation. And I would consider David's precedent a justification for escape, if escape could be effected. Though I may seem extreme by modern standards in my regard for the first commandment with promise, by the standard of historic biblical interpretation, I'm not even on the scoreboard.

But enough about me. What about Jonathan? Was he out of his mind to submit as he did? One way to judge Bible stories is by the way things turn out. On the negative side, Jacob deceived his father; he was deceived in turn by Laban. On the other hand, David submitted to Jesse; Jesse sent him to Goliath right on schedule. In our story Jonathan submitted to Saul—and God preserved him from death. I do not require you to act the part of Jonathan. But I think his story is one of many biblical examples that encourage submission to authority which has exceeded its God-given prerogatives.[12]

The Loyal Friend

Do you remember the rule of thumb I mentioned earlier? *Obey your parents until they instruct you to break the Ten Commandments.* Jonathan seems to have used it.

> Now Saul told Jonathan his son and all his servants to put
> David to death. But Jonathan, Saul's son, greatly delighted in
> David. So Jonathan told David saying, "Saul my father is

> seeking to put you to death. Now therefore, please be on
> guard in the morning, and stay in a secret place and hide
> yourself." (1 Sam. 19:1–2, NASB)

When his father told him to kill a righteous man, Jonathan disobeyed his father. More than that, and this is important to observe, he spoke the truth in love to his sinful parent:

> Then Jonathan spoke well of David to Saul his father, and said
> to him, "Do not let the king sin against his servant David,
> since he has not sinned against you, and since his deeds have
> been very beneficial to you. For he took his life in his hand
> and struck the Philistine, and the Lord brought about a great
> deliverance for all Israel; you saw it and rejoiced. Why then
> will you sin against innocent blood, by putting David to death
> without a cause?" And Saul listened to the voice of Jonathan,
> and Saul vowed, "As the Lord lives, he shall not be put to
> death." Then Jonathan called David, and Jonathan told him
> all these words. And Jonathan brought David to Saul, and he
> was in his presence as formerly. (1 Sam. 19:4–7, NASB)

What a mixture of boldness and diplomacy! Boldness to say, "Let not the king sin"; diplomacy in appealing to the parent's own standards: "*You* saw it and rejoiced." How many parents might be deterred from sin, as Saul was, if they were addressed by their children in this manner!

The peace effected by Jonathan lasted until David's next successful campaign. Then "the evil spirit from the Lord was upon Saul" again (1 Sam. 19:9). He tried to kill David, and David ran for his life. Later, David met secretly with Jonathan and asked him, "What have I done? what is mine iniquity? and what is my sin before thy father, that he seeketh my life?" (1 Sam. 20:1). Take note of Jonathan's response: "By no means! You shall not die! Indeed, my father will do nothing either great or small without first telling me. And why should my father hide this thing from me? It is not so!" (1 Sam. 20:2). Do you see how Jonathan thought the best of his father? He remembered Saul's promise to him (19:6), and he was slow to believe that it could be broken so soon. Matthew Henry comments:

> Jonathan, from a principle of filial respect to his father, was
> very loth to believe that he designed or would ever do so
> wicked a thing. . . . As became a dutiful son, [he] endeavoured to cover his father's shame, as far as was consistent
> with justice and fidelity to David.[13]

"Oh that my words were now written! Oh that they were printed in a book! That they were graven with an iron pen and lead in the rock for ever!" (Job 19:23–24). If only these words, if only this reverence, were inscribed on the tables of our hearts, then it might be well with us! How many disasters we might avoid! How many sorrows might be unknown to us! If only we were swift to believe the best, and slow to think the worst, of our parents!

> But from that mark how far [we] rove we see,
> [By] all this waste of wealth and loss of blood.[14]

How often I have sat with a young or middle-aged adult, whose life has been wrecked by drugs, divorce, and sins too shameful to mention—only to discover that one of the root causes was thinking the worst of a parent. How often I have counseled mature Christians, whose personal and spiritual life has been blighted by failing to follow Jonathan's example. The way of blessing is so simple—communicate, communicate, communicate!—but few there be that find it. Enter at this narrow gate; it leads to abundant life. Let your parents know you, and seek to know your parents.[15] Don't give up on them or hide your heart from them. Let Jonathan be your guide, that you may prosper in all you do.

Let's review what Jonathan has taught us. When our parent encourages us to sin, we appeal to our parent. Putting aside our fears, we speak the truth in love, in terms our parent can understand. If, after initial success, and promises of amendment from our parent, we hear rumors of a relapse, we think the best *until we have indisputable evidence* that he or she has failed to perform what was promised. We must consider the evidence against our parent, but when we do let us proceed as Jonathan did.

Having heard David out, having considered that the worst could be true, Jonathan said to him, "Whatever you say, I will do for you" (1 Sam. 20:4, NASB). They prudently decided that David should hide from Saul, while Jonathan tested the troubled waters of his father's soul. See how Jonathan expressed it: "When I have sounded out my father" (20:12, NASB). Well, now, . . . have you ever sounded out your own father? Have you fathomed the depths of his soul? If not, you must be judging him by appearances. Please do not assume the worst about a man you hardly know.

In the end Saul exploded in anger and cast a spear at Jonathan. "Then Jonathan arose from the table in fierce anger, . . . for he was grieved over David because his father had dishonored him" (20:34, NASB).[16] What can we learn from this?

The Courage to Honor

Some people might say, "We should learn not to take the risks that Jonathan took. If a parent is likely to get angry, leave that parent alone. Becoming a target for parental aggression is bad for everyone involved." This makes a lot of sense. Let me explain why I must give you different advice.

A wise pastor once said:

> *The Christian of all men needs courage and resolution.* Indeed there is nothing he does as a Christian, or can do, but is an act of valour. A cowardly spirit is beneath the lowest duty of a Christian: "Be thou strong and very courageous, that thou mayest . . ."—What? stand in battle against those warlike nations? No, but that thou mayest "observe to do according to all the law, which Moses my servant commanded thee" (Joshua 1:7). It requires more prowess and greatness of spirit to obey God faithfully, than to command an army of men; to be a Christian than a captain.[17]

It takes great courage to keep the first commandment with promise. It takes great courage to honor our parents with real communication, to allow them to know us and to seek to know them. But there are some very practical reasons why we should welcome the risks involved in real communication.

We all know the risks of confrontation—anger, accusations, and hurt feelings are among them. (These risks may be lessened by a humble spirit.) But how many of us have counted the cost of taking the safe way out? Let me tell you what I have learned about it. Nothing is more common in our culture than people who have given up on their parents. Though outwardly they may show them respect, inwardly they have dismissed their parents, deciding that they are unable or unwilling to meet their deepest needs. Yet these rejecters have not, like Jonathan, accomplished a diligent search for the truth. Instead they have assumed the worst in a moment of stress or sin. Having hidden the pain they feel, they have denied their parents the opportunity either to change their sinful ways or to defend their actions.

Consider what happens in appeals court if the convicted person had no opportunity to present a defense at his trial. *The verdict of the lower court is thrown out.* By this standard, most of us would have to throw out the guilty verdicts we have pronounced upon our parents.

Once we have rejected our parents, all things are possible for us. Rebellion, drugs, perverse relationships, divorce, mistrust of authority—all things are ours. But the truth is that often fear, if not coward-ice, is the root of all these troubles. We fear to act the part of Jonathan; we take the easy way out—and we never realize the price we have paid. But if taking the seemingly safe way out is your first priority, what business do you have naming the name of Christ? Was the cross the easy way out? Was the lion's den or the dungeon of Jer-emiah? Who told you that you could be a Christian without the cour-age of Jonathan?[18]

Fringe Benefits

On a more positive note, there is much to be gained from risking real communication with your parents. You might make a friend who knows more than you do.

You couldn't be more distant from your parents than I was from mine in my mid-twenties. Yet when my father died (nearly two decades later), I was surprised to see how much I missed him as a friend. I hadn't thought of him that way before, but we had really become friends. As soon as he was gone, it was only too apparent. Losing a friend is a painful experience, but I'll always be glad that I took the risk of opening up to him again. Getting on the right side of the Ten Commandments would have been enough reward. But I soon found, as you will, that the Lord adds fringe benefits to sweeten the deal.

If Ever a Son . . .

When Jonathan "sounded out" his father, did he tell him a lie?

> David's place was empty; so Saul said to Jonathan his son, "Why has the son of Jesse not come to the meal, either yester-day or today?" Jonathan then answered Saul, "David earnestly asked leave of me to go to Bethlehem, for he said, 'Please let me go, since our family has a sacrifice in the city, and my brother has commanded me to attend. And now, if I have found favor in your sight, please let me get away that I may see my brothers.' For this reason he has not come to the king's table." Then Saul's anger burned against Jonathan. (1 Sam. 20:27–30, NASB)

I used to think that Jonathan made this up, but Matthew Henry and Dr. Gill, among others, think David really did go to his family's sacrifice at Bethlehem. I am happy to concede the point to those who presume the best about our biblical heroes.[19]

See how shamefully Saul speaks to Jonathan: "You son of a perverse, rebellious woman! Do I not know that you are choosing the
son of Jesse to your own shame and to the shame of your mother's
nakedness?" (1 Sam. 20:30, NASB). If ever a son had reason to rage at
his father, Jonathan did. Yet see how he replied: "Why should he be
put to death? What has he done?" (20:32, NASB). He said nothing
about Saul's slanders against himself and his mother. He did not
accuse; he inquired. When Saul answered with a javelin, Jonathan
left "in fierce anger" (20:34), but he did not lash out at his father,
either physically or verbally. He knew how to be angry and sin not.
Let us strive to be like him.

Jonathan is our great example of self-control when dealing with
an abusive parent.[20] Satan will do everything he can, and the Lord
for our good may allow him, to tempt us into responding with hostility, anger, and blame. Let us not be ignorant of his devices.

After this incident we hear of Jonathan only once more before his
death. He makes a secret visit to David to "strengthen his hand in
God" (1 Sam. 23:16). Obviously he didn't tell Saul where he was
going. Being loyal to his father, to his friend, and to his God, he
knew where to draw the line on the first commandment with promise. We may have such knowledge too—*after* we have graduated
from that institution of higher learning, the school of Jonathan, the
son of Saul.

CHAPTER 7

The Example of Jesus

The Incarnation of our Lord is a sublime mystery, a fact, like light shining out of darkness, which we cannot explain. Comprehensible to faith, it transcends reason. There is no sensible reaction to it, none except awe and humility. We are standing on holy ground. Let us take our shoes from our feet, and pray that, unlike the bashful shepherd before the burning bush, we'll be quick to obey God's holy revelation.

"And the Word became flesh and dwelt among us" (John 1:14). God made Himself a man. He "made Himself of no reputation, taking the form of a servant, and coming in the likeness of men" (Phil. 2:7). He Himself became our great example.

What kind of a Man was this incarnate God? He was poor; He was humble; He was compassionate; He was fearless. He was the bane of hypocrites; He was the friend of sinners. He was all things to all people. The obvious question for us is this: How did He deal with His parents? I would skip the subject if I could; it is so far beyond me. I venture into it for my readers' sake.

Jesus is a good model for our time because He grew up with a stepparent. As close as He was to His Father, He lived in His stepfather's house. Therefore, we shall explore all of His parental relationships—with His Father in heaven, with His stepfather on earth, and, last but not least, with His mother.

"I Honor My Father"

When Jesus was disputing with the Pharisees, they asked Him:

> Say we not well that thou art a Samaritan, and hast a devil?
> Jesus answered, I have not a devil; but I honor my Father, and
> ye do dishonor me. (John 8:48–49)

This interchange inspired Matthew Henry to remark: "Though God has promised that those who honour Him He will honour, He never promised that *men* should honour them."[1] Or, as Jesus put it: "Remember the word that I said unto you, The servant is not greater than his lord. If they have persecuted me, they will also persecute you" (John 15:20).

The Lord Himself has assured us that, if we honor our parents by doing their will, we may expect to be insulted for it. Have you endured this kind of persecution? If you have, I congratulate you on your successful imitation of Christ. If you have not, may I suggest that you are missing something of value? Rather than dreading this form of derision from man, we should look forward to it, that in all things we may be like our Master.[2]

Let's get practical. Are your parents different? Are they immigrants with outlandish customs? Are they richer or poorer, more godly or more sinful, than your friends' parents? Do they have odd habits or eccentric ideas? These parental peculiarities, which seem so painful to the untutored adolescent—or adult—look more like opportunities when we have learned the mind of Christ. God blesses us for accepting the parents He gave us, whether they seem normal or peculiar. If the insults of man are more real to us than the blessing of God, we have much to learn about the Christian life. May God instruct us gently!

The subject of how Jesus honored His Father is worthy of a chapter of its own. Since time is short, and because it *was* a special situation, I shall simply point out the salient features of our Lord's observance of the first commandment with promise.

1. *Jesus did the will of His Father.* "I can do nothing of My own self . . . I do not seek My own will but the will of the Father who has sent Me" (John 5:30, MKJV). "The Father has not left Me alone, for I always do those things which please Him" (John 8:29, MKJV).

2. *Jesus spent time with His Father.* "And it happened in those days, that He went out into a mountain to pray, and He was spending the night in prayer to God" (Luke 6:12, MKJV). Notice that at this

time Christ had a decision to make—selecting the men who would establish the church and evangelize the world.

3. *Jesus poured out His heart to His Father.* He always obeyed Him; and in fulfilling His obedience, He expressed to His Father all that He was feeling.

> Then saith he unto them, My soul is exceeding sorrowful, even unto death: tarry ye here, and watch with me. And he went a little farther, and fell on his face, and prayed, saying, O my Father, if it be possible, let this cup pass from me: nevertheless not as I will, but as thou wilt. He went away again the second time, and prayed, saying, O my Father, if this cup may not pass away from me, except I drink it, thy will be done. (Matt. 26:38–39, 42)

4. *Jesus spoke well of His Father* and of their special relationship, too. "My Father love[s] me" (John 10:17). "I and my Father are one" (John 10:30). "My Father is greater than I" (John 14:28). "The cup which my Father hath given me, shall I not drink it?" (John 18:11). "Thinkest thou that I cannot now pray to my Father, and he shall presently give me more than twelve legions of angels?" (Matt. 26:53). "I appoint unto you a kingdom, as my Father hath appointed unto me" (Luke 22:29). Does any of this sound like your speaking about your parents?[3] "Faithful are the wounds of a friend" (Prov. 27:6).

There is one verse in particular that I would bring to your attention:

> All things are delivered unto me of my Father: and no man knoweth the Son, but the Father; neither knoweth any man the Father, save the Son, and he to whomsoever the Son will reveal him. (Matt. 11:27)

True, the incarnate God is a special case, but He is also our great example. Do you desire this kind of intimate relationship with your parents, to know them better than others do? God is pleased by such desires. If you don't feel that way, have you fully and humbly explained to your parents the real reasons you are not close to them?

Much more could be said about Christ's "I honor My Father," but it's enough to grasp the general idea. As Jesus said, "Go, and do thou likewise" (Luke 10:37).

The Example of Joseph

When it comes to "the honor that comes from the only God" (John 5:44), no man has acquired more of it than Joseph, the stepfa-

ther of Jesus. Though these three men, Noah, Daniel, and Job, were
with me; though Moses and Samuel stood before me; yet I would
maintain that Joseph excels them all. Why? God conferred on him an
honor beyond our comprehension—to be the parent and the teacher
of his own Messiah. Nor was Joseph selected at random for this
honor. No, as Matthew Henry has often remarked, "Those know best
how to command that know how to obey."[4] Joseph was such a man.
To judge from his behavior, and from the blessing of God upon him,
he was a man who honored his parents.

We know very little about Joseph. We know that he was poor, that
he was a carpenter, and that he was a just (or upright) man (Matt.
1:19). He was never "disobedient to the heavenly vision" (Acts
26:19).

> Then Joseph being raised from sleep did as the angel of the
> Lord had bidden him. (Matt. 1:24)

> Behold, the angel of the Lord appeareth to Joseph in a dream,
> saying, Arise, and take the young child and his mother, and
> flee into Egypt . . . When he arose, he took the young child
> and his mother by night, and departed into Egypt. (Matt.
> 2:13–14)

> But when Herod was dead, behold, an angel of the Lord
> appeareth in a dream to Joseph in Egypt, Saying, Arise, and
> take the young child and his mother, and go into the land of
> Israel: for they are dead which sought the young child's life.
> And he arose, and took the young child and his mother, and
> came into the land of Israel. But when he heard that Arche-
> laus did reign in Judea in the room of his father Herod, he
> was afraid to go thither: notwithstanding, being warned of
> God in a dream, he turned aside into the parts of Galilee.
> (Matt. 2:19–22)

Whatever God told him to do, Joseph did. It's as simple as that.
And that, I believe, was his chief qualification for the awesome task
God gave him. Simple obedience. Where do you suppose he learned
it? Not at school, for it's likely he never went to school.[5] He learned
obedience where most people do. He learned it at home.

No, I can't prove to you that Joseph honored his parents from his
youth. But it surely looks that way to me. I see it in the fruit of his
own life, and I see it in his Son's.[6]

The Temple Incident

Coming now to Christ's treatment of His earthly parents, we begin with the temple incident (Luke 2:41–51).

Jesus could have told His parents that He must be about His "Father's business" in the temple, but He didn't. Dr. John Gill suggests:

> He did not ask leave of them, since his stay was about an affair of his heavenly Father's; and therefore this action of Christ is not to be drawn into an example, or precedent for children, to act without consulting, or asking leave of their parents.[7]

Let us notice what we can about Christ's first recorded conversation with His mother. "His mother said to Him, 'Son, why hast thou thus dealt with us? behold, thy father and I have sought thee *sorrowing*'" (Luke 2:48, emphasis added).[8] The Greek word we translate *sorrowing* means more literally "greatly *distressed*" (*Interlinear Bible*). It is used three more times in the New Testament.

> And [the rich man] cried and said, Father Abraham, have mercy on me, and send Lazarus, that he may dip the tip of his finger in water, and cool my tongue; for I am *tormented* in this flame. But Abraham said, Son, remember that thou in thy lifetime receivedst thy good things, and likewise Lazarus evil things: but now he is comforted, and thou art *tormented*. (Luke 16:24–25, emphasis added)

> And they all wept sore, and fell on Paul's neck, and kissed him, *Sorrowing* most of all for the words which he spake, that they should see his face no more. And they accompanied him unto the ship. (Acts 20:37–38, emphasis added)

A word used to describe the torments of hell and the sorrow of close friends at their final parting—'tis a heavy word indeed. Suppose the Hope of the human race were committed to your care— and you lost Him! How would you feel?

Jesus makes clear by His reply that He has done nothing wrong. Obviously, He is delivering some kind of message to His parents. Let those who are able reduce it to writing![9]

What is more manageable—and more important for us—is the upshot of the whole affair: "And he went down with them, and came to Nazareth, and was subject unto them" (Luke 2:51). I love Matthew Henry's comment on this verse:

> Herein he hath given an example to children to be dutiful and obedient to their parents in the Lord. Being *made of a woman,* he was made under the law of the fifth commandment. . . . Though his parents were poor and mean [i.e., lowly], though his father was only his *supposed* father, yet he was *subject to them;* though he was *strong in spirit,* and *filled with wisdom,* nay though he was the Son of God, yet he was subject to his parents; how then will *they* answer it who, though foolish and weak, yet are disobedient to their parents?[10]

A question to be asked.

By now you should know better than to protest, "But *my* parents aren't like Joseph and Mary!" Neither were mine; but I dare say they were a lot closer to that holy couple than I am to the perfect Lamb of God.

Before we leave the temple story, we should notice the verse that follows (or concludes) it. Just after we hear of Christ's being subject to His parents, we are told: "And Jesus increased in wisdom and stature, and in favor with God and men" (Luke 2:52). It's too late for most of us to increase in stature, but if we desire to increase in wisdom and favor, we would do well to remember our Savior's example.

We have all fallen short of the glory of God; we have all been disobedient to our parents. Most of us can admit as much; but few of us, I think, have any idea that past disobedience may be causing current difficulties in our lives. The easiest way to determine if it is, is to examine our younger years, to note our disobedience, to express appropriate repentance to God (and to others, if our parents are still living), and to bring forth fruit worthy of repentance (see chap. 14). Then simply wait and see what changes.

I didn't take a simple or easy route to discovering that my past actions and attitudes were still hindering my growth in the Lord. But I can say without doubt that, whatever degree of wisdom has been granted to me, it has come in the years since I began to repent of rebellion against my parents.

Jesus and His Mother (John 2:1–12)

Before Jesus performed "this beginning of miracles," He had His only other recorded conversation with His mother.[11]

> And when they wanted wine, the mother of Jesus saith unto him, They have no wine. Jesus saith unto her, Woman, what

> have I to do with thee? mine hour is not yet come. His mother
> saith unto the servants, Whatsoever he saith unto you, do it.
> (John 2:3–5)

I wish we had this one on tape, because the tone of His words would be very revealing. The only thing that's clear to me is that these two had a very special relationship. Christ seems to have had two goals in mind—honoring His Father in heaven and honoring His mother on earth. (And you think *you've* got it tough because your parents are so different from each other!)

My favorite comment on this passage, though it won't satisfy everyone, is: "He reproved not His mother by what He said, who honored her by what He did."[12] We don't know for sure what He meant by His words, but we know that she trusted Him and that He did what she wanted.

We do well to remember this incident ourselves. When dealing with a child who understands the first commandment with promise, parents don't need to be bossy. They can just point out the problem and allow the child to be creative about the solution. I know Jesus was more creative than our kids are; but if His Spirit dwells in them, we shall be pleasantly surprised when we employ the methods of Mary.

Do you have (or did you have) this kind of special relationship with your parent, conveying much in a few words, and leaving other people guessing? Probably not. But if you *want* to have such a relationship—if you *wish* you had had such a relationship—you are well on the way to honoring your parent.

Who Is My Mother?

> There came then his brethren and his mother, and, standing
> without, sent unto him, calling him. And the multitude sat
> about him, and they said unto him, Behold, thy mother and
> thy brethren without seek for thee. And he answered them,
> saying, Who is my mother, or my brethren? And he looked
> round about on them which sat about him, and said, Behold
> my mother and my brethren! For whosoever shall do the will
> of God, the same is my brother, and my sister, and mother.
> (Mark 3:31–35)

This passage gives us opportunity to practice two fine arts—thinking the best of other people, and comparing Scripture with Scripture. Some commentators fail to practice the first art to their advantage. They assume that Mary and company were wanting to assert fleshly authority over Christ, to draw Him away from His ministry, and other such things—not one of which can be proven.

Here's how I look at it. For some reason, which has been hidden from us, Mary and Jesus' relatives came to see Him. Matthew 12:40 tells us specifically that they were "desiring to speak with [Him]." In anyone else this would be counted a virtue: should it be counted a sin for Mary? I don't see why. But Mark 3:31 adds another significant detail: ". . . they sent unto him, calling him." They didn't just stand and wait; they sent Him word that they were there. They interrupted His teaching. Was this a sin? Jesus never says so. Why should we? Thinking the best of Mary, she had what she considered an important reason to see Him, one that justified her in interrupting His lesson. That's all we know. Did she want Him to paint the fence back home? Did she come because of some family crisis? Was she worried about Him?[13] Your guess is as good as mine. But remember: Our guesses reveal a lot about us, but they don't tell us much about Mary.

Jesus used the interruption to make a point to His disciples. (What that point was, we'll discuss in a minute.) Then one of several things happened. He went right out to see His family, then continued His lesson; or He kept on teaching till the end of His lesson, then went out to talk to them; or at this time He never spoke to His mother. Of these three options, I like the first one best, I can live with the second well enough, and I don't care for the third one at all. But my preferences stem from my ideas about the message Christ was teaching by example.

"For whosoever shall do the will of God, the same is my brother, and my sister, and mother." Jesus was saying that everyone who obeys God is a member of His spiritual family. But how does Jesus treat that family? Well, how did He treat His natural family at this particular time? To me it seems likely that Christ encouraged His disciples with this teaching, and then *demonstrated* its meaning by going out to see His natural family. If this is what He did, a disciple might have observed, "I am a member of Christ's family. No matter how busy He is, no matter how surrounded with multitudes, He will take time for me. When I come to Him with a need, He will meet that need. He will not disown His near relations or put them off with excuses."

Although my idea is different from most interpretations of this passage, please consider it for a moment. Remember that Mary was a member of Christ's spiritual family too: "[Then] Mary said, Behold the handmaid of the Lord; be it unto me according to thy word" (Luke 1:38). She was one who did the will of God. If He didn't go out to see her, He won't go out to see you either, when you come to Him with a need. But hear what the Scriptures say: "Come unto me all ye that labor and are heavy laden, and I will give you rest" (Matt. 11:28). How will He give you rest, if He won't come out to see you? "If any man thirst, let him come unto me and drink" (John 7:37). How will you drink, if you can't get near the River? How shall we come boldly to the throne of grace, if Mary (the obedient disciple) couldn't get a word with her Son? Jesus stopped what He was doing to heal a blind beggar; I think He was willing to do as much for His mother.

"Ah!" you say, "away with this indirect reasoning: it's *direct evidence from Scripture* we need. You can't prove what you're saying from the words in the Bible." Perhaps not, but I can come a lot closer to it than you think. Consider the evidence:

> For whosoever shall do the will of God, the same is my brother, and my sister, and mother. And he *began again* to teach by the seaside: and there was gathered unto him a great multitude. (Mark 3:35—4:1, emphasis added)

We have two pieces of direct evidence to support what I am saying. First, none of the evangelists reports any further teaching of Jesus in that same location. They all pick up the narrative again by the sea. Second, Mark says clearly that Jesus "began again" to teach by the sea. What makes this remarkable is that these Greek words appear together *nowhere else in the New Testament*. Both words are used dozens of times, but only here are they used together. If Mark's meaning were, "Once more Jesus was teaching by the sea," we might expect to find the expression used elsewhere, for Jesus often taught by the sea.[14] Mark is the only evangelist who uses the expression, "began to teach," and he uses it several times.[15] Yet only here does he say that Christ "began *again* to teach," as if He were continuing after an interruption.

Putting the evidence together, I find that my positive interpretation of the passage fits well with the language of Mark. Jesus encouraged His disciples, went out to see His mother, and, possibly after some rest and refreshment, continued His teaching in a new location, where there was room to accommodate the crowd.

One of the cardinal principles of this book is that parents are innocent until, in the language of the courts, they are *proven guilty beyond a reasonable doubt*. Have I been able to produce a reasonable doubt in your mind that Mary did anything wrong? Then you are bound to hold her innocent, or else to discard my teaching. Please, if you can, do the former.

Before we leave this difficult passage, let's approach it from another angle. Jesus said of Himself, "A greater [One] than Solomon is here." Jesus was like Solomon, only greater (and, of course, without sin). Well, what about the day Solomon's mother came to see him?

> So Bathsheba went to King Solomon to speak to him for Adonijah. And the king arose to meet her, bowed before her, and sat on his throne; then he had a throne set for the king's mother, and she sat on his right. (1 Kings 2:19, NASB)

Jesus acted very differently from Solomon, if, as many people think, He spurned His mother when she called for Him.[16]

Instead of applying this passage negatively toward Mary, why don't we apply it positively toward ourselves? Let us rejoice that we are members of Christ's family. Let us rest secure in our relationship with Him. And while we're at it, why not grant Mary the same privileges her Son bestows so freely upon us?

Mary at the Cross

In our first three incidents Mary took the initiative. In the temple, at the wedding, and while He was teaching, she communicated with Jesus first. But at the cross she had nothing to say. At the cross she was silent. No doubt she communicated by her looks, but only Jesus spoke.

> When Jesus therefore saw his mother, and the disciple standing by, whom he loved, he saith unto his mother, Woman, behold thy son! Then saith he to the disciple, Behold thy mother! And from that hour that disciple took her unto his own home. (John 19:26–27)

In His dying agony Jesus provided for His mother. He thought not of His own interests, but of the interests of others (Phil. 2:4). But of all the others in the world, on the cross He mentioned only three individuals—Mary, John, and the thief. Some of His utterances from the cross were necessitated by the Scriptures: there were prophecies He must fulfill.[17] There was no prophetic necessity, as far as I can see, behind His words to these three individuals. However, notice that immediately after He provides for Mary, Scripture tells us: "After this, Jesus *knowing that all things were now accomplished*" (John

19:28, emphasis added). This seems to give added significance to His last words to Mary and John. Caring for His mother—and also for His bride[18]—was essential: all things were not accomplished till this last work was done.

If you have an older parent without visible means of support, you should be providing for that parent (see 1 Tim. 5:8). Perhaps you have a parent who needs your time or your emotional support. If your priorities are like Christ's on the cross, your parent's needs will rank with the essential things of life.

CHAPTER 8

The Teaching of Jesus

Christians and tightrope walkers have a lot in common. They need to keep looking where they're going; they have to concentrate on every step they take; and they need to remember that they can't fly. That's what motivates them to keep their balance.

A tightrope walker who's always losing his balance may not fall to the ground, but he'll sure take a long time to get where he has to go. That's why Satan tempts us to focus on one part of Scripture, while ignoring some others. By keeping us off balance, he can render us ineffective. He tempted Jesus the same way in the wilderness, but for our sakes the Messiah kept Himself erect. He knew how much we would need His example.

Christ clearly upheld the first commandment with promise, but He always balanced it with "the first and great commandment" (Matt. 22:36–38). In teaching His disciples to honor their parents, He focused their minds on their Father in heaven. We'll look first at His teaching to keep our commandment; then we'll look at the limits He placed on its keeping.

Jesus Upholds the Commandment

With the Pharisees

The Pharisees were pious men who had lost their spiritual balance. In the time of the Maccabees, when most of the Jews were hankering after the ways of the world, the Pharisees had remained faithful to the Old Testament law: "The [original] Pharisees were men of strong religious character; they were the best people in the nation. Subsequently Pharisaism became an inherited belief."[1]

The Gospels reveal the condition of the later Pharisees. Their religion was external, more of the hand than the heart; their leaders were vain, the persecutors of Christ. Though good men could still be found among them, Jesus and John the Baptist both referred to the group as a "generation of vipers" (Matt. 3:7; 23:33).

When He was challenged by the Pharisees, our Lord could have named a hundred sins of theirs. Yet He mentioned only one.

> And he said unto them, Full well ye reject the commandment of God, that ye may keep your own tradition. For Moses said, Honor thy father and thy mother; and, Whoso curseth father or mother, let him die the death: But ye say, If a man shall say to his father or mother, It is Corban, that is to say, a gift, by whatsoever thou mightest be profited by me; he shall be free. And ye suffer him no more to do aught for his father or his mother; Making the word of God of none effect through your tradition, which ye have delivered: and many such like things do ye. (Mark 7:9–13)

The Pharisees loved money. One way they obtained more of it was by teaching that giving to the temple took precedence over giving to one's parents. These men, who loved to devour widows' houses (Matt. 23:14), were equally happy to consume the sustenance of aged parents. If they had been simple armed robbers, Christ would have had less to say to them. But when they cloaked their thievery in the righteousness of His Father's house, it was more than He could bear.

Did you notice that Jesus upheld the death penalty for a man who cursed his parents? Think about that. Say what you will about the Jews being under the law, being children of the Old Covenant, etc., yet the fact remains. Our Lord considered cursing one's parents a capital offense.[2] I am not suggesting that we hang every adolescent who curses his father. I am suggesting that you "Let this mind be in you which was also in Christ Jesus," and that you give due reverence to your father and mother.

In this passage Christ also taught that we must provide for our parents.[3] His emphasis was on financial needs, but we need not limit His teaching to economics. Some of us have parents who are wealthier than we are. Have we no obligation to them? Look at it this way. We think poorly of a parent who has provided his children all that money can buy, but who has withheld from them his time, his affection, or his love. What, then, of the adult child who pays his parents' bills—or because they are wealthy, does nothing—but deprives them of his (or his children's) company and love? Is this fulfilling the first commandment with promise? You know what I think.

Considering the emphasis Christ lays on our commandment, we could hardly be too careful in making sure that we have not broken it. If we give to our church or its members the time, the energy, the money, or the affection that should be going to our parents; if we are too busy with "the Lord's work" to render honor or obedience to our father or mother; then we may be guilty of the sin for which Christ rebuked the Pharisees. I can't decide this issue for you. But you could spend your time a lot worse than in thinking and praying about it.

With the Rich Young Ruler

Everyone knows the story of the rich young ruler. Not everyone keeps in mind his original question: "Good Master, what good thing shall I do, that I may have eternal life?" (Matt. 19:16). Brushing aside the theological thickets of faith and works, I point to Jesus' reply: "If thou wilt enter into life, keep the commandments." If you want to enter into life, honor your father and mother. You may not accept all my ideas on the observation of this duty; but I hope my efforts stimulate you to ponder the subject for yourself.

In all three accounts of this story, Christ places the first commandment with promise *after* the other commandments. Commentators have different explanations (none too convincing) about this departure from the usual order. The one I like best is by Alexander Jones:

> [Jesus] doubtless surprises the youth when he lays down as necessary conditions the elementary prohibitions of the Decalogue. . . . But *he passes then to positive commands* that admit of degrees of perfection in their observance. First, the young man's duty to his parents . . . ; secondly, the great precept of charity toward one's fellows.[4]

Whether or not Jones' is the proper explanation, he makes a very important point. Our commandment is a positive commandment.

However you count the Ten Commandments (see introduction), you will find that eight of the ten are prohibitions. Only two of the commandments, keeping the Sabbath and honoring parents, are positive duties. Christians have differing ideas about how our observation of the Sabbath is modified under the New Covenant, but they all agree that it has been changed. Yet no one, as far as I know, has suggested any modification of the first commandment with promise. Ours, then, is the only positive command in the Decalogue with unchanged New Testament support. Does this seem like nit-picking to you? To me it seems like another important honor Scripture pays to our commandment, one I had missed entirely in my research for this book.

The great commands of Jesus are positive commands:

> Jesus said unto him, Thou shalt love the Lord thy God with all thy heart, and with all thy soul, and with all thy mind. (Matt. 22:37)

> Thou shalt love thy neighbor as thyself. (Matt. 22:39)

> Love one another. (John 13:34; 15:12, 17)

> This do in remembrance of me. (Luke 22:19)

> Go ye therefore, and teach all nations. (Matt. 28:19)

Of all the words Jehovah spoke publicly from Mount Sinai, only the first commandment with promise remains positive and unchanged. It keeps company with the great commands of Jesus. It is a commandment with staying power. How appropriate that the words which promise us length of days have such a long life of their own!

Jesus Limits the Commandment

To increase their power and wealth, the Pharisees had distorted a basic truth: God's honor must come before our parents'. Undeterred by their sinful application of it, Jesus taught us how to observe this priority.

> He that loveth father or mother more than me is not worthy of me: and he that loveth son or daughter more than me is not worthy of me. And he that taketh not his cross, and followeth after me, is not worthy of me. He that findeth his life shall lose it: and he that loseth his life for my sake shall find it. (Matt. 10:37–39)

> If any man come to me, and hate not his father, and mother, and wife, and children, and brethren, and sisters, yea, and his own life also, he cannot be my disciple. And whosoever doth not bear his cross, and come after me, cannot be my disciple. (Luke 14:26–27)

Forsaking one's family for the Lord's sake can be a great trial for a Christian. If it is done according to the will of God, it is a true spiritual sacrifice. It is a form of bearing the cross, of following Christ, of losing one's life for the Lord. Believers must support and strengthen those Christians whose walk with the Lord requires them to break away from their families. How else shall they receive "a hundredfold now in this time . . . brethren, and sisters and mothers and children . . . with persecutions" (Mark 10:30)—unless we become their family and friends?

I wish I were the only believer whose self-righteous "zeal for the Lord" had ever caused him to sin against his parents. If you came to Christ from an unbelieving family, and honored your father and mother in the process, you have far excelled this poor author. You should be teaching me. It takes wisdom to implement Christ's warning without falling into sin, and not every new Christian abounds in such discernment. (If only as mature believers we exercised that grace!) It's easy to abuse our Lord's teaching that we must put Him first, and hard to keep it without sinning against others. May God guide us in loving Him more than our parents—and keep us from violating the first commandment with promise!

Jesus taught us by example how to "hate"[5] our father and mother (see chap. 7). He put "His Father's business" before all else; He put spiritual relationships before natural ones; and He was careful always to do the will of His Father in heaven. Yet He submitted himself to His parents and their authority; He did not (as I see it) deny the bonds of nature; and He provided for His mother before He died. It is no small assignment, I know, but let us strive for the same balance in our own lives.

"No One Is Good but One"

While I was writing this chapter, a young man stopped by my office, seemingly just to visit. But as he soon referred to serious trouble in his marriage, we drifted into informal counseling. He admitted that at home, at work, and in general, continual conflict with women was making his life miserable. It was not well with him. When I inquired about his relationship with his mother, things heated up in a hurry. He blamed her for his parents' divorce when he was young, and that blame dominated their relationship. It certainly seemed clear to me why he was having trouble with women.

Then I asked him for evidence—that would stand up in court, of course—that the divorce was really his mom's fault. There was none at all. This got me to thinking: *Why does he blame his mother, when his father deserted the family? Why not blame Dad, or at least divide the blame between them?* It took some time to get to the bottom line, but when we did, it went something like this: "I'm a man, just like my dad. If my dad's bad, I must be bad, too. But if it's my mom's fault, I could still be good." He thus had, according to the sinful logic which flesh is heir to, a vital reason to dishonor his mother.

This intelligent, conscientious, Christian young man was unconsciously breaking the commandments of God. He was, in effect, ascribing his righteousness to his earthly father, and not to Christ. No matter how you slice it, no matter who falls into it, this is idolatry. Idolizing his father caused him to dishonor his mother. Dishonoring his mother, in turn, ruined his relationships with women. As I saw it, the root of his problem was loving his father more than God. Persisting in this unconscious sin, he found himself in bondage. Thank God that our righteousness is in Christ, and not in ourselves or our parents! "Why do you call Me good? No one is good but One, that is, God" (Matt. 19:17; Mark 10:18; Luke 18:19). There is freedom in such teaching, which we too often take for granted.

Not Peace, but Division

Of course there are more obvious ways to put our parents before the Lord. We may fail to receive Christ or fail to confess Him publicly, because we fear our parents. We may choose a profession or a spouse that pleases them but denies our calling from God. Would David's mother have urged him to go forth against Goliath? Did Matthew's father suggest leaving a lucrative practice to follow a no-account Prophet? (In chaps. 12 and 13 I suggest a Christian approach to such dilemmas.) We must do the will of God when it differs from the will of our parents. But I caution you: it is more common today for young people to miss the will of God by forsaking their parents' instruction, than to miss His will by putting their parents first.

Our Lord was careful to help us count the cost of following Him:

> Suppose ye that I am come to give peace on earth? I tell you, Nay; but rather division: For from henceforth there shall be five in one house divided, three against two, and two against three. The father shall be divided against the son, and the son against the father; the mother against the daughter, and the daughter against the mother; the mother-in-law against her daughter-in-law, and the daughter-in-law against her mother-in-law. (Luke 12:51–53)

If you wonder, as I have, why the mother-in-law/daughter-in-law combination is singled out, I propose a practical solution. When a woman was widowed, she was likely to move into her son's home. Over the years of her widowhood, there would be abundant opportunities for conflict with her daughter-in-law, particularly if only one of the two were a Christian. As widows were more numerous and more dependent than widowers, Jesus was merely emphasizing the domestic trials most likely to occur.

For the Lord's sake, we must be willing to endure division, strife, or separation from our loved ones. We must make it clear to them that Christ is the Lord of our lives. But we must do it humbly; we must suffer, if need be, charitably. We must return good for evil, guarding our hearts against holier-than-thou hypocrisy. If we do all these things, still honoring our parents when they dishonor the Lord, then the blessing of God shall rest upon us.

The Cost of Discipleship

I shall close this chapter with two of our Lord's more difficult teachings.

> And he said unto another, Follow me. But he said, Lord, suffer me first to go and bury my father. Jesus said unto him, Let the dead bury their dead: but go thou and preach the kingdom of God. And another also said, Lord, I will follow thee; but let me first go bid them farewell, which are at home at my house. And Jesus said unto him, No man, having put his hand to the plow, and looking back, is fit for the kingdom of God. (Luke 9:59–62)

Most commentators agree that in the first situation the disciple was literally about to bury his dead father. Alfred Edersheim comments feelingly on this passage:

> No doubt Christ had here in view the near call to the Seventy—of whom this disciple was to be one—to "go and preach the Kingdom of God." When the direct call of Christ to any work comes—that is, if we are *sure* of it from His own words, and not (as, alas! too often we do) only infer it by our own reasoning on His words—then every other call must give way. For, duties can never be in conflict—and this duty about the living and life must take precedence of that about death and the dead. Nor must we hesitate, because we know not in what form this work for Christ may come. There are critical moments in our inner history, when to postpone the immedi-

> ate call is really to reject it; when to go and bury the dead—
> even though it were a dead father—were to die ourselves![6]

An author honors such teaching by adding nothing to it; a reader, by pausing to ponder it.

For me it has been no easy matter to reconcile the second part of Christ's teaching with the calling of Elisha.

> So he departed thence, and found Elisha the son of Shaphat, who was plowing with twelve yoke of oxen before him, and he with the twelfth: and Elijah passed by him, and cast his mantle upon him. And he left the oxen, and ran after Elijah, and said, Let me, I pray thee, kiss my father and my mother, and then I will follow thee. And he said unto him, Go back again: for what have I done to thee? And he returned back from him, and took a yoke of oxen, and slew them, and boiled their flesh with the instruments of the oxen, and gave unto the people, and they did eat. Then he arose, and went after Elijah, and ministered unto him. (1 Kings 19:19–21)

It is not good to take Scripture piecemeal. If we would be well grounded in God's Word, if we would make proper interpretation of a particular verse, we must seek out related passages, and by them test our teaching. If we would comment on the would-be disciple, we must compare him to Elisha. For as Rev. John Trapp wrote on this occasion, "Christ here happily alludeth to that which Elisha did, 1 Kings 19:19."[7]

After much thought and some prayer on the proper relationship of these two stories, it seems to me that the deciding factor between them is the call of God. Elisha was called to his work; the would-be disciple in Luke, as far as we know, was not. His case is therefore entirely different from Elisha's—and from the man's whose father had just died. There is little difference in their requests; there is a great difference in their circumstances.

You cannot call yourself to preach the gospel.[8] When you are called, you may say or do what you will. You may make excuses, as Moses and Jeremiah did; you may grieve over your sins with Isaiah; you may sail for Tarshish with Jonah; you may feast with Matthew and Elisha; or, you may simply leave your nets and follow the Lord. God knows that He will have His way in your life at last. However poorly you respond at the beginning, He will not reject you.[9]

The would-be disciple was not called.[10] With this self-disqualifying statement, he put himself forward as a disciple of the Master: "Lord, I will follow You, but . . . . " Charles Spurgeon devoted an entire sermon to these words, to dissuade his hearers from ever using them. We, too, should train ourselves to avoid them. If they never come into our minds, they will never come out of our mouths.

In any event, it is clear that respect for parents can be, but need not be, a hindrance to those who serve the Lord. It is idolatry to place a parent's wishes before the call of God. However, as we see from the case of Elisha, the man whose heart belongs to his Maker will be granted occasion to honor his parents.

CHAPTER 9

The Apostle Paul's Teaching

There is commonly one good result that comes from dishonoring our parents. Sometimes when we upset them, they utter things they never planned to tell us. When the apostle Paul was provoked by his wayward children in Corinth, and felt he had to defend his apostleship, he told them he had been "caught up to the third heaven. . . . [I] was caught up into Paradise and heard inexpressible words, which it is not lawful for a man to utter" (2 Cor. 12:2, 4). His experience must have been beyond all human imagining, for Paul was given a "thorn in the flesh," "lest I should be exalted above measure by the abundance of the revelations" (v. 7). When I consider what a thorn in his flesh the Corinthian church was already, I marvel that any additional ballast was needed to keep the apostle from soaring too high.

Though his thoughts were often in the clouds, Paul could be very down-to-earth. He had plenty of practical advice for the disciples of the Lord. He taught us more about the first commandment with promise than all the other apostles put together.[1] We shall examine his doctrine under three separate headings—obedience and respect, gratitude, and spiritual relationships.

Obedience and Respect

We have already examined Paul's reiteration of our commandment (see chap. 3). Here we shall look at it in more detail, and compare it to related passages in the apostle's letters.

> Children, obey your parents in the Lord: for this is right. Honor thy father and mother; which is the first commandment with promise; That it may be well with thee, and thou mayest live long on the earth. And, ye fathers, provoke not your children to wrath: but bring them up in the nurture and admonition of the Lord. (Eph. 6:1–4)

> Children, obey your parents in all things: for this is well-pleasing unto the Lord. Fathers, provoke not your children to anger, lest they be discouraged. (Col. 3:20–21)

Perhaps the first question that occurs to you is, "What does Paul mean when he says, 'Obey your parents *in the Lord*'?" Here is Dr. Gill's comment on the emphasized words:

> [They] may be considered either as a limitation of the obedience, that it should be in things that are agreeable to the mind and will of the Lord; or as an argument to [perform] it, because it is the command of the Lord, and is well-pleasing in his sight, and makes for his glory, and therefore should be done for his sake.[2]

The words "in the Lord" both limit and incite our obedience. We should refuse to obey commands or requests which will cause us to sin, and we should be quick to obey in all other matters. *In doubtful matters, we should obey our parents.* The Lord knows how to make our duty clear in those uncommon times when we must disobey them.

Notice that in both Ephesians and Colossians, our commandment is followed by advice to fathers on how to raise their children.[3] Parents are to encourage, discipline, and instruct their offspring; they are not to frustrate or provoke them. Have your parents failed to do their part? You are still obliged to do yours. The Lord blesses His children who honor their sinful or negligent parents.

Perhaps the easiest way to illustrate this principle is to look a little further into the contexts of our commandment. In both cases the apostle speaks next of servants and masters (see Col. 3:22—4:1 and Eph. 6:5–9). There is a parallel passage in 1 Peter, which may well be applied to children and parents:[4]

> Servants, [be] subject to [your] masters with all fear, not only to those good and forbearing, but also to the perverse ones. For this [is] a grace, if for conscience [toward] God anyone endures grief, suffering wrongfully. For what glory [is it] if you patiently endure [while] sinning and being buffeted? But if you suffer [while] doing good, and patiently endure, this [is] a

> grace from God. For you were not called to this? For Christ
> also suffered on our behalf, leaving us an example, that you
> should follow His steps, He who did no sin, nor was guile
> found in His mouth, who when He was reviled did not revile
> in return. When He suffered, He did not threaten, but gave
> [Himself] up to Him who judges righteously. (1 Pet. 2:18–23,
> MKJV)

I know full well that, in asking you to honor a harsh parent, I am
asking a hard thing. Passages like this one cause us to see our inadequacy and make us cry out to God for His grace. Yet a Christian
should never be dismayed because the commandments of God seem
impossible to perform. He who sent Moses to Pharaoh, who
watched over Daniel in the lion's den, who commanded His fisher
friends to take on the world—may He not fitly ask you to bear with
your parents?

If your parents are unbelievers, unkind, or unjust—or just believers whose actions disgrace their calling—I have a word of encouragement for you. When God gave you to them, He knew what He
was doing. He knew full well that you would come to believe in
Christ, and that your faith, for better or for worse, would become visible to your parents. Have you ever thought of yourself as God's personal messenger to your father and mother? Whether He sent you to
them for their salvation, their instruction, or their being without
excuse on the last day—you are a messenger from Him. Your actions
and attitudes, as well as your words, should be revealing His light in
the dark places of the earth. The greater the darkness of the family
you were born into, the greater the honor you have received from
God. He has trusted you with this difficult assignment. He knows
better than you do how inadequate you are for the task. Instead of
complaining about the misery you were born into, try waking up to
the special honor such misery implies. As you do, I am confident
that you will draw closer to God, regretting that you have not been a
better ambassador, and rejoicing that He has trusted you to be a light
for Him.

I must insert a word here about dealing with severely abusive parents. Whether the abuse is physical or emotional, God does not
require children to simply grin and bear it. "To every thing there is a
season, a time to every purpose under the heaven" (Eccl. 3:1). There
is a time to flee or take refuge from abuse.[5] There may even be a
time for self-defense. I can do no better than to refer you to chapter
6, to the examples of Jonathan and David. "So David fled, and
escaped, and came to Samuel to Ramah, and told him all that Saul

had done to him. And he and Samuel went and dwelt in Naioth" (1 Sam. 19:18). Be sure that your flight, if there must be one, is to a godly and responsible person—one capable, as Samuel was, of telling you your faults.

Disobedient to Parents

Twice in his epistles St. Paul employs the phrase "disobedient to parents." In both instances it occurs in a list. If we may know a man by the company he keeps, we ought to consider the company in which Scripture casts this phrase:

> And even as they did not like to retain God in their knowledge, God gave them over to a reprobate mind, to do those things which are not convenient; Being filled with all unrighteousness, fornication, wickedness, covetousness, maliciousness; full of envy, murder, debate, deceit, malignity; whisperers, Backbiters, haters of God, despiteful, proud, boasters, inventors of evil things, *disobedient to parents*, Without understanding, covenantbreakers, without natural affection, implacable, unmerciful. (Rom. 1:28–31, emphasis added)

> This know also, that in the last days perilous times shall come. For men shall be lovers of their own selves, covetous, boasters, proud, blasphemers, *disobedient to parents*, unthankful, unholy, Without natural affection, trucebreakers, false accusers, incontinent, fierce, despisers of those that are good, Traitors, heady, high-minded, lovers of pleasures more than lovers of God; Having a form of godliness, but denying the power thereof: from such turn away. (2 Tim. 3:1–5, emphasis added)

Are you or your friends disobedient to or disrespectful of your parents? Then you are likely to be heir to some of the other qualities listed here. While all of them are hateful to a godly soul, let me draw your attention to the last one mentioned.

"Having a form of godliness but denying its power"—this is a dangerous condition. The Pharisees cloaked their sins with a form of godliness, and our Lord warned them, "Verily I say unto you, That the publicans and the harlots go into the kingdom of God before you" (Matt. 21:31). The obvious sins of the flesh are more easily known and abhorred than the self-righteous sins of the hypocrite. A condemned murderer is more likely to repent than a proud and successful pastor.

The Greek word for "disobedient," which Paul employs in "disobedient to parents," also occurs in Titus. Speaking there of reprobates, the apostle says, "They profess that they know God; but in works they deny him, being abominable, and *disobedient*, and unto every good work reprobate" (Titus 1:16, emphasis added). It is bad enough to be disobedient, but trebly so when we justify our sin. If we have a form of godliness—if we profess to know God, but use our religion to excuse our disobedience—our condition is truly perilous. Yet I testify to you that that condition is a common one among modern Christians. There are many today who imagine that they are mature in Christ, but who live in violation of the first commandment with promise. (Before you conclude that I cannot be speaking of you, please examine chap. 10.)

We Respected Them

Authors of Christian books are always looking for Scripture to support their arguments. This makes us susceptible to "proof-texting," or wrenching verses from their context to strengthen our pet theories. This can be accomplished in a number of ways. One, which I particularly dislike, is to treat a passing reference to a subject as if it were a direct teaching on that subject.

You will have perceived from this introduction that I am about to present a secondary teaching. It occurs in Hebrews 12, a passage on God's discipline and His dealing with us as His sons. In the midst of it, the apostle adds:

> Furthermore we have had fathers of our flesh which corrected us, and we gave them reverence: shall we not much rather be in subjection unto the Father of spirits, and live? For they verily for a few days chastened us after their own pleasure; but he for our profit, that we might be partakers of his holiness. (Heb. 12:9–10)

Obeying parents is not the issue here, but we can glean some practical wisdom from this passage. "We have had human fathers who corrected us, and we gave them reverence." I infer that among religious Jews of the first century it was normal to accept paternal correction, to respect the fathers who applied it, and to live in subjection to them. What interests me most is the Greek verb for "give reverence" or "pay respect." It comes from a root meaning *to turn*, and a scholarly Greek lexicon gives the meaning here as "to turn toward something or someone, have regard for, respect."[6] The image that comes to mind for me is of a small child, having received a spanking, turning to embrace the parent that applied it.

As we learn to respect our parents, we turn toward them when they correct us; we deal with them face to face; we communicate openly and honestly with them. We do not bury our feelings; we do not assume that our parents cannot understand or sympathize with us; we do not obey them outwardly and despise them inwardly. In other words, I believe we have much to learn from the Hebrew Christians who received this life-changing letter.

Do Not Rebuke

From Paul's advice to Timothy, we can glean further guidance on how to treat our parents:

> Rebuke not an elder, but entreat him as a father; and the younger men as brethren; The elder women as mothers; the younger as sisters, with all purity. (1 Tim. 5:1–2)

We are to treat our spiritual family as we ought to treat our natural family. We should esteem the elder members of our church, as we esteem our parents. In truth, the more you keep the first commandment with promise, the more you will be a blessing to your congregation. The less you keep the first commandment with promise . . .

The Greek word for *entreat* in this passage means "appeal to, urge, exhort, encourage."[7] The word for *rebuke* means "strike at, rebuke, reprove." Could the difference be much clearer? Dr. Gill makes a number of interesting observations here.

> Now an ancient man, a member of a church, is not to be rebuked in a sharp and severe way; the word here used signifies to smite or strike . . . meaning not with the hand, but with the tongue, giving hard words, which are as heavy blows . . . *but entreat* him *as a father,* as a child should entreat a father, when he is going out of the way: give him honour and respect, fear and reverence, and persuade him to desist; entreat and beseech him to return to the right path of truth and holiness.[8]

I hope you have treated your parents in this way. If you have not, it can hardly be well with you until you repent.

Later in the same chapter, Paul counsels us: "Do not receive an accusation against an elder except before two or three witnesses" (1 Tim. 5:19, MKJV). Here he is speaking not of aged Christians, but of the leaders who must rule in the church. For our current purposes this makes little difference: Parents have positions of authority in our lives, as well as greater age. When someone makes an accusation against your father or mother (whether living or dead), do not receive it. If the evidence presented seems sufficient, you may investigate the truth of the charge; but be careful to hold your parent innocent until he or she is proven guilty.

Gratitude

Between the two passages we have just studied, Paul encourages gratitude to parents.

> Honor widows that are widows indeed. But if any widow have children or nephews, let them learn first to show piety at home, and to requite their parents: for that is good and acceptable before God. (1 Tim. 5:3–4)

Here Paul reinforces Christ's teaching that caring for needy parents is among the first duties of a Christian. I am guilty of understatement. Though Jesus spoke clearly and forcefully on this point, Paul goes further still: "But if anyone does not provide for his own, and especially his family, he has denied the faith and is worse than an infidel" (1 Tim. 5:8, MKJV). "Worse than an unbeliever"! May none of us be guilty of this sin!

Most of us have heard the saying, "Charity begins at home." Yet few of us know its original context:

> *Charity begins at home,* is the voice of the World . . .
>   That a man should lay down his life for his Friend, seems strange to vulgar affections, and such as confine themselves within that Worldly principle, *Charity begins at home.*[9]

Despite such negative reviews from wise old Sir Thomas Browne, it may be that this "Worldly principle" is but a distortion of the scriptural truth: "Let them first learn to show piety at home and to repay their parents." If we should lavish money on ourselves and our relatives, while ignoring the destitute members of Christ's Body, we should prove Sir Thomas right. We would be imitating the tax collectors (Matt. 5:46) rather than the repentant Zacchaeus.

On the other hand, Christ and Paul are both emphatic that, before we give to others, we must first care for our parents. We should not, however, make our parents—or anything else—an excuse for not tithing to the church. Thus, we come to Rosenbaum's corollary: *Charity begins at home, but it never ends there.*

I note with interest that in the same paragraph in which he decries "Charity begins at home," Sir Thomas refers to the subject of this book. "I hope I do not break the fifth Commandment," he says, "if I conceive I may love my friend before the nearest of my blood, even those to whom I owe the principles of life." The first commandment with promise is often in the thoughts of a righteous man.

A Good Inheritance

Paul begins his second letter by reminding Timothy of the great spiritual blessings they had both received from their ancestors.

> I thank God, whom I serve from my forefathers with pure conscience, that without ceasing I have remembrance of thee in my prayers night and day . . . When I call to remembrance the unfeigned faith that is in thee, which dwelt first in thy grandmother Lois, and thy mother Eunice; and I am persuaded that in thee also. Wherefore I put thee in remembrance that thou stir up the gift of God, which is in thee by the putting on of my hands. (2 Tim. 1:3, 5–6)

Before he speaks about what he himself has done for Timothy, he remembers the "pure conscience" of his own forefathers and the "unfeigned faith" of Lois and Eunice. This is the proper order for a Christian. We should seek out teachers like Paul, who honor the godly souls who went before us in this life. If we are thankful as we should be for an ancestor who built up the wealth of our family, how much more should we remember those who have provided a spiritual heritage for their descendants?

Unthankful

We have already examined 2 Timothy 3:1–5, where "disobedient to parents" occurs in a descriptive list of the perils of the last days. Now we will consider more closely the word, "unthankful," which immediately follows that phrase. As Paul's word order makes clear, disobedience and ingratitude are usually found together. Has Satan, since his fall, ever been grateful to God? The more we count our blessings, the more likely we are to obey.

At the end of his life, Moses warned Israel in a prophecy that is relevant to the subject at hand:

> Because thou servedst not the Lord thy God with joyfulness, and with gladness of heart, for the abundance of all things; Therefore shalt thou serve thine enemies which the Lord shall send against thee, in hunger, and in thirst, and in nakedness, and in want of all things: and he shall put a yoke of iron upon thy neck, until he have destroyed thee. (Deut. 28:47–48)

A grateful spirit is the best of all preservatives. In this world we shall have tribulation, it is true. But insofar as we are able to salt away our blessings, what keeps them from spoiling is a glad and thankful heart.

Whether we were blessed with little or much in our family life, the principle given by Moses applies to us today. Those who focus on the negative, and dismiss the positive side of their upbringing, are most likely to rebel against their parents. The usual result is that, after forsaking their parents' authority, they wind up in a worse situation.

Consider the example of a young man who is fed up with life at home, so he enlists in the military. When he discovers that a Marine drill sergeant has taken the place of his father, he begins to have second thoughts. Others think, as I once did, that a cult or a close friendship will meet their needs better than the family God gave them. A decade later, sadder but wiser, their perspective is likely to be different.

I know a woman who rebelled against her father's rule in her early teens. Her life since leaving home has been a history of false starts and disappointments. Even though she is now a Christian, the effect of her broken relationship with her family is still a major force in her life. How different her abbreviated life at home looks to her now! How she wishes she had been grateful for the love that was there! Won't you say a prayer for her, or someone you know like her (perhaps even yourself), to experience the blessings of the first commandment with promise?

If you study the derivation of the Greek word for *unthankful*, you will find that it boils down to something like "not cheerful." God knows it is difficult to be cheerful when there is serious trouble in your family life. Yet sometimes the situation we find so distressing would be less harmful if our own attitude were different. And how soon—after we've been in bondage to those who do not love us, and after we've repented of our sins—the family life we once renounced looks like "the abundance of all things"!

There is, of course, a classic example of all this in Scripture—the parable of the prodigal son.[10] When your repentance is complete as the son's, then you can compare your parents to his father. I have learned, and I keep on learning, that a clear view of our own sins will give us a charitable view of the sins of others.

Spiritual Relationships

It would be easy to write a whole chapter on spiritual parent-child relationships in Scripture. We could hardly do justice to the first commandment with promise if we ignored the reality of such connections. A Christian who honored his natural parents, but despised those who "begot him in the gospel," would be a contradictory creature indeed. And from Paul's comments on spiritual parenthood, we may draw practical hints on how to honor our fathers and mothers.

This is not the place to unravel the theological complications involved in our being children of God (Rom. 8:16), even while Paul is saying, "In Christ Jesus I have begotten you through the gospel" (1 Cor. 4:15). We shall simply accept the fact that the apostle speaks frequently about such spiritual begetting, about his many "beloved children" (1 Cor. 4:14), and we shall apply these passages to our own lives. What Paul was to Timothy, other believers have been to us. Whether we consider them as our parents in the Lord, or as spiritual midwives and nurses to us, the fact remains that we were all converted and/or brought up in the Spirit through the agency of other Christians. Let us speak of them as Scripture does and honor them as God directs.

Abraham was physically the father of many nations. Spiritually, however, he is the father of all who believe.

> We say that faith was reckoned to Abraham for righteousness. . . . that he might be the father of all them that believe, though they be not circumcised; that righteousness might be imputed unto them also: And the father of circumcision to them who are not of the circumcision only, but who also walk in the steps of that faith of our father Abraham, which he had being yet uncircumcised . . . Abraham; who is the father of us all. (Rom. 4:9, 11–12, 16)

Faith, and walking in that faith, are the sure marks of spiritual descent. Those who are of the faith of Abraham, and who walk in the steps of that faith, are the children of Abraham. Jesus explained this to the unbelieving Jews, though they could not understand it. They did not "walk in the steps of that faith of our father Abraham"; therefore, they could not be his children (John 8:37–59).

We may observe the same pattern of descent among the disciples of Paul.

> For this cause have I sent unto you Timotheus, who is my beloved son, and faithful in the Lord, who shall bring you into

> remembrance of my ways which be in Christ, as I teach every-
> where in every church. (1 Cor. 4:17)

> But ye know the proof of him, that, as a son with the father,
> he hath served with me in the gospel. (Phil. 2:22)

> To Titus, mine own son after the common faith: Grace, mercy,
> and peace, from God the Father and the Lord Jesus Christ our
> Savior. (Titus 1:4)

> I desired Titus, and with him I sent a brother. Did Titus make
> a gain of you? walked we not in the same spirit? walked we
> not in the same steps? (2 Cor. 12:18)

Paul discipled Timothy and Titus; he may also have led them to Christ. These two young men shared the faith of their master, and they walked in his steps. Let's take a minute to think about what this means for us today.

Perhaps there was a Paul in your life. Perhaps an older, ever-faithful believer led you to repentance or instructed you in the Christian life. If so, you should still be thanking God for him (or her) today. Your actions should still remind others of your parent's ways in Christ. Can you be recognized as a chip off the old spiritual block? Are you still walking in the same spirit as your parent? Are you walking in the same steps?

I'd love to know more about what Paul was thinking, when he said that "as a son with his father [Timothy] served with me in the gospel." Here is one worthy commentator's idea of what he meant.

> *He has served with me as a child with the father,* that is to say,
> that he had yielded to him, in the work of the Lord, all the
> obedience, reverence, subjection, and love that the best son
> could have yielded to his father, remaining always attached at
> his side in all his painful and dangerous expeditions, soften-
> ing the labors of his apostleship by his continual assistance,
> flying where he sent him, refusing no danger, whether by sea
> or land, but taking as kindnesses all those labors in which St.
> Paul employed him, religiously obeying all his orders, without
> ever infringing any of them. Indeed, if you read in the Acts
> the history of the apostle left us by St. Luke, you will every-
> where find Timothy with him; or if he sometimes quits him, it
> is by his command to execute his orders elsewhere.[11]

If you were able to read this quotation without a pang of sorrow for your sins of omission, whether toward your natural or your spiritual parents, you must be either less culpable or less discerning than I am. I trust it is the former.

You Do Not Have Many Fathers

Just before he called Timothy "my beloved and faithful son in the Lord, who shall remind you of my ways in Christ," Paul wrote to the Corinthians:

> I write not these things to shame you, but as my beloved sons I warn you. For though ye have ten thousand instructors in Christ, yet have ye not many fathers: for in Christ Jesus I have begotten you through the gospel. Wherefore I beseech you, be ye followers of me. For this cause have I sent unto you Timotheus, who is my beloved son, and faithful in the Lord, who shall bring you into remembrance of my ways which be in Christ, as I teach everywhere in every church. (1 Cor. 4:14–17)

However many Christian teachers you have, you do not have many fathers in Christ. However many friends or instructors you have had in this world, your father and mother were the source of life God gave you. Though your natural or your spiritual parents fall short of St. Paul, the Lord still requires you to give them special honor. The apostle honored his spiritual father in front of all the Jews ("brought up in this city at the feet of Gamaliel" [Acts 22:3]), and we do well to imitate him.

Paul devotes several chapters of 2 Corinthians and Galatians to a defense of his ministry.[12] I had read these passages many a time, but I had never before seen their relevance to parent-child relationships. Reading them from this new perspective, I have been deeply, and sometimes sadly, moved. May God give me grace to make them plain to you!

"I am become a fool in glorying; ye have compelled me: for I ought to have been commended of you" (2 Cor. 12:11). Soon after Paul's departure, false apostles came in (2 Cor. 11:13), who seduced his congregations into believing their lies. Instead of commending Paul to these imposters, the newborn Christians either forgot him or believed the worst about him. With great energy and fervor, Paul exerted himself to show his children the truth. What a sad commentary on the loyalty of Christians it is, that Paul had to defend his ministry to those he had begotten in the gospel.[13]

How many parents (whether natural, step, or spiritual) have been in Paul's situation! Though we should have commended them, we rejected their instruction and followed other teachers. In Paul's words, we "suffer fools gladly" (2 Cor. 11:19). As there are false apostles in the world, there are also false parents—persons ready to usurp our parents' place without honoring them or acknowledging their authority in our lives. How we need to be wary of these usurpers! We shall be, if we understand and implement the first commandment with promise.

But those who ignore it are fair game for such imposters. Rebellious or ignorant children fall into their clutches and shall not easily escape. "For ye suffer, if a man bring you into bondage, if a man devour you, if a man take of you, if a man exalt himself, if a man smite you on the face" (2 Cor. 11:20). A true parent will not abandon his child at such a time but will plead with him, as Paul did, to save him from destruction. Woe to the child who then turns a deaf ear!

Did your foolishness ever compel your parent to vindicate his or her authority in your life? If you were like me, you may well have thought the worst of your parent at such times. You may have said, "He (or she) doesn't really care about me. He just wants to control me, so that I'll live up to his expectations." I assure you, it is much more likely that your parent was grieving for you as Paul grieved for his children. His chief concern was not himself or his expectations, but your welfare.

> For I am jealous over you with godly jealousy. (2 Cor. 11:2)

> I will not be burdensome to you: for I seek not yours, but you: for the children ought not to lay up for the parents, but the parents for the children. And I will very gladly spend and be spent for you; though the more abundantly I love you, the less I be loved. (2 Cor. 12:14–15)

> Now I pray to God that ye do no evil; not that we should appear approved, but that ye should do that which is honest, though we be as reprobates. . . . For we are glad, when we are weak, and ye are strong: and this also we wish, even your perfection. (2 Cor. 13:7, 9)

Do you find it hard to believe that your parent was capable of such motivation? Perhaps you have yet to fulfill the old adage: "By the time you're old enough to think your dad was right, you'll probably have a son who thinks you're wrong."

If your parent accused you of indifference and ingratitude, if he or she spoke sometimes of "all I've done for you"—then your parent is in the very best company, the apostle Paul's. However negatively you may have reacted to such criticism in the past, please stop now and consider it again. Was your parent's motivation really selfish, or was it selfless like St. Paul's? Was he or she naturally given to complaining, or did your own foolishness force your parent to such "foolish boasting"? Compare your parent's pleas to St. Paul's, and consider how much your own behavior resembled the Corinthians'. Then, if you find reason to repent, remember that "godly sorrow works repentance to salvation, [which is] not to be regretted" (2 Cor. 7:10).

Our Heart Is Wide Open

I shall close this chapter with the most touching, and for our purposes the most helpful, of Paul's pleadings with his children:

> O Corinthians, our mouth is opened to you, our heart has been enlarged. You are not restrained in us, but you are restrained in your own affections. But for the same reward, (I speak as to children), you also be enlarged. (2 Cor. 6:11–13, MKJV)

It is a most instructive exercise to read a number of good commentaries on this passage. Here are a few selections.

> Paul here says nothing but what we every day experience, for when we have to do with friends, our *heart is enlarged*, all our feelings are laid open, there is nothing there that is hid, nothing shut,—nay more, the whole mind leaps and exults to unfold itself openly to view.[14] (John Calvin)

> [Paul] addresses the members of the church in a very pathetic manner, saying *our mouth is open unto you*; to speak our minds freely to you; we shall hide and conceal nothing from you, we shall deal with you with all plainness and faithfulness. . . . *Our heart is enlarged*; with love to you, and eager desires after your good; and it is from the abundance of our hearts, and hearty affection for you, that our mouth is open so freely to communicate to you . . . [v. 12]. Our hearts are so enlarged with love unto you, that they are large enough to hold you all; an expression setting forth the exceeding great love, and strong affection the apostle bore to the Corinthians: when, on the other hand, they had but very little love to him comparatively.[15] (John Gill)

> A heart full of love will give vent to its feelings. There will be no dissembling and hypocrisy there. . . . *I speak as unto my children*. I speak as a parent addressing his children. I sustain toward you the relation of a spiritual father, and I have a right to require and expect a return of affection.[16] (Albert Barnes)

> *O ye Corinthians* is simply "Corinthians" in Greek. This is the only place in which he addresses them by name. . . . 12. There is plenty of room for you in my big heart; but in your

> heart there is no room for me; you are too full of suspicion
> and resentment. . . . 13. By way of exchange . . . let your heart
> also be enlarged, i.e., reciprocate my love for you.[17] (Charles
> Callan, O. P.)

Open communication is a chief part of honoring a parent. Suspicion and resentment, or dissembling and hypocrisy, make it impossible to communicate in this fashion. Whether or not you think your parent's heart is, or was, open unto you, your heart should be open to your parent.

Needless to say, most of us have not laid all our feelings open to our parents. Our minds have not leaped and exulted to unfold themselves openly to their view. But Paul said this is how it should be between parents and children. And I say that your parent's capacity for loving communication is probably much greater than you think. If I had not seen parents, time and time again, revealing this hidden capacity as their children opened their hearts to them, I would never have written this book.

Part Three:
Absorbing the Teaching

CHAPTER 10

Piercing the Armor

After we have examined Scripture on a subject, the next step should be to apply what we have learned to our own lives. But some people, who are glad to be hearers of the Word, have difficulty doing what it says. Others may say to themselves, "Why should I read further? I don't have a big problem with my parents." If only all who thought so were correct! My experience counseling Christians (and others) has shown me that there are many who are at least partially blind to their sins against their parents. They need, as the Scripture says, to be *convinced* (or convicted) of their sin. This chapter is meant to be the acid test which shows you the true condition of your heart. It is designed to motivate you to complete the good work you have begun. Please do not pass over it lightly.

Armored and Disguised

When Ahab went to Ramoth-gilead, he protected himself against the judgment of God by wearing both armor and a disguise (1 Kings 22:30, 34). Is it possible that you are like him? Many Christians today are both armored and disguised against the convicting power of the first commandment with promise. Their disguise takes the form of Christian maturity. They are settled in the faith; they have overcome sin; others look to them for guidance. Surely they know and keep the Ten Commandments. And if one should be so bold as to question their disguise, he soon discovers the armor underneath it. The armor is made of memories, memories of all the bad things (real or imagined) which their parents did to them. If they have any resentment or coolness toward their parents, they use the memories to justify their attitude. They pride themselves on their forgiveness toward their parents, thinking themselves virtuous where they are most in sin.

We all need to be wary of the deceitfulness of sin. If we have been deceived in an area of our Christian life, it does not mean that we are not saved. It does not mean that we have failed as Christians; it does not invalidate any of our good thoughts or good deeds. What it means is that we need help. But that can be the hardest thing for us to admit, especially when it comes to dealing with our parents.

Consider the current wisdom of our time, which goes something like this: "Most people have feelings of inadequacy, of insecurity, or of inferiority. Some people hide them better than others: Their success in the world may be just another way of coping with the problem. And where did they get those feelings? Wasn't it from their parents? If their parents did not abandon or abuse them, then surely they criticized them or judged them unfairly. Whatever hurts they may have received from their peers, their fundamental anxieties probably stem from family life." This, I believe, is a common idea today, and there is truth in it. The trouble is that it's a half truth, and a very dangerous one.

It's true that our basic feelings of inadequacy are likely to have come from troubles with our parents. But that is not the whole truth. The whole truth is that parents love their children, because men are created in the image and likeness of God. However much the divine image may have suffered from sin and unbelief, certain vestiges remain; chief among them is the love of the parent for the child.[1] God loves His children enough to die for them, and so do most parents. But how many of us really feel such intense love from our fathers and mothers?

God created the family. Therefore, the devil is always at work to destroy it. The alienation of husband and wife is what he desires most. Next to that he seeks to estrange children from their parents. Although long-range planning is not Satan's strong point, in the shorter term he is a master. He knows that a child alienated from his parents will soon be fertile ground for the seeds of discord and divorce. If he can separate parent and child, all things (as we know to our sorrow) will be possible for him in the next generation.

How It Usually Works

A subtle strategy pleases the devil most. Outright abuse on the parent's part will damage a child; but where the harm and its causes are easily determined, the need for a cure may be felt. Where the need is felt, a remedy is likely to be found. It is better for the destroyer if both parent and child are deceived, either by thinking that all is well or by mistaking the real cause of the trouble. This sort of deception is all too common in our families. Here is how it usually works.

Most people can remember a time in early childhood when they felt loved and protected by their parent.[2] Though even then life had its troubles, they recall it as a time of confidence and hope. But some incident in childhood or teenage years brought about the end of their childlike trust. The incident itself is often, from the parent's point of view, a very minor thing: It could be only a passing remark, an insensitive moment, or a forgotten promise. Sometimes, of course, it takes the form of serious mistreatment or abuse. In any event, *the key to the broken trust is not the incident itself, but the child's response to the incident.*

At some point the child gives up on the parent and no longer communicates his true feelings. It may be that at first the child attempts to speak the truth, but feeling rebuffed, he shuts down emotionally. He begins to conceal how he really feels and develops a secret inner life the parent knows nothing about. All future incidents tend to get filtered through the first one, until the child's judgment of the parent becomes a kind of self-fulfilling prophecy. The child gets used to thinking like this: "You're being nice to me now, but I know I can't trust you. If I let you, you might hurt me again the way you did *then.*" Or, it could be, "You say you love me, but you really only care about yourself. All your seeming concern for me is just concern for your own reputation. You don't love me, or you would never have done *that.*"

Once this kind of thinking begins—and is kept hidden from the parent—it is easy to find more incidents to confirm the original impression. The parent is guilty until proven innocent, and he cannot prove himself innocent no matter what he does, because he is denied the right to confront his accuser. In fact, the parent does not even know that he or she is on trial. Outwardly nothing is wrong. The parent may sense something but cannot put a finger on it. He may try to talk to the child, but the child no longer trusts him enough to share what is in the heart. This state of distrust and secret judgment on the child's part is what I call a *broken relationship* with the parent.

Frost-Free . . . and Ready to Explode

The broken relationship is as much a part of family life in our culture as the frost-free refrigerator. And the child who carries it—whether he is ten years old or fifty—resembles that appliance more than he knows. On the outside it is shiny and clean; it runs smoothly and quietly for a long time. Whatever is put into it, no matter how spicy or warm it may be, becomes chilled or frozen solid in a short time. Being frost-free, it removes excess ice automatically and never seems to need attention. But sooner or later the thing breaks down. Whatever is frozen thaws; whatever is chilled warms up. Things rot and ferment. Jars become fermentation tanks, which, having no vent, may explode. You don't know what odious means until you've encountered such a broken-down fridge. It's an experience you're not likely to forget. Woe, woe to the man who first opens the door!

Refrigerators break down because they are machines. But a child with a broken relationship is under a curse. He has violated the first commandment with promise, whether he knows it or not, and it cannot be well with him. Something is rotten on the inside, and the longer it is hidden the more sickening it becomes. The only remedy is to bring it all to the light, clean up the insides (which can take a while), repair the broken part, and monitor it carefully in the future. It takes courage and hard work to deal with the mess, but he who begins the task brings a blessing to his family.

It is no honor to be outwardly polite to a parent we inwardly despise. A child who is secretly disappointed or resentful cannot be a blessing to his parents, no matter how many Mother's or Father's Day cards he dispatches. Remember Christ's warning about the hypocrisy of the Pharisees: The outside and the inside must be in true accord.

It's been said: "It is a great step toward cure to know the extent and the inveteracy of the disease."[3] It will soon be well with us, once we can admit that we have sinned against our parents. It is a sin:

- not to have spoken the truth to them in love.

- not to have expressed our grievances—and given them opportunity to defend themselves or to apologize to us.

- to have *assumed* that they were trying to hurt us, or that they didn't care about us, without even asking them what they were *trying* to do.

- to have cut ourselves off from them without telling them what we were feeling.

- not to have taken them seriously.

- to have thought the worst of them when we might have thought the best.

Am I being too hard on you? I admit it's asking a lot of a child to speak the truth in love, especially when he has had little encouragement (and much provocation) from adults. I do not condemn you—I am in no position to throw stones!—if you fell into such a sin when you were young. But you are no longer a child if you are reading this book. And now you have Scripture to encourage you. Why should you go on living under the shadow of an old error, when you can see the light? You are growing in the Lord; it is time to put away childish sins.

However we may sympathize with those who have broken their relationship with a parent, we must not say that they have not sinned. We should not condemn them for their past, but we must insist that they accept responsibility for what they thought and did. To require less will deprive them of the cure and blessing their heavenly Father has stored up for them. The medicine may taste bitter, but if it can heal a dread disease, only a fool will refuse it. It will not be well with those who continue to focus on their parent's sin. Let them take the beam out of their own eye first. Then, *if* there is a speck in the parent's eye, they can deal with that later.

Nothing Secret About It

I have spent a lot of time on the secret broken relationship, because it is so common and so insidious. But trouble with our commandment can come in other forms. For some people the relationship is broken, but there is nothing secret about it. They may be openly expressing their hostility, or they may have broken off all contact with the parent. Though either way it cannot be well with them, there is more hope for such open sinners than for those whose sin is hidden even from themselves. At least part of the conflict is out in the open. There may well be awareness of the need for healing. But even where the hostility is open, the real cause may still be hidden. Withdrawal from or anger toward a parent may help us to see we have a problem. The resolution of it will still require us to face our own sin and to speak the truth in love.

Some of us have sinned in deed as well as in thought. We may have seriously disobeyed our parents. We may have cursed them or hurt them or neglected them in time of need. Whatever we did, the key to healing is to stop justifying our sin. We justify it by looking at what our parents did to us. But Christians should know that the sins of others can never free them from their own. After all, that line of defense was first tried in the Garden. . . . Until we stop blaming others, we can hardly be free to receive the Lord's pardon. When we cease to blame our parents, the Holy Spirit will instruct us about repentance and forgiveness.

Do You Honor Your Parents?

Here are a few simple ways to measure your level of honoring your parents. [Circle one answer for each question. If you really have mixed feelings, you may circle two answers for some questions. You should take the quiz separately for each parent.]

- When someone says something derogatory about my parent, I am most likely to:

    A. Agree with the accuser.
    B. Think my parent could not have done such a thing.
    C. Suspend judgment until I get both sides of the story.

- When I cannot reconcile an accusation against my parent with what I know of him or her, I will probably:

    A. Not care which party is telling the truth.
    B. Ask my parent to help me figure out the truth.
    C. Investigate the matter without telling my parent.

- In the language of the courts, I will do my best to:

    A. Prosecute my parent to the full extent of the law.
    B. Defend my parent, no matter what the cost.
    C. Hold my parent innocent until he or she has been proven guilty beyond a reasonable doubt.

- If things are still unclear, as a last resort I would be willing to:

    A. Take a nap.

B. Tell my parent what rumors I have heard, what suspicions I have entertained, and what I hope the truth is.

C. Hire a private investigator—or go to a counselor myself.

- If it should be established beyond a reasonable doubt that my parent has done something wrong, I would probably feel:

    A. Vindicated in my low opinion of him or her.
    B. Grieved that my parent has sinned.
    C. That I need to forgive my parent and make the best of it.

- When I think about my parent, what comes to mind first are his or her:

    A. Sins or annoying habits.
    B. Virtues or noble qualities.
    C. Accomplishments or abilities.

After you have jotted down your answers to the questions, see the endnote for the evaluation.[4]

Perhaps you are used to thinking, "Well, really, Mom (or Dad) was not a very good parent, but I suppose she did the best she could." This kind of attitude may be healthy or harmful, depending on the motivation behind it. All too often it is a way of demeaning the parent. It makes her into a kind of emotional cripple, *who could never have met your real needs anyway.* This is very dishonoring. It's like saying, "She tried hard, but what could you expect from an imbecile?"

The honoring thing to say would be something like this: "I see the sins that oppressed my parent. And I see how my own sins made a bad situation worse. Yet beyond the current (or past) distress, I perceive the parent that still can be (or could have been) a blessing to her children. I'm grateful for the love and strength that were there for me, at least potentially, and I regret that I was not better at encouraging them and drawing them out."

Do you see the difference? It's one thing to look on a poorly designed, substandard house and to say, "How tacky! This thing should never have been built!"—and quite another to gaze at the ruins of the Parthenon exclaiming, "How magnificent! I wish I could have seen it in its glory!" Believe me, the parent God gave you had the ability to meet your real needs. If it didn't happen, it doesn't mean that it couldn't have happened under different circumstances. And if your parent's sins got in the way, as they surely did, remember your own sins before you start throwing stones.

There is a charitable way of saying, "They did the best they could." The child who is charitable uses the same words, but he uses them to honor his parents. He emphasizes the positive side of what they did, or wanted to do, *for* him. He thinks about how much they loved him, not how much they failed him. When you say, "They did the best they could"—what do you mean by it? Are you damning your parents with faint praise? Or are you really singing their praises?

CHAPTER 11

What It Means:
Specifics of Honoring

"The reason why so few good books are written," said a practical man, "is that so few people that can write know anything."[1] Hmm. Those with faith should add virtue to it; those with a fine style of writing should add knowledge. It is good to have hands-on experience of the subject we're talking about. Let us mix down-to-earth knowledge with our meditations on Scripture.

We've spent many pages preparing ourselves to get practical. What, then, are the specific requirements of honoring our parents? In this chapter I shall lay out, as best I can, the duties involved in keeping our commandment; in the next, the limits God has placed upon those duties.

Honor to Whom Honor Is Due

Our first question: "Who are the people whom I am supposed to honor? Natural parents, step-parents, in-laws, relatives—to whom does the commandment apply?" (See chap. 5, endnote 9).

Natural Parents

I am confident that we should begin with our natural parents, and that we should not extend the commandment to others until we have learned to honor them.

Perhaps, due to death, adoption, or desertion, you do not even know who your natural parents are. Does the commandment not apply to you? O, it does—as much as to anyone alive. God used your biological parents to bring you into the world, and He wants you to honor them for it. As you do, you worship the Lord who gave you life. If you do not, you reveal your lack of faith in His power and benevolence.

If you do not know who your parents are, you are still able to think the best—or the worst—of them. Without positive proof to the contrary, you should assume that they loved you and that they wanted only what was good for you. Did they give you up to be raised by others? You should assume that they did the best they could for you, according to the light they had and the circumstances they were in. Did they desert you? Until you know the whole story, from unprejudiced sources, you should assume that they left you with sorrow, a sorrow that may still be with them today.

I know a man whose father abandoned his family while he himself was an infant. For many years he assumed that his father had completely rejected him. It wasn't until he had children of his own, and difficulties in his own marriage, that he began to see things differently. He realized that a man could love his children deeply, but still be tempted to leave them, to escape a situation that seems unbearable. This man made a wiser choice than his father. He stayed with his family and "encouraged himself in the Lord his God" (1 Sam. 30:6).

But he learned something of value from his trials. He realized that, despite the sin of abandonment, his father might have loved him, just as he himself cared for his own children. Later in life, he located his father, visited him, and experienced a wonderful restoration. When he came back from that visit he told me, "I felt like a big piece of myself, that had always been missing, was finally there." He was glad he had taken the risk of visiting a parent he hardly knew.

Perhaps you also were abandoned by a parent, but he or she is now deceased or unwilling to see you or impossible to locate. You may still obtain the blessing in our commandment—by doing what you can do and leaving the rest to God. Honor the memory of a deceased parent. Reach out in love and humility to a parent who has been unwilling to see you (see chaps. 14 and 15). Try to locate a parent whose address you do not know.[2]

Most of us know who our natural parents are—and there's the rub. We know their sins, their fears, and their weaknesses. It's a fine art, learning to honor them. But I can think of no form of education that is more rewarding. Needless to say, millions of people with advanced degrees are dunces in this essential field of learning. May we not be among them!

Step-Parents, Foster Parents, and Guardians

Once we have begun to honor our natural parents, we should learn to honor the substitute parents in our lives as well. If one of your natural parents has married another person (or a succession of such persons), honoring your step-parent is a part of honoring your parent. If, for example, your mother is living with her fourth husband, you are no longer bound to honor husbands two and three, but you must do your best to honor your current step-father. This kind of situation may require special grace, but "Is anything too hard for the Lord?" (Gen. 18:14). He will bless you as you seek to do His will in a difficult situation.

Having directed a school for delinquent boys, where intact families are rarely encountered, I know the value of a devoted step-parent or foster parent. If you were blessed by having such a person in your life, you should be thanking the Lord for him or her and joyfully rendering the honor that is your duty. But you must be careful not to neglect or despise the natural parent whose place your step-parent has taken. Though your step-parent is kind, loving, generous, and devoted; though your natural parent seems abusive or uncaring; you must beware of honoring the one and despising the other. In the flesh it would be only natural to do so, but in God's economy it is sinful to neglect or despise the source of the life He gave you.

If you had guardians or other persons *in loco parentis*, you should have rendered them the honor that is due to parents. If they abused their authority, you should have followed the examples of Jonathan and David. If you flew to someone for refuge (whether emotional or physical), it should have been someone like Samuel—mature, responsible, and, most important, *capable of telling you your faults*. David didn't run off to the local home for wet puppies; he went to a fearless prophet. If your authority figure became abusive like Saul, did you look for a comforter as uncompromising as Samuel?

Grandparents, In-Laws, Uncles, and Aunts

All of these are parents-once-removed to us. By descent, by marriage, or by kinship, all these persons we are bound to honor. If, as often happens, there is serious conflict among them, we must try to think the best of all parties. We must not allow these other figures to usurp our parents' authority and honor. Yet we must not despise the claims of the "secondary parents" in our lives, either. When you are caught up in one of these family dilemmas, seek the Lord first, and then the advice of the Samuel in your life. Make sure that your Samuel has mastered our commandment, that he or she has learned to honor the parents that God gave him.

The Duties of Our Commandment

Whether you are sixteen or sixty, you should pay attention to the specifics of this section. What I have written here, I have written both to teach older believers what they should have done, and to teach younger ones what they should be doing.

Obedience

Fasten your seat belt while I tell you the filial duties God required of us. Until we married or found our calling from the Lord,[3] we were bound to obey our parents in all things, except those that were directly sinful or dangerously abusive. Let me list for you some things that were *not* directly sinful or dangerously abusive.

- Taking out the trash.
- Doing the dishes.
- Mowing the lawn.
- All of the above.
- Having less of something than your friends had.
- Not playing with Johnny; or not going out with Johnny.
- Not dating before you were sixteen.
- Not hanging out at the mall.
- Not driving when your friends were driving.
- Visiting relatives.
- Spending time with your parents.
- Not attending the school you thought was best for you.
- Not having the job you wanted.
- Not marrying until you had your parents' blessing.

I am quite serious about all this. God has long been blessing those who did these things in a spirit of obedience. If your friends' approval or your own pleasure were more important to you than the blessing of God, your knowledge of Scripture (and of godly living) must have been slight.

I stand by the rule of thumb I gave earlier: *You should have obeyed your parents until they told you to break the Ten Commandments.* But consider: outward obedience coupled with inward rebellion could bring only a curse into your life, not a blessing. What should you have done, when you knew you ought to have obeyed a parent, but you hated to do the thing he or she required?

You should have communicated. As respectfully as possible, you should have let your parent know how you felt about the duty that seemed so burdensome to you. Often it would have been best to do this after you had completed the task, or endured the deprivation, assigned by your parent. Sometimes it would have been better to speak up beforehand.

What I cannot emphasize enough, however, is that at such a time almost everything depended upon your attitude. Were you an obedient and usually respectful child who was momentarily distressed? Or were you a rebellious one who bridled at any limit authority imposed? Even an insensitive parent can tell the difference between these extremes. In the first case, especially if the child is patiently insistent, the parent will be likely to hear and to reconsider the situation, though rarely as quickly as the child desires. But where the parent senses a defiant spirit, he or she is likely to react with sternness or with anger.

If you did not trust your parent, you would hardly have been able to communicate effectively in such situations. You must first go back to the causes of the broken trust, and deal with them (see chaps. 14 and 15), before you can hope to implement the advice I am giving here.

But if you were able to see your parent as benevolent—and if you made it clear that, much as you hated it, you would do what he or she required—then I trust your parent would have been willing to consider your point of view. But were *you* able to consider your parent's? Did you really try to see things from your parent's perspective? Blessed are those who listen, for they shall be listened to.

Did obeying your parents in all things (Col. 3:20) seem burdensome to you? If you want to get on with the Christian walk, you should get used to obedience. The Christian life is a life of submission. The employee is subject to the employer (Col. 3:22); a wife, to her husband;[4] a man, to civil and church authorities and to Christ.[5] The submission God required of you as a child, He still requires of you in other ways as an adult.

If you knew someone who had every opportunity for a good education, but, due to his intractability in childhood, was still learning to read as an adult, how would you feel? Perhaps you would sorrow that he was so backward, so humbled—and yet rejoice that he was finally learning his lessons. "To obey is better than sacrifice," said the prophet (1 Sam 15:22); it is also more important than reading, writing, and 'rithmetic. The home or homes that you were raised in were God's school of obedience for you. You may complain to Him about His concept of education, if you choose, but do not fail to learn the lesson He assigned you there.

Friends, School, and Work

As Jesus grew in wisdom and stature, He remained subject to His parents (Luke 2:51–52). As His size and His powers increased, His obedience did not diminish. We, who have fallen short of His example, can still wish we had been more like Him. As we encountered the changes of adolescence and early adulthood, our obedience should have been one of the constants in our lives. Though we failed in that obedience then, we need not fail in our repentance now. Remember that David's sins, humanly speaking, were worse than Saul's. It was Saul's lack of repentance that cost him his kingdom.

God gave you your parents to protect you and to train you in His ways. Many parents, who know little or nothing of God, still perform His will in protecting and training their children. This is particularly true when it comes to the choice of friends. What motive, other than his child's welfare, does a parent have for restricting friendships?[6] Usually none. Jonathan continued a friend to David, when Saul forbade their friendship; but meanwhile he served his father loyally, and hardly ever saw his friend. If you were truly in Jonathan's situation, you might have followed his example. But was your friend really as good as David? And was your parent unreachable as Saul? Many grown children are tempted to answer yes to this last question. But in my experience nearly all of them are wrong.

You would not believe, until you have seen it, how the child's obedient spirit opens the heart of the parent. Sensing that his or her requirements will be obeyed, the parent listens more carefully to the appeals of the child. If you accepted parental authority in your youth, if you communicated lovingly the anguish in your heart, you not only pleased God, but you helped your parent to respond wisely to your plea. When you bridled at restrictions, when your friends seemed more important to you than your parents, you were incapable of the obedient spirit that is required to appeal. Wise (and not so wise) parents often change, or at least modify, their policy at the request of obedient children. Only foolish or fearful parents give in to the demands (or the manipulations) of rebellious sons and daughters.

In the same way, we should have honored our parents in choosing our school activities or jobs. If your mother wouldn't let you play football, if your father wouldn't let you take art, you must have gone through a great trial. If only our thoughts at such times had been of God! Instead of thinking about what we would lose by obedience, we might have thought about what we would gain. We might have put the Lord's blessing in the scales with the pleasure, the esteem, or the expertise we had hoped to acquire. We might have taken a long-term view of what would be best for us, instead of concentrating on the deprivations of the moment. Then we might have been able to communicate with and appeal to our parents in a way that would have caused them to change their minds.[7] But the bottom line must be, unless we had a clear and recognizable calling from God, we should have conformed to the will of our parents.

Yes, it would have been hard not to take the summer job you wanted, not to have attended the college of your choice. That we can see clearly. What we often fail to see is the disastrous consequences (in the long run) of thinking that we knew better than our parents. The author of Proverbs made it clear: a parent is someone who knows more than we do. To which I add, even an ignorant parent may be used by God to guide us into the way of blessing. Our parents did not have to prove their expertise before they directed us. We ought to have proved ours, before we started thinking they needed guidance from us.

Dating and Marriage

Nothing is harder today for parents to do with their children than to cooperate with them in the process of finding spouses.

The biblical model, as I understand it, is that parents and children work together to ensure the survival of loving, stable, and godly families in future generations. Over and over again in the Bible, though in different forms, we see the generations cooperating in finding a spouse for the child. The stories of Isaac and Rebekah, Jacob and Rachel, Moses and Zipporah, Ruth and Boaz—all witness to the necessary union of the parent's consent with the heart's desire of the child.[8] Even among the mysteries of the Song of Solomon, we find the same pattern:

> Go forth, O ye daughters of Zion, and behold king Solomon
> with the crown wherewith his mother crowned him in the day
> of his espousals, and in the day of the gladness of his heart.
> (Song of Sol. 3:11)

Where either the parent or the child is excluded from the process of selection, as has often happened, the resulting relationship may well be unloving or may fail altogether. We moderns should, however, note that the consequences of excluding the parent have proved worse than the consequences of excluding the child. "What?" you ask. "Would you have liked your parents to arrange your marriage for you?" Frankly, no; but let us reason together. Please consider the evidence for my assertion that the parents' role is at least as vital as the child's.

In former times, in many pagan lands and even in some Christian cultures, the child's consent was considered of less importance than the parents', or even of no value at all. While surely this arrangement resulted in some unhappy marriages, those marriages usually lasted till death intervened, *and the cultures themselves were preserved for centuries.* Under our present system—where the preference of the child is the main thing, and the parents' blessing, if desired at all, is considered less than essential—what is the permanence of marriage? Divorce is as likely as not, and many of the marriages that endure lack the stability that was taken for granted in previous centuries.

Though we have thoroughly sown the wind of dishonor and divorce, we have only begun to reap the whirlwind that must follow from our sins. As the generations of children from broken homes mature, as we drift further from the norm of stable family life, our productivity, our morals, and our safety will all continue to decline. Our Lord's saying applies to methods as well as to men: "You shall know them by their fruits." The harvest of evil is not yet fully gathered for our culture. When it is, when it has brought us either to repentance or to destruction, we will no longer deny parents their crucial interest in the marriages of their children.[9]

There's always more to learn about the first commandment with promise. Let me tell you what happened to me while I was writing this chapter.

I knew that my father's parents were married by the arrangement of their families.[10] But I didn't know how much choice, if any, they had had in the matter. So I called my elderly aunt in New York to ask her about it. She told me that my grandparents met only once before their wedding. Did they go out for pizza and a movie? No. Brought together by their *shadkhen* (a professional matchmaker hired by the parents), they saw each other briefly, said little or nothing, and that was that. My aunt believes that if either one of them had hated the sight of the other, they would have been able to escape the marriage contract. Evidently, they looked all right to each other, for they were married soon after.

My aunt went on to say that my grandparents had a wonderful relationship: "They loved each other dearly and would do anything for each other." Since they died before I was born, I had never really thought about the quality of their married life. I had just assumed that they were like the couple in *Fiddler on the Roof*, who never talked about love until their children ran off and got infected with modern ideas. So it was wonderful for me to hear my aunt speaking about their love for each other. Though her father had been dead for half a century, her parents' good marriage was still alive in her mind. I wish I could describe to you the glow and the blessing I felt after speaking to her. It's a wonderful thing to discover that your heritage of love is richer than you thought.

Caring for Older Parents

As our parents cared for us when we were young and helpless, we need to care for them as they grow old and helpless. Even if they failed to do their part, or failed to do it well, we should still do ours, with our eyes on the Lord. As Jesus on the cross provided for His mother, we should do what we can to comfort elderly parents.

For many of us, honoring our parents in this way requires a lot of time or effort or money. I cannot tell you what God wants you to do in your particular situation. But I think I can offer two guiding principles to help you to know and to do His will.

First, try to see the burdens that come to you as opportunities and honors from the Lord—opportunities, I mean, to glorify Him and learn more of His ways. How does your emptying the bedpan, paying the bills, or buying the groceries glorify Christ? It exhibits some of His virtues—humility, desire to serve others, gratitude, and faith-fulness. If you fall short in these areas, serving your parents may well be the school in which God intends to teach you the fruits of His Spirit. "Blessed is the man whom thou chastenest, O Lord, and teachest him out of thy law" (Ps. 94:12).

It is an honor to be chosen to serve the Lord. Whoever says to Him, "Here am I; send me"—whether he ends up prophesying to the nations or shopping for his parents—is the servant of the Lord. The psalmist said, "I had rather be a doorkeeper in the house of my God, than to dwell in the tents of wickedness" (Ps. 84:10). Whether you are slaying Goliath or buying a pizza, what's the difference when you're serving the King of kings? The least chore in His kingdom is greater than the highest honor the world can bestow. If we really believe it, we may feel a sense of honor when it's our turn to empty the bedpan.

Second, in doubtful situations—serve your parents. Your duty to them is so clearly expressed in Scripture, that you should not leave them in time of need, unless you have a clear call from the Lord to do something else. If you have yearnings and desires, talents and abilities, that could be used in God's service—wait for His call. He can make it crystal clear that you should leave your parents to serve Him some other way. If you wait till He does, you may expect a blessing in your new field of service.[11]

CHAPTER 12

Limitations

Sir Thomas More and Martin Luther both had fathers who wanted them to be lawyers. More, who loved scholarship and found the monastic life attractive, did his father's will and became a practicing lawyer; he continued his other interests on the side. The result? He soon became the chancellor of all England, a famous writer, and, later, a martyr for his faith. Luther, on the other hand, suddenly joined a monastery, before his father had opportunity to forbid him. He might have found a better way to begin following his calling, but becoming a lawyer for his father's sake would have amounted to denying his Father in heaven.[1]

Some of us find God's will for our lives expressed through the desires of our parents, rather than through our own desires. Others of us have to resist parental commands in order to be faithful to our Maker.

We have seen in chapters 6 and 8 that unbounded devotion to parents may lead to sin. God and God's laws must come before the orders and desires of our parents. From this premise arise all the limitations on the first commandment with promise. But practically speaking, how are we to determine when our duty to God overrules our duty to man?

The answer to this question cannot be found in any one passage of Scripture. From my knowledge of the Bible as a whole, supplemented by my observations of godly Christians through the ages, I shall determine it as best I can. You may work out your own answer with fear and trembling. I trust that if you do, yours and mine will have some things in common.

As I see it, there are three broad areas in which our duty to God may overrule the first commandment with promise. I have already referred to the first limitation, which applies to children and to many young adults: Obey your parents *until they tell you to break the Ten Commandments*. The other two areas are for adults only. These are, *in caring for your own family* and *in following your own calling from God*, you may have to disobey or disregard your parents.[2]

Breaking the Ten Commandments

Suppose a mother calls her employer, says she's sick, and then goes out to shop at a one-day-only sale. What should her child do if her employer calls? Should he lie and say she's too sick to come to the phone? Should he tell the truth, even if it costs his mother her job? Let's use this situation to test our first limitation: Obey your parents *until they tell you to break the Ten Commandments*.

I believe we should apply the Ten Commandments broadly in such situations. Though the child might not be bearing false witness *against* his neighbor, he would certainly be giving false witness *to* the employer if he lied to him about his mother's whereabouts. I would not think less of the child if, caught by surprise the first time it happened, he stammered out a falsehood; but he would be violating the Ten Commandments. He ought to make it plain to his mother that he will not tell lies for her, because God's law comes before man's. The parent may react with anger in such situations, especially if she feels convicted by her own conscience. But the child must stand firm to his Christian principles. I do not see any alternative.

The same thing applies to situations where a parent asks a child to lie to grandparents, to the police, to a stepparent, or to the other natural parent. If you think Jacob was justified in deceiving Isaac because his mother told him to, you may take a more liberal line with such falsehoods than I do. But I cannot condone them. I think Jacob was wrong, and we must not imitate his bad example[3] (see chap. 5).

Let's look at some other common situations. A father is addicted to tobacco, and he asks his daughter, home for her college vacation, to buy him some cigarettes. (A child under age, of course, should refuse.) What should she do if she is convinced smoking is bad for him? Unless he is likely to become ill from using the products she purchases for him, I think she should obey her father. If she knows he has emphysema or some other lung condition, she must not help to make it worse. She must not kill; neither should she be an accessory to manslaughter. But otherwise, much as she may hate it, I think she should do his will. It is not a violation of the Ten Commandments to buy cigarettes. Therefore, she should obey her parent.

However, she should let her father know how she feels about his smoking. This does not mean lecturing him about what *he* should be doing, but rather letting him know how his smoking affects her and her relationship with him. Ultimately, she must make a distinction between her father's sins[4] and her sins. She cannot stop him from sinning, and she must not allow him to cause her to sin.

But she is not the Holy Spirit. It is not her job to convict her parent of sin. As she honors her father, by obeying him against her own wishes, she is doing the will of God. Her example will, I think, do more to help him come to his senses, than her lectures could ever accomplish. And as he sees her yielding spirit, he will be more open to hearing her account of how his smoking hurts and saddens his children.

A Christian man I know is distressed by his mother's New Age beliefs. His criticisms of her religion have often caused tension between them. Recently he took his own family and his mother on a camping trip. "We had a wonderful time," he told me. "I didn't say a word about religion." In other words he lived his faith by honoring his mother, and he chose to say nothing about her sinful religious practices. I have no doubt that in his case, and for most of us generally, such an approach will bring more of the blessing of God into our families.

If you were once pregnant and your parent insisted that you get an abortion, you should have disobeyed. If your sister or cousin was pregnant and your parent wanted you to help her obtain an abortion, again you should have disobeyed. The commandment is "Thou shalt not kill." It's as simple as that. God blesses us for putting His law before our parent's and for repenting of those times when we failed to honor Him.

Until we have discerned our calling from the Lord, we should place our parents' authority above that of teachers or employers. If you ever experienced a conflict between your parent and the authorities at school or work, it is likely that at some point you failed in filial esteem. Probably, on the inside at least, you cringed when your parent expressed his or her concerns. A parental point of view can be peculiar or even wrong, but still be a legitimate expression of his or her God-given role as your primary protector and educator. Did feelings of embarrassment at such a time seem weightier than the first commandment with promise? It might be time to reconsider your ways and to express to your parent your new point of view.

The essential thing, in such trials as I have been rehearsing, is to keep one's eyes on the Lord. Children should not obey because parents tell them to; they should obey because God has commanded it. If we really believe that, His peace will sustain us in difficult situations with parents or other authorities.

It's a Family Affair

Before there were any children in the world, this truth was established: When a man and a woman are married, a family is created. "Therefore shall a man leave his father and his mother, and shall cleave unto his wife: and they shall be one flesh" (Gen. 2:24).

Why did God emphasize the man's leaving home, rather than the woman's? No doubt there are several answers to this question,[5] but a chief one must be this: At marriage the husband assumes the leadership of a new household. How can he "know. . . how to rule his own house" (1 Tim. 3:5), unless he is free from his parents' authority? He must stand before God as the head of the house, even as his father did—or should have done—before him. Whether or not he takes his parents' or his in-laws' advice, he alone is responsible for ruling his family well.

Does this mean he has no obligation to his parents? No. It means that *in matters relating to his family*, he stands before God, not his parents. He must follow his own light, as God gives him light, in ruling his family, and he is under no obligation to obey his parents. But God still requires him to honor, to esteem, and to help his parents as much as he can, without neglecting his own wife and children. The new husband must weigh the demands on his energy, his finances, and his time, and distribute them wisely. He is one with his wife; therefore she must ever be his closest companion. He must clearly establish that she is his first love in this world, and that she ranks even higher with him than his parents do. But if she should urge him to neglect his parents, in the name of God he must resist her.

What about the newly married wife? What of her obligations to her parents? She belongs to a new order now. Her husband, not her father, is or should be the head of her family. The newlyweds must work out their own salvation with fear and trembling. The wife ought to obey her husband, unless he requires her to break the law of God. She may not go to mate-swapping parties, and she may not neglect her remaining duties to her parents. If her husband should require her to cut her ties to her parents, she must experience the sorest of trials. At such a time, her conscience—not her husband, and not her fears—must be her guide. If it's clear her husband is telling her to break the first commandment with promise,[6] in obedience to God she should refuse to obey him. In doubtful cases she should do what her husband requires. May the Lord spare us from such dilemmas and give us wisdom if He chooses not to spare us!

We must be careful not to despise our in-laws. Husbands or wives should not be advancing their natural parents' claims against those of their in-laws. Each married person has four parents to honor, whether they are living or dead, and we should recognize their separate claims to our allegiance. If we love one parent more easily than another, we must be careful to honor each person to whom honor is due. Thus we inherit the full blessing of God.

What dilemmas are likely to occur when married people try to honor their parents? I shall examine child-rearing, finances, parents in the home, and religious differences. These areas should suffice to give us the lay of this difficult and promising land.

Child-Rearing

Some couples have conflicts with their parents over how they raise their kids. This is a difficult subject, but let's put first things first. It is the young couple's right and responsibility to raise their children before God. They do not have to listen to anything their parents say on the subject—and some couples don't. Whether they are wise to ignore the advice of their elders is another question.

Grandparents are often dismayed by the parenting methods of their children. They see their grandchildren as abused or indulged, as neglected or doted on, as pressured too much or not stimulated enough. Not every grandparent is supplied with the diplomacy and discernment which help families to deal with such differences. Therefore conflicts arise. What do you do when your parents or your in-laws think you're too strict with your kids—or that you're spoiling them rotten?

Communicate; communicate; communicate. You shouldn't do anything until you know what your parents are thinking, until you understand their motivation. And if you think their motivation is simply to make your life miserable, you're not ready to talk about raising kids, or anything else. You must first come to a better—and more honoring—understanding of your parents, if you want to be blessed.[7] The vast majority of grandparents sincerely desire a good life for their children and grandchildren. Such benevolent motivation, coupled with long life experience, ensures that grandparents' criticisms and suggestions will be worth listening to.

If you have a teachable spirit and if you seek after truth, then search for the grains of wisdom in your parents' teaching, and sift patiently through the chaff, if need be, to find them. You can open up some interesting dialogue with parents, by asking how well they practiced what they are preaching to you now.[8] You may discover that their doctrine grew from remorse at their own mistakes in raising you. Or you may learn the blessed experience behind their principles of parenting. Either way, you will find reason to value what they say.

If you find you cannot agree with your parents on how their grandchildren should be raised, there is a fine art to communicating your decision. Your parents ought to feel that you took what they said seriously, that you considered it carefully, and that you had important reasons for choosing not to follow it. If their criticisms were hasty or ill-tempered, be careful not to follow their example. If you really believe your principles are based on God's Word, you ought to have His peace in presenting them to your parents.

When grandparents treat kids differently from the way their parents treat them, the parents may feel undermined or think it's bad for the kids. Usually this takes the form of the grandparents being more indulgent than the parents. Too much TV, too many treats or presents or special trips, too little discipline—"It takes me two days to calm them down when they get back from Grandma's," groans the mother. The trick in this situation is to determine what is really damaging to the children. (Some television programs unquestionably are.) Were you ever indulged by an uncle, an aunt, or a grandparent? I was. Do you look back on those times as the cause of your troubles later in life? I don't. I treasure the memory of them. I have even taken my kids and their cousins to places that kids love and parents suffer through, simply because I remember how much I enjoyed such visits as a child.

Forbidding grandparents to see their grandchildren, though it is in the proper powers of the parents, must be the very last resort. Being spoiled or being treated too strictly is less harmful to kids than being deprived of their grandparents' love. In severe situations—such as if the grandparent has a history of child abuse or is grossly negligent—parents may need to be present at all times, but they should never cut off the relationship, except in the most dire emergencies. By the way, the same principle applies to divorced or separated spouses. Hard as it may be, a wise parent will encourage visits between the estranged spouse and their mutual children, even when it makes the parent's life more difficult afterwards. How shall our children learn to honor their absent parent, if we make it impossible for them to know one another?

I have known cases where the parents considered a grandparent to be neglectful or untrustworthy. Fearing for the safety of their children, they would not leave them under the grandparent's supervision. The question here is this: How realistic are the parents' fears? Are they thinking the best or the worst of the grandparent? In most cases, a loving communication of parental concern, combined with trial experiments of the grandparent's abilities, will yield surprising results—to the parents.[9] It is a refreshing experience, I assure you, to counsel a couple on this subject, and years later to meet the grandparent in question at a playground—with a flock of her grandchildren in tow.

Finances

Financial issues often cause conflicts between the generations. Where a child is still under his parents' authority by biblical standards,[10] he ought to obtain his parents' advice and consent before making major gifts, purchases, or investments.[11] But where the child is no longer under parental authority, what obligations, if any, does he or she have to the parents?

Jesus made it clear that the obligation to support needy parents is fundamental to the Christian religion (see chap. 8). The only exceptions I can think of are a parent who is able but unwilling to work and parents who will waste the money you give them. Let's start with the lazy parent. Paul said, "For even when we were with you, this we commanded you, that if any would not work, neither should he eat" (2 Thess. 3:10). The emphasis here is on a willingness to work,[12] to contribute in some meaningful way to the welfare of others. Where an able-bodied parent is unwilling to work or to be useful in some other way, I do not see that he or she should be excepted from Paul's commandment. If you have doubts in this area, consult your pastor or the deacons of your church.

What if your parent is an alcoholic, a drug user, or a compulsive spender? You are still obliged to support your parent, but you ought to do it prudently. You may need to give your parent food or clothing instead of money. You may need to pay his or her bills yourself, instead of trusting your parent to do it. You are not obligated to deprive your wife and children so that your parent can vacation in Hawaii. On the other hand, if you are keeping your children in expensive colleges while your parent lives in poverty, I doubt that you have the mind of Christ in this matter.

Some parents have medical conditions which require expensive treatment. You, not your parent, must decide how much you should contribute toward such treatment. If you make major contributions toward medical expenses, you ought to have some role in deciding what treatment is best or necessary, just as your parents did for you when you were little. I cannot give specific guidelines here, but I can say that the historic Christian position is opposite to the "quality of life" arguments one hears about today. You need not bankrupt yourself to pay for some highly technical treatment for an aged parent. But if you think it proper to deprive your parent—comatose or conscious—of food, water, or basic medical care, remember:

> For we know him that hath said, Vengeance belongeth unto me, I will recompense, saith the Lord. And again, The Lord shall judge his people. It is a fearful thing to fall into the hands of the living God. (Heb. 10:30–31)

Last but not least, what about parents who disapprove of how you spend, invest, or give away your money? Before you respond, "That's none of their business," please hear me out on the matter. I would rather you say, "That's not their decision to make." Yes, it is up to you what you do with your money. But that doesn't mean that it's none of your parents' business. Finances are a vital area of life. How can those who love you and want the best for you, even when you think they don't, not be concerned, if they see you taking dangerous risks or passing up choice opportunities? And if, perhaps, their own economic future is bound up with yours, they have an additional reason to be interested in your well-being.

If your parent says something to you about money, don't dismiss it out of hand. The Lord could be speaking to you through the voice of your parent. Many of the proverbs lend support to this kind of thinking (see chap. 4). It's true that God may be leading you in a way that your parent cannot understand at the moment, but that's not the only possibility.

When we moved to California in the early 1980s, my mother-in-law suggested, on one of her visits, that we might do well to buy a home, even though prices were so much higher than we were used to. I chose instead to follow the advice of some financial newsletter writers, who said that the price of California real estate was inflated. These writers had more degrees in business and economics than my mother-in-law, but by the end of the decade, I was sorry to have neglected her advice.

Parents in the Home

Nowadays few people choose to have their parents live with them. When a parent moves into the home, it's usually because she or he cannot live independently or lacks the money to do so. In other words, we are not accustomed to thinking of a live-in parent as a blessing.[13] But from the beginning it was not so.

Paul instructed Timothy: "If any widow has children or grandchildren, let them first learn to show piety *at home* and to repay their parents; for that is good and acceptable before God" (1 Tim. 5:4, emphasis added). In other words, the widow in question would normally be residing in the house of one of her children or grandchildren.[14] This was probably the case for Naomi, who seems to have passed her widowhood in the house of Boaz and Ruth. Boaz was "a . . . man of wealth" (Ruth 2:1), who could easily afford a condo for his child's legal grandmother. But the Scriptures tell us: "And Naomi took the child, and laid it in her bosom, and became nurse unto it" (Ruth 4:16). Does it sound as if she lived outside the home?

Peter's mother-in-law lived in his house.

> And he arose out of the synagogue, and entered into Simon's house. And Simon's wife's mother was taken with a great fever; and they besought him for her. And he stood over her, and rebuked the fever; and it left her: and immediately she arose and ministered unto them. (Luke 4:38–39)

While some commentators think she served Christ simply to show her gratitude, I think she was resuming her normal household duties. She contributed to the welfare of her family (as every able-bodied person should) by serving, just as Martha served the disciples in her house at Bethany.

A parent or in-law who lives in the house must abide by the rules of the house.[15] She or he must live under the authority of the head of that house. She should have a position of honor, of course, but she also needs to know the duties that attend her position and the rights and privileges of other family members.

Asa, the righteous king of Judah, illustrates for us the principle that "parents do not have an absolute claim to honor."[16]

> And Asa did what was right in the sight of the Lord, like David his father. He also put away the male cult prostitutes from the land, and removed all the idols which his fathers had made. And he also removed Maacah his mother from being queen mother, because she had made a horrid image as an Asherah; and Asa cut down her horrid image and burned it at the brook Kidron. (1 Kings 15:11–13, NASB)

As head of the kingdom, and as head of his own family, Asa was responsible to God. He removed his mother from her position of honor, because her idolatry was offensive to the Lord. He did not put her to death, as he might have done,[17] but (in Matthew Henry's words) "he banished her from the court, and confined her to an obscure and private life." He showed her mercy, in sparing her life; he continued to support her, though not in the style to which she was accustomed; and he showed publicly that "the first and great commandment" takes precedence over the first commandment with promise.[18] We may profit from Asa's example.

Governing a household of three (or more) generations is definitely one of the fine arts. Every family member's patience and obedience will be tried as the head of the house "learns the ropes" of his calling. If you grew up with a live-in grandparent, you probably know what I'm talking about. When your parents failed to deal with that grandparent effectively—whether they were too lenient or too severe—did you support and honor them in those difficult times? Or did you focus on their failings and think the worst of them? Remember: "Blessed are the merciful, for they shall obtain mercy."

Religious Differences

There may be problems between different kinds of Christians, or between Christians and non-believers. In our family we have had first-hand experience with both situations. My wife and I are Christians; my parents were non-believers. We are evangelical Protestants; my in-laws are Greek Orthodox. (Never a dull moment, you might say.) What does the first commandment with promise mean when applied to circumstances like ours?

When God said, "Honor your father and mother," He could have added any number of qualifying clauses—*if they love Me; if they keep*

My commandments; if they worship Me in spirit and in truth. But He didn't. He gave it to us straight. Whether your parents are atheists, cult members, New Agers, or model Christians, your duty to them in most things is the same. The proverbs about heeding your parents' instruction still apply to you. It's only when they command you to sin or to participate in demonic religion, that you must refuse them.[19] But the vast majority of parental commands, requests, and instructions have little to do with these exceptions.

If you are still living under your parents' authority and they forbid you to attend any church or to have any Christian fellowship, I cannot easily tell you what to do. You would certainly have grounds for disobeying their injunction,[20] but you might be wiser not to, for a time. Such cases must be decided individually. If your parents forbid you to tithe your income to the Lord, see if they will allow you to give a smaller amount or give the same amount in a different way. I doubt that God will be displeased with a cheerful giver who reduces his tithe at his parents' command. What discipline He might mete out to the parents—that's another question!

If your parents are or seem hostile to your faith, the manner and spirit in which you respond to them are just as important as your actions.

> But the fruit of the Spirit is love, joy, peace, long-suffering, gentleness, goodness, faith, Meekness, temperance: against such there is no law. And they that are Christ's have crucified the flesh with the affections and lusts. If we live in the Spirit, let us also walk in the Spirit. Let us not be desirous of vain glory, provoking one another, envying one another. (Gal. 5:22–26)

What you do, or refuse to do, with a Christlike spirit is likely to please God and may even find favor with your parents. What you do in a different spirit won't get the same results.

This is particularly true when your parents or in-laws belong to a Christian church that is quite different from your own.[21] You should view that church as you ought to view them, as Shem and Japheth viewed Noah, emphasizing the good points and refusing to dwell on the weak or unscriptural ones. It was a great moment in my relationship with my in-laws when I finally asked their forgiveness for having judged their church, for not having thought the best of their faith. They didn't respond, "Oh, we don't know what you're talking about." They knew only too well, yet they graciously forgave me and never mentioned the matter again.

Do you think I am the only Christian who ever needed to apologize in this way? I wish that I were. I would have kept my shame to myself, if I thought none of my readers could learn from my experience.

The Call of God

I have a friend who is a globe-trotting evangelist in his sixties. He has been successful as a pastor, a church planter, a missionary, and a seminary professor. Now he is a consultant on church growth with very large churches on several continents. It's wonderful work, and he loves it, but it has its complications. He mentioned to me recently the difficulty he feels about not being able to care for his aged parents when he is out of the country. They would like him to be around more, and although they try not to make a fuss about it, his travels are a real burden to them.

When he finished telling me his troubles, I replied facetiously, "You're on the verge of having your own calling from God. Soon you'll be able to justify your absence on that basis." You should have seen the look he gave me! But there was method to my madness. His parents weren't asking him to break the Ten Commandments. The fact that he was married and had his own family was not a valid reason for him to be out of touch with his parents. Only his calling from God could justify his absence.

If any man has a valid calling, with evidence and credentials to support his claim to it, my friend does. Why then did I joke about his being "on the verge of his own calling"? I was trying to get him to see the situation from his parents' point of view. His father had been very active in Christian ministry and was still not fully retired. He felt the need of his son's help in prolonging his own usefulness in the Lord's work. From the perspective of a man still trying to fulfill his own calling, I surmised, his son's calling might seem less impressive or less compelling than it was to other people. Of course my friend was justified in what he was doing. But he also needed, I thought, to appreciate his parents' perspective and to deal with them gently while helping them to understand his own.

My friend found a way to help keep his father's ministry going without compromising his own busy international schedule. His willingness to help his parents, I believe, is one reason that his own work has been extraordinarily fruitful in recent years.

Before they died, both my parents were past eighty and had extremely serious medical conditions. They lived on the east coast of the United States (as do my in-laws), but for nearly a decade I and my family had been living out west. Though I visited them twice a year, I often agonized over the distance between us. Yet the reason that distance existed was my belief that God had called me to live and to write in California.[22] A few years ago, my wife and I consulted and prayed with our pastors about moving back east. They agreed with us that both in terms of family needs and economics this would be the sensible thing to do, unless the Lord directed otherwise. Yet even as they spoke, I had a clear conviction of God's wanting us to stay where we were. So we remained, ever mindful of Winston Churchill's dictum, "Play for more than you can afford to lose, and you will learn the game."

We finally moved back to Virginia when my father fell and broke his hip. With both parents bedridden and no children living nearby, I knew what my duty was. Since at the time I was writing this book, I said to my dad, "Well, I could stay in California and win the Hypocrite of the Year Award." To which he replied, "There's a lot of competition for that award."

Age, Recognition, and Evidence

It's easy to tell when a man and a woman are married: Their marriage certificate is proof of their condition. But the documentary records of our personal callings are stored up in heaven. It's much harder to determine if the Lord has called a man or a woman to a particular work. What criteria should we follow in discerning whether we or other people have a valid call from God? The chief ones, I think, are age, recognition, and evidence. Allow me to explain.

When Abraham responded to the call of God, he was no spring chicken. "So Abram departed, as the Lord had spoken unto him; and Lot went with him: and Abram was seventy and five years old when he departed out of Haran" (Gen. 12:4). Clearly Abraham was old enough to have a calling; but he had no approval from the United Temples of Babylon, and the evidence of his relationship with God was a long time coming. The miraculous birth of Isaac, foretold from heaven, was more-than-sufficient proof of his father's peculiar calling. But during the twenty-five years between his departure from Haran and the birth of Isaac, who could be certain that Abraham was not deluded? Age and maturity alone may not be enough to establish the fact that we are called by God.

Moses was eighty years old when the Lord told him to return to Egypt (Ex. 7:7). "Then Moses answered and said, 'But, behold they will not believe me, nor hearken unto my voice: for they will say, "The Lord hath not appeared unto thee"'" (Ex. 4:1). So God gave Moses signs to convince the elders of Israel that He had really called him. By the time of the Exodus, Moses had the approval of the elders and the ten plagues to prove that he was a prophet from God. He had age, recognition, and evidence in abundance. But if you know his story, you know that wasn't enough to make his job easy.

Turning to the Book of Acts, we find:

> Now there were in the church that was at Antioch certain prophets and teachers; . . . As they ministered to the Lord, and fasted, the Holy Ghost said, Separate me Barnabas and Saul for the work whereunto I have called them. And when they had fasted and prayed, and laid their hands on them, they sent them away. (Acts 13:1–3)

Paul and Barnabas had sufficient age and the blessing of the church when they left Antioch. They started collecting evidence at their first stopping place, Cyprus. Before long, they would have a mountain of evidence that God had sent them out.

The Harder Cases

So far, so good. If we're not spiritually blind, it's easy to see that some people are called by God. What about the harder cases in Scripture? What about the Davids, the Jeremiahs, and the Amoses in our lives?

When David saw Goliath and thought it strange that no one was willing to fight with him, Eliab questioned his younger brother's motivation. "Why camest thou down hither? . . . I know thy pride, and the naughtiness of thine heart; for thou art come down that thou mightest see the battle" (1 Sam. 17:28). A few minutes later, of course, no one would be doubting David's motivation—or his calling; but how did things stand *before* he slew Goliath? Eliab was present when Samuèl anointed David as the new king of Israel (1 Sam. 16:13); He knew that godly authority had ordained David to great things. But he may have thought that David was not yet old enough for his royal role, and he may not have known that David had slain a lion and a bear.[23] When we seem to have only one of the three basic supports for our calling, we should not be surprised when people doubt our motivation.

If you think it's tough for a young king, well, things are worse for young prophets. Jeremiah had neither age nor evidence in his favor, and his calling was revealed to no one in authority.

> Then said I, Ah, Lord God! behold, I cannot speak: for I am a child. But the Lord said unto me, Say not, I am a child: for thou shalt go to all that I shall send thee, and whatsoever I command thee thou shalt speak. Be not afraid of their faces: for I am with thee to deliver thee, saith the Lord. (Jer. 1:6–8)

Until God gave him miraculous signs, which seem to have been a long time coming, even the best of men might have doubted Jeremiah. I find nothing before the death of the false prophet Hananiah which might have caused skeptics to believe "the weeping prophet." But Jeremiah had been prophesying some three decades before that confirmation came to pass![24] Imagine the abuse he suffered in those years!

What Jeremiah said agreed with the words of Isaiah, who *had* been confirmed by miraculous signs. But that was long before, and the bulk of Isaiah's prophecies had yet to be fulfilled. Moreover, there were plenty of false prophets to mislead the people. Small wonder, then, that men rejected Jeremiah and his dismaying message from the Lord.

In one respect Jeremiah had an advantage over Amos: Jeremiah was a priest. He might be supposed to know something about spiritual things. When Amos was told not to prophesy in Israel any more,

> Then Amos answered and said to Amaziah, "I am not a prophet, nor am I the son of a prophet; for I am a herdsman and a grower of sycamore figs. But the Lord took me from following the flock and the Lord said to me, 'Go prophesy to My people Israel.'" (Amos 7:14-15, NASB)

Amos was absolutely without credentials. To make matters worse, he was sent from his own people to prophesy to the neighboring kingdom of Israel. Do you think it's likely that his parents approved of this arrangement?

We are not told what the parents of the prophets and the apostles thought about their sons leaving their flocks, their nets, or their tax tables. To me it seems certain that some of them went forth without their parents' blessing. When God calls, we must go. To heed our parents' commands instead of God's would be nothing short of idolatry. The question is this, How do you know that you are called by God, especially when your parents think you're not?

Since we have an exceedingly clear command to obey our parents, the call from God must be equally clear before it can justify any disobedience on our part. I do not say that it must be clear to *them*, for some parents may never grasp what God is telling you to do. But you should be very cautious about stepping out on your own, without your parents' approval. David was anointed by Samuel himself, but he stayed home with the sheep, until Jesse sent him to the battle. Are you sure that you're wiser than David or that your situation is radically different from his?

Do you believe God has called you to do something your parents cannot understand? Then put your burden on the Lord. Ask Him to make your calling clear—to you, to your parents, and to the leaders of your church. If neither elders nor parents witness to your calling or to your timing in responding to it, you are taking your life in your hands to step out on your own authority. No one can say for sure that you are wrong to do so: you could be a Jeremiah or an Amos. But for every real prophet like them, there are too many young people eager to "do something for the Lord," but unwilling to wait for His direction, which is often expressed though the blessing of parents, even parents who do not know Him.

CHAPTER 13

Miss Barrett
and Her Father

It's easy to come up with ideas about what the Bible means. It's harder to apply them to real situations. The life of Elizabeth Barrett Browning provides an excellent case study for testing the limits of our doctrine. I have been challenged, intrigued, and humbled as I have sought to apply the standards of this book to Miss Barrett and her father. Their story has much to teach us about trust and honesty and communication between parent and child. As we study the Barretts, may God grant you discernment—about them, about my teaching, and about you and your parents.

Long before they met each other, Elizabeth Barrett and Robert Browning were recognized as gifted poets. Their secret courtship and marriage, and their subsequent escape to Italy, became (in literary circles at least) the most famous love story of the nineteenth century. Two factors in particular have preserved that fame: Miss Barrett's love poems to her future husband, the *Sonnets from the Portuguese*[1]—and the public perception of her father as a heartless tyrant.

Was Mr. Barrett the "inhuman monster" depicted in the popular play, *The Barretts of Wimpole Street?*[2] Or is there another side to the story?

Was Elizabeth justified in marrying and leaving home without her father's permission? How well did she observe the first commandment with promise?

The Facts of the Matter

Let's begin with the facts that nearly everyone agrees on. From about the age of fifteen, Elizabeth passed a secluded life, partly because of illness. Except for intervals at the seashore for her health, she lived in her father's house until she was forty. Mr. Barrett encouraged his daughter in all her literary pursuits, and since she had never found a young man who interested her romantically, they both assumed that she would never marry.

After Miss Barrett made some complimentary remarks about Robert Browning in her poetry, he wrote her a letter.[3] They corresponded for a few months, and then (in May 1845) he came to visit her. He fell in love with her virtually at first sight; after that he came to see her every week. Over the next year, she came to accept and to return his love and, despite her weak health, to think it possible that she could marry him. Meanwhile, they pretended to everyone that their friendship was limited to a mutual interest in literature.

When Elizabeth was forty years old, she and Browning were married in a secret ceremony. She parted from her husband at the church door, visited a friend as if nothing unusual had happened, and returned home to live with her family as before. A week later, she sneaked out of the house with her maid, met her husband, and embarked for Italy.[4] She informed her family of her marriage and departure only by letters that arrived after she had left London. Her father disinherited her and declared that their relationship was ended. (He put her books in storage, and the bill was sent to her.)

The Brownings' deep love for each other never diminished. Making Italy their home, they visited England several times. Elizabeth saw her siblings on those trips, but she never had any direct contact with her father. They were still unreconciled when he died in 1857. The final decline in her health began soon after her father's death, and she finally succumbed to chronic respiratory disease in 1861.

Popular and Scholarly Views

When the Brownings' son (and only child) published their love letters in 1899, the image of Mr. Barrett as a tyrant became firmly established in the public mind. Two films, a play, and dozens of books later, it lingers on today among those who still remember the drama of Wimpole Street.

Perhaps the best gauge of current opinion is the articles on Elizabeth Barrett Browning in our popular reference works. The *Encyclopedia Americana* tells us that Mr. Barrett was "tyranically jealous" and that he "never forgave his daughter."[5] *World Book* states that "Elizabeth's father violently opposed [the Brownings'] marriage."[6] Both of these accounts are less than accurate. Worse still, they ignore completely Mr. Barrett's many virtues. He is known to posterity only through a gross distortion of his worst traits. (God help us not to see our parents so!)

In fact Mr. Barrett did forgive Elizabeth.[7] And contrary to the *World Book* article, Mr. Barrett had absolutely no knowledge of the Brownings' marriage (or their love for each other) until a week after the wedding. (How can one "violently oppose" what one knows nothing about?)

When two standard reference works give out erroneous information about a man, and make no attempt to present a balanced picture of his character, is it any wonder that he is not admired? As you get to know Mr. Barrett better, you may form your own estimate of his worth as a parent and as a Christian. You may also learn how to avoid drawing distorted conclusions about your own parents.

In the Hands of the Scholars

Mr. Barrett has been treated better by the scholars.[8] The longer, the more detailed, and the more recent a biography of his famous daughter is, the better Mr. Barrett looks. In the last three decades thousands of Barrett family letters and documents have come to light, and many of them have been published. Biographer Margaret Forster tells us, "It is Mr. Barrett who gains most" through our knowledge of these documents.[9] "Truth will come to light," said Shakespeare, ". . . in the end, truth will out."[10] Nearly a century after the publication of the love letters portraying him as a tyrant, a fuller picture of Mr. Barrett—and his daughter—is beginning to emerge.

Seeking the Whole Truth

Let us try to "speak the truth in love" about Elizabeth and her father. Let us treat Mr. Barrett as we ought to treat our own parents, thinking the best of him, without denying his sins.

Mr. Barrett's chief virtue was his great capacity for love, which can hardly be separated from his devout Christian faith. Mr. Barrett loved his wife and children intensely, especially his firstborn, Elizabeth. He was very devoted to his children after the death of their mother, and he hated to be away from them. He was a very loving father.[11]

Mr. Barrett's greatest fault, I believe, was his inability to show weakness. You may call it pride, if you prefer.[12] This took several forms.

> [Mr. Barrett] could never bring himself to say either that he had been wrong or that changed circumstances had altered his opinion.[13]

> [Elizabeth] knew that he prided himself on never showing emotion, especially not misery. . . . Confronted with her father so near to breaking down Elizabeth's one thought was to help him preserve his dignity: it was this anxiety that prevented her and everyone else from ever questioning Mr. Barrett directly. All his children conspired to let him keep them in the dark not out of fear but out of respect and love.[14]

Remember, it is not the parent's sin, but the child's reaction to that sin, that is all-important (see chap. 5). What started as an innocent desire to protect Mr. Barrett from having to show his weakness, soon grew into a conspiracy that was positively sinful. To spare him and themselves pain, his children began to hide their feelings from their father, to close off their hearts to him. They began to dissemble. While Mr. Barrett's inflexibility and anger might make his children's sin seem prudent at the time, they could not escape the consequences of their deception.

Mr. Barrett's foremost misfortune was being raised without a father. Only in infancy did he live with both his parents. The marriage failed, and the children were raised by their mother. Meanwhile their father begot children by three other women. During this time, he had only slight and distant contact with his son.[15]

> From the beginning [Mr. Barrett] could have no balanced conception of what it meant to be a father. Through his own lack he had developed an exaggerated conception of the importance, of the dimensions, of fatherhood.[16]

When Elizabeth was just out of her teens, Mr. Barrett lost much of his fortune, and his wife died unexpectedly (in 1828). Soon he had to sell his beloved property. He could still afford servants; but the transition from a prosperous gentleman to a widower in reduced circumstances was certainly a keen one. He bore it all without complaining, with great concern for his children, and, of course, with little show of emotion.

Mr. Barrett's now motherless family remained intact until 1840, when accident and illness claimed the two oldest sons. Both of them were far from home when they died, and the death of the oldest son is a part of our story.

Elizabeth's doctors in London had ordered her to the seashore for her health. Though Mr. Barrett was reluctant to send her away, he sent three of her siblings with her to help her get settled in the resort of Torquay. Elizabeth could not bear to part with her oldest brother when, after many weeks had passed, their father expected him back in London. As Elizabeth later described it to Browning,

> When the time came for him to leave me . . . my aunt . . . wrote a letter to papa to tell him that he would "break my heart" if he persisted in calling away my brother . . . And Papa's answer was—burnt into me, as with fire, it is—that "under such circumstances he did not refuse to suspend his purpose, but that he considered it to be *very wrong in me to exact such a thing.*" So there was no separation *then.*[17]

But there was to be a dreadful separation later.

For two more years her beloved "Bro" stayed on with Elizabeth in Torquay. Then, one fateful day in August, he went sailing with his friends. Their boat sank in calm seas, and all of them were drowned. Elizabeth was devastated. She blamed herself for keeping "Bro" with her, but her father "was generous & forbearing in that hour of bitter trial, & never reproached me as he might have done."[18]

Slowly recovering her strength, Elizabeth returned to London and her father's house on Wimpole Street. There she dwelt as a near recluse and began picking up the pieces of her literary life.

Elizabeth's seclusion at Wimpole Street was largely of her own making. She had a highly abnormal fear of normal social intercourse, and she used her poor health, her literary work, and her father's protectiveness to ward off unwelcome visitors and invitations. She was not her father's prisoner. Her isolation was convenient for her—until a starry-eyed young poet came to call. Hence Forster concludes, "Her father could not be blamed for thinking she wanted only to stay in her room, reading and writing, and wished nothing else from life except her family around her."[19]

Nearing forty, Elizabeth lacked the courage to tell her father that love had changed her life for ever. She assumed, fairly enough, that Browning, who had no income and was six years her junior, would not satisfy Mr. Barrett as a son-in-law. This brings us to the vexed question of Mr. Barrett's attitude toward marriage, which Forster calls "extremely puzzling."

> He found in the Bible the evidence he wanted—in this case, to confirm that a father had authority over his children in all respects—and ignored any that conflicted with his opinion. . . . He never at any time issued an edict saying his children could under no circumstances marry. . . . *In fairness to him, it is true to say that few Victorian fathers would have approved the matches which his children proposed.*[20] (Emphasis added)

More than once his children had applied unsuccessfully to Mr. Barrett for permission to marry, and Elizabeth assumed, whether fairly or not, that no satisfactory candidate could ever be found. In any event, there was only one candidate for her affections—Robert Browning.

The Pisa Conflict

After Browning had declared his love to Elizabeth, but before they had resolved to marry secretly, Miss Barrett and her father suffered a severe, but unacknowledged, break in their relationship. The incident that appeared to cause the break was (in Forster's words) "the failure of the Pisa plan." For years friends and relatives had been urging Elizabeth to winter in Malta or Italy, or some other place with a climate likely to improve her health.

> But Elizabeth's answer, though she was sorely tempted and would have liked nothing better, had always been the same: she could not and would not break up her father's home again, as she had done when Dr. Chambers insisted on her going to Torquay.[21]

But under Browning's influence she overcame her fearful memories, and appealed to her father for permission to winter in a warmer climate. Pisa (of Leaning Tower fame) became her goal, and for weeks she waited anxiously for her father's decision.

We can trace the development of the broken relationship in Elizabeth's letters to Browning.

> [September 6, 1845] Now that the [trip] comes so near . . . in this dead silence of Papa's . . . it all seems impossible.
>
> [September 23] I have spoken again, & the result is that we are in precisely the same position,—only with bitterer feelings on one side. If I go or stay they *must* be bitter: words have been

said that I cannot easily forget, nor remember without pain. . . .
He complained of the undutifulness & rebellion (! ! !) of everyone in the house. . . . And I could not get an answer.

[September 29] DON'T think too hardly of poor Papa—You
have his wrong side . . his side of peculiar wrongness . . to
you just now. When you have walked round him you will
have other thoughts of him. [Forster comments: "But Robert
was never given any chance to do any walking around: Elizabeth kept him as far from meeting her father as ever."]

[October 13] . . . *I do not go to Italy* . . it has ended as I feared.
. . . [Papa] said that I "might go if I pleased, but that going it
would be under his heaviest displeasure." . . . <u>The bitterest
'fact' of all is, that I had believed Papa to have loved me more
than he obviously does.</u>[22]

Two months after her marriage, in a long letter to a friend, Elizabeth wrote her most detailed defense of her break with her father.
There we learn more about what she calls "the Pisa conflict of last
year."

I never had doubted but that papa would catch at any human
chance of restoring my health. . . . His manner of acting
towards me last summer was one of the most painful griefs of
my life. . . . Now if he had said last summer that he was reluctant for me to leave him . . . I was ready to give up Pisa in a
moment, and I told him as much. Whatever my new impulses
towards life were, my love for him (taken so) would have
resisted all—I loved him so dearly. But [instead] . . . I was
wounded to the bottom of my heart—cast off when I was
ready to cling to him.[23]

"He that is first in his own cause seemeth just; but his neighbor
cometh and searcheth him" (Prov. 18:17). In Elizabeth's case her
"neighbors" are her careful biographers. Here is Forster's view of the
Pisa conflict:

A tremendous struggle of wills was taking place, a struggle
complicated by the fact that neither she nor her father spoke
plainly. She found it impossible to tell him that she was in
love with Robert Browning and that she wished to change her
life in more ways than merely wintering abroad. And *her
father*, in so brutally resisting the innocuous sounding idea of
escaping to the sun, *was challenging her to tell him the whole
truth*. He remembered perfectly well how, in the last three
winters . . . she had sided with him, proclaiming she was "just
as well off" in her own warm room and that it was not worth

the upheaval [of wintering abroad]. Suddenly, the upheaval
was worthwhile. Why?[24] (Emphasis added)

Concerning the Pisa crisis, there are two points I wish to under-
score. The first is that it was the central incident in Elizabeth's broken relationship with her father. After Pisa, she concluded that he
did not really love her. That assumption, and her refusal to question
it, made her secret marriage and flight inevitable. Outwardly Elizabeth's great adventure was just beginning. Inwardly, with respect to
our commandment, the drama was practically over. The tragedy was
already complete.

The second point is that, if I were on a jury of Mr. Barrett's peers,
I would find him not guilty of the charge his daughter laid against
him. He was guilty of many things, I'm sure, but lack of love for his
children was not among them.

Coming to Conclusions

Did Mr. Barrett say he did not love Elizabeth? No. Could his
behavior in the Pisa conflict be interpreted in a loving way? Yes. Forster thinks he was challenging Elizabeth to tell him the whole truth.
Others think he could not bear the risk of losing more of his children. Did Mr. Barrett's "displeasure" about Pisa, and Elizabeth's decision not to go there, injure her health?

"The winter came, with its miraculous mildness." (The words are
hers.) Staying in her father's house, without going to Pisa, Elizabeth's
health continued to improve. Yet she did not rethink her decision
about her father; she did not give him the benefit of the doubt.
Though she had very reluctantly followed his advice and been
blessed in doing so, still she concluded that he could not love her.
That was very dishonoring.

Elizabeth justified her secrecy, saying that she would have col-
lapsed under Mr. Barrett's anger, if he knew that she loved Browning. Perhaps she would have. But if she had not discounted her
father's love, she might have been able to bear his anger better.

In any event, Elizabeth's focus was on herself. Her first question
was not, "What is right?" but rather, "What is possible for me?"
Assuming that she could not tell her father the truth and survive it,
she found other justifications for her actions. Her bottom line seems
to have been that children have the right to marry whom they will,
regardless of parental objections.

I am not saying that it was wrong for the Brownings to marry. I can hardly conceive of their not marrying. To imagine English literature without the Brownings' marriage is a little like imagining the Great Lakes without Niagara Falls. And since Mr. Barrett never approved a marriage for any of his eleven adult children, one may reasonably argue that some of his prohibitions must have exceeded his authority as a father. Robert and Elizabeth could have disobeyed him on the grounds that in "forbidding to marry" (1 Tim. 4:3) he was usurping the will of God.

What I *am* saying is that the deception of Mr. Barrett was unjustified, and that it was based on false premises. First, Mr. Barrett still loved his daughter. Not allowing his daughter to go to Pisa hardly proves he did not love her. Second, the two poets could have married publicly.

> There were . . . no legal or economic obstacles to the match; nor was there any question of physical force being exercised by Mr. Barrett against his daughter. . . . Browning and Elizabeth Barrett might have married and settled in London (or abroad, if they chose, for the sake of Elizabeth Barrett's health) openly and with perfect freedom.[25]

Elizabeth prevented Robert from approaching Mr. Barrett because she thought she could not bear his reaction. She was thinking of herself more than of her father or her siblings.[26] Her fear made her selfish, and her selfishness proved costly to herself, her husband, and to everyone around her.

Jeannette Marks has written perceptively of Elizabeth and her siblings:

> She was incapable of intentional falsification, yet she swung from deification of her father to the conviction that he was less than human in his attitude towards her. . . . Over the years his children had *given* [Mr. Barrett] a right of way straight through the very heart of their own independence and self-respect. At the worst there had been hysterical scenes *but never year after year any persistent, courageous, and independent development of their own lives.*[27] (Emphasis added)

Nor had there been any persistent, courageous, and independent development of a real relationship with Mr. Barrett. There was no David or Jonathan in this house, no one who would take the continuing risk of communicating with the father, of challenging his distorted ideas and exposing them to the light.

Elizabeth, I believe, had been guilty of idolizing her father, of putting him to some extent in the place of God. She had said publicly that he had "sustained and comforted" her existence as well as "given" it.[28] He was never to be challenged, lest he should become angry. He was either to be worshiped or cast off entirely. There was no middle ground. There was no room for Mr. Barrett to be simply human. As Elizabeth told Browning shortly before their marriage, "Anything but his *kindness*, I can bear now."[29]

We must not make idols of our parents, lest, when they fail us (as they certainly will) we should reject them altogether. We should honor our parents, speaking the truth in love to them about their faults, when those cannot be safely or honorably ignored. If our parents cannot bear to hear their faults mentioned, if honest dialogue becomes impossible, we must seek out a Samuel, a prophet-like person with spiritual authority, to search us and know us, before we resort to deception or disobedience. We should follow David's example, rather than Elizabeth Barrett's.

The End of the Matter

Elizabeth's married life was haunted by her father's rejection. "The happier she was with Robert, the greater the emphasis she laid on her unhappiness over her father."[30] Nor was this a matter of a year or two. Her unhappiness remained past her father's death, until her own end was fast approaching.

I think Elizabeth's preoccupation with her father was the flower of her guilt. If she had confronted her father in love, if she had plumbed the depths of his soul and possibly of his anger, if she had moved in the light of day with her brothers' approval at least, she would not have suffered as she did.[31]

Elizabeth never admitted that there had been a better way to deal with her father. She continued to justify her sin: Her lack of peace was merely the outward sign of her inward lack of repentance.[32] If she had not deceived her father, she might have had peace, however rough the road to it proved. If she had ever fully repented—ever fervently wished that she had done things differently—she might have had peace also. As it was, the peace she attained came more from her father's growth than her own.

Like a drowning person clutching a life ring, Elizabeth clung to the news that her father had forgiven her at last. She wrote her married sister, who was also disinherited, after Mr. Barrett's death:

[Papa had written to a family friend] that he "had forgiven" [us]—that he "even prayed for our well being and well doing."—Those were the words. Let us hold them fast, beloved Henrietta. He prayed for us. Our poor little children had so much from him. And when we pray, may thank God for so much comfort.[33]

If she had possessed the Lord's peace, Elizabeth would have rejoiced more for her father's sake than her own. She would have been glad to see this token of his true Christian spirit overcoming at last his rigid views and actions. But she needed the "comfort" in order to live with herself, as a salve for her own troubled conscience. May it not be so with us!

Elizabeth, however, was not the first Barrett to have trouble with the first commandment with promise. Our story would be incomplete if we ignored Mr. Barrett's sins against *his* father.

After I had written this chapter, I discovered Dr. Peter Dally's recent biography of Elizabeth. He tells us, "At no time in his life did [Mr. Barrett] have anything good to say of his father." Moreover, "When his father died in 1819 he showed no regret." And most significantly—"His Achilles' heel was his fear of failure. In his mind he had to be the perfect husband and father . . . the very opposite of his father."[34]

Mr. Barrett didn't have to search for his father's faults: they were only too evident.[35] But I trust you remember my teaching: *it is not the parent's goodness or wickedness that determines whether the child shall be blessed or cursed; it is the child's reaction to the parent that is crucial* (see chap. 5). Mr. Barrett focused on his father's sins, while ignoring (or not searching for) good points.[36] *At no time in his life did he have anything good to say of his father*—a sure sign of breaking the first commandment with promise.

Dally links "fear of failure" to Mr. Barrett's determination to be "the very opposite of his father." Had he been sympathetic toward his father, had he perceived his good points as clearly as his faults, Mr. Barrett would have been a more tolerant person. His standards for himself and his children would have been more attainable, more realistic. Mr. Barrett "could have no balanced conception of what it meant to be a father,"[37] not because his father had left the family, but because he had rejected his father.

We have reason to be charitable to Mr. Barrett. Brought up with his mother's presumably negative impressions of an adulterous father, who also pilfered his son's estate, it is hardly surprising that Mr. Barrett focused on his father's faults. Yet I maintain that he sinned against his father, and that his sin—unrecognized and therefore unrepented—predisposed his children to do the same to him. Mr. Barrett never sounded out his father, as Jonathan did Saul. He never, when he came to maturity, got his father's side of the story or shared his hurt feelings with him in any vulnerable way. Instead of appealing to his father's good side, he tried to protect himself from his bad side.

Did not Elizabeth do the same to him? She shied away from confronting her father in love and strove to protect herself from his anger. When she concluded that her father did not love her, she gave him little opportunity to explain his actions.

We should be charitable to Elizabeth too, recognizing the influence of her father's bad example, but we may not excuse her. God has instructed each of us to honor our parents; their failures in no way diminish our duty.

Though Elizabeth was wrong to deceive her father, God was just in visiting Mr. Barrett's sin upon him. He who thinks the worst of his parent may expect his own children to think the worst of him. So today, in many a family, God is visiting the parents' sins upon them in the form of rebellious or disrespectful sons and daughters. May I remind you that He often does it in love to turn us from our sins? "Before I was afflicted I went astray, but now have I kept thy word" (Ps. 119:67).

Let us hope that near the end of his life Mr. Barrett recognized his sin against his father and thus was able to forgive the children who had offended him.

And, last but not least, let us recall that Elizabeth always respected her father. Though she thought he did not love her, she never despised him. The best evidence of her respect for Mr. Barrett was her wonderful marriage to Robert Browning. A woman who despises her father is likely (sooner or later) to despise her husband too. A woman who, like Elizabeth, thinks the worst of her father at times, but who respects him still, may share a strong and lasting love the world will long remember.

Part Four:
Making It Right

CHAPTER 14

The Key to It All

To those readers who looked at the table of contents and skipped to this chapter, the key to it all is repentance. Why did I wait thirteen chapters to tell you? Because I cannot make you repent. Only the Spirit and the Word of God can do that. This book was written to prepare you for repentance. I hope and pray that you will make the most of it.

The people I have been able to help in counseling have been the ones who were brought to repentance. I have learned by experience that most of us have plenty to repent of, but we need to be instructed or guided or challenged or provoked before we will recognize and deal with our sin. If you can read the first twelve chapters of this book without any pangs of conscience, you must be quite free from the sins depicted there—or very hardened in them. Those chapters were written to help you open up, so to speak, to the Holy Spirit, to offer yourselves to Him and the work He wants to do. A humble and repentant spirit will enable you to obtain maximum benefit from the rest of this book. Without that spirit, your efforts to get along better with your parents will probably make things worse.

I do not forbid you to start the book here and to take the practical steps I recommend in the remaining chapters. But if things don't go well for you afterward, please have the decency not to blame me.

For the Rest of You . . .

Now for the rest of you, those who have read the book through . . . You should rejoice to hear that repentance is the key to it all. Why? Because no one has the power to keep you from repentance; no one can hinder you along the path of blessing. Though you may need to express your repentance to others, their reaction, whatever it may be, will never control your life. The promise attached to our commandment will take effect in your life as soon as you repent. It's as simple as that.

In its emphasis on repentance, this book differs from most books on family counseling. You may easily find books that tell you to forgive your parents; there are lots of them around. And I rejoice that that portion of the truth is so thoroughly published. We *do* need to forgive our parents the wrongs they have done us. It will never be well with us until we do. Why, then, have I said so little on that important subject?

When we forgive others, we cannot help thinking of their sins against us. However briefly, we must focus on their iniquities. If we do this with our father and mother, before accomplishing a full repentance ourselves, we may hinder the healing process in our family. First of all, some of the "sins" we think we must forgive may be either figments of our own (or someone else's) imagination—or else they are gross distortions of the truth. For example, has not the truth about Mr. Barrett been grossly distorted? Before we forgive, we ought to be sure that our parents are really blameworthy.

Second, even when our parents' sins are as red as scarlet, focusing on them makes it hard to see our own.

> And why beholdest thou the mote that is in thy brother's eye, but perceivest not the beam that is in thine own eye? Either how canst thou say to thy brother, Brother, let me pull out the mote that is in thine eye, when thou thyself beholdest not the beam that is in thine own eye? Thou hypocrite, cast out first the beam out of thine own eye, and then shalt thou see clearly to pull out the mote that is in thy brother's eye. (Luke 6:41–42)

There are too many Christians whose forgiveness of their parents is tainted by hypocrisy. May we not be among them!

I do not mean to suggest that whoever tells you to forgive your parents is giving you bad advice. Far from it. But if your counselors go no further than that, their advice is incomplete. I hope you will receive mine as a kind of supplement to theirs. It may look like bitter medicine; but if God is calling you to repentance, its taste will be sweet in your mouth[1] (see Ezek. 2:8—3:3).

Finally, getting in touch with our own sin is the surest route to being able to forgive others. If you have had difficulty forgiving your parents, if your resentment keeps popping up time after time, God may be telling you that you're still part of the problem. There's a kind of tangled anger which settles in our souls when our involvement in a sin is greater than we know. Is there a demanding tone to your forgiveness? Do you feel strongly that your parents still owe you something? These symptoms indicate that something is hindering you in your attempts to forgive. It could be incomplete repentance. Instead of spending years fussing and fuming about your parents, why not spend a little time looking at yourself? It could be the quickest way to the peace you long for.

Like Good Cooking

The requirements for repentance are the same as for good cooking. You have to have the right ingredients, and you have to take your time. The thunderbolt from heaven may fall in a moment, but usually on a heart that God has seasoned for a while.

> Now when the wife of Uriah heard that Uriah her husband was dead, she mourned for her husband. When the time of mourning was over, David sent and brought her to his house and she became his wife; then she bore him a son. But the thing that David had done was evil in the sight of the Lord. *Then* the Lord sent Nathan to David. (2 Sam. 11:26—12:1, NASB, emphasis added)

As professors Keil and Delitzsch interpret the text,

> The Lord left David almost a whole year in his sin, before sending a prophet to charge the haughty sinner with his misdeeds, and to announce the punishment that would follow. . . . Not only was the fruit of the sin to be first of all brought to light . . . but God would first of all break his unbroken heart by the torture of his own conscience, and prepare it to feel the reproaches of His prophet. . . . Nathan's reproof could not possibly have borne this saving fruit, if David had still been living in utter blindness as to the character of his sin at the time when the prophet went to him.[2]

Our situation is both like and unlike David's. We too must experience the fruit of our sin. We too must be troubled in our conscience. And we need to be prepared for the reproaches of the Holy Spirit.

The difference is that most of us have been suffering the consequences of our sin for some time. We have violated God's law, and it has not been well with us. If now at long last we can hear the Lord's reproaches and come to repentance, we may soon find a blessing instead of a curse. We can look forward to real improvements in our lives if only we can recognize our sin and accept the discipline that God has laid upon us.

The first step is to offer ourselves to the Holy Spirit. This means taking time to pray and wait, to review our lives, and to consider if we have sinned against the holy law of God. Look over chapter 10 of this book and any other chapter that specially challenged you. Read the Scriptures referred to in those chapters and any other portions of the Word the Spirit leads you to. Make a diligent search for your own sin, and look away from the sins of your parents.

Having trouble coming up with a list of your sins? If you are feeling brave and even humble, you might ask your parents how you have been ungrateful, disobedient, or dishonoring to them. (Have pen and paper ready. And don't use the word "sin" unless it's part of their vocabulary.) If your parents are deceased, you might ask their surviving relatives or friends for some perspective on the matter. Ask the ones who thought well of your parents, and skip the ones who often ran them down. I myself have no personal experience with this method; my sins were too apparent.

Ask the Holy Spirit to convict you of your sin. Be persistent, like the widow in Luke 18, but try not to be impatient. My wife prayed for two weeks before she was ready to call her father. Our friend in chapter 1 took two years to come to repentance. In my ignorance I thought she took too long, but God's timing is different from ours. When we wait for the convicting power of the Holy Spirit, however long it takes, then we are really being most efficient. Never think the time wasted you spend waiting on God.

How will you know when your prayers are answered? In my experience there's no mistaking the real thing. It's a heart-rending sorrow; it's the essence of regret. Whether or not you give way to tears, you'll have reason to weep when it comes. And when it does, you won't be thinking of someone else's sin.

It's hard to face the pain you've caused your family and yourself. And it's harder still to see that you might have had a better relationship with your parent if only *you* had been different. But when these things need to be faced, God will give you grace to bear them.

> Sing unto the Lord, O ye saints of his, and give thanks at the remembrance of his holiness. For his anger endureth but a moment; in his favor is life: weeping may endure for a night, but joy cometh in the morning. (Ps. 30:4–5)

The Nuts and Bolts of Repentance

If you're a practical, nuts-and-bolts kind of person, you may feel disappointed by my advice thus far. "Praying and waiting—is that all? What if I don't get anywhere that way? Can't you give me something practical to do?" Well, you could fast; that often accelerates the things of the Spirit. But let me tell you what I would do if you came into my office for counsel. . . .

Remembering my advice at the end of chapter 1, I would not ask you if you have honored your parents. Instead I would inquire about your troubles; I would seek to know whether or not it is well with you. Then I would look for patterns that exhibit the common effects of the first commandment with promise. If you were having conflict with your spouse, I would ask you about your relationship with your parent of the opposite sex. If you were having trouble getting along with authority figures (whether teachers, bosses, pastors, or police), I would look at your relationship with your father (or whoever was the authority to be reckoned with in your family).[3] I would try to determine if you had unfairly judged your parents and whether your uncharitable judgment might be related to your current troubles. My goal would be to show you very real and recognizable sins against your parents—and their connection with the obvious troubles in your life.

Sometimes the link between dishonoring one's parents and one's current troubles is easy to see, at least for outside observers. Sometimes it is subtle and hard to detect. Usually I can discern a likely connection between a person's troubles and the first commandment with promise.[4] The goal of such counseling is to identify attitudes or events that were clearly sinful, that both you and your parents can recognize as wrong.

You may need someone else's help in coming to grips with your sin or concluding in all fairness that you have little to repent. Pack up your troubles and your thoughts after reading this book, and take them to a trusted friend or counselor. Ask that person to help you put the pieces together. Your helper should be someone who under-stands and obeys the first commandment with promise, someone who clearly holds his or her parents in esteem. A plumber who hon-ors his father and mother will be more help to you than a trained counselor who resents or despises his parents.[5] When the blind lead the blind, credentials are of little use. What you need is a man or a woman who can see.

When you have come to a clear knowledge of your sin, when the Holy Spirit has added His convicting power to your knowledge, then you are ready to take the next step. Then you are ready to "bear fruits worthy of repentance" (Matt. 3:8; Luke 3:8). Then you are ready to start "making it right."

Fruits Worthy of Repentance

A number of people whom I counseled years ago have been bear-ing fruit worthy of repentance. Before we get into the specifics of making things right with your parents, let me encourage you with a few examples.

My counselees' sorrow for sin was not very visible on the outside; if there were floods of tears, I rarely saw them. Theirs was repen-tance from "the hidden man of the heart" (1 Pet. 3:4). Their faithful adherence to the principles of this book led over time to the healing of old wounds, to friendlier relations with their parents, and to a number of "fringe benefits."

Of Shorts and Slacks

I like to try foods I have never eaten before, and I like counseling situations that are new and different. One couple came to me because the wife found it hard to relate to her father. That was hardly new or different. What made the story unusual was that the elements I had learned to expect in such cases were missing. There were no lies, no rebellion, no drugs, and no sexual sins involved. Just a sincere and very strict Christian parent, whose grown daughter found it hard to visit him. The apparent issues between them were that she sometimes wore shorts and slacks and that she and her chil-dren had married Christians of other persuasions. Dad rode these issues so hard and so relentlessly that it was hard for family members to have a civil conversation with him.

It took me a while to get acclimated to the problem, but when I did, I encouraged the couple to think the best of her father. They and he agreed on the basics: A woman's clothing should be modest and different from a man's. The disagreement was only about where to draw the line between the sexes. Since the difference, as I saw it, was one of interpretation, not of principle, what would be the harm in visiting Dad dressed in clothing he approved of? At least we could see if Dad was just looking for a fight: If he were, he would immediately find some other issue to complain about.

With her husband's consent, the daughter started visiting Dad with her hair and her clothes in the styles he liked best. She started spending more time with her father and being more generous to her parents, who were just getting by financially. How much one, or all, of these new approaches did to convince Dad that she was serious about honoring him, I can't say; but he soon became less irascible. He did not look for another issue to argue about, and somehow he became more tolerant of his descendants' marriages. He began to show more interest in the grandchildren, and their spouses, from whom he had seemed so distant.

This woman reached out in love to her father—without compromising herself or her values—and Dad noticed and responded. She dealt with an issue that was important to him, and he mellowed on the one that was important to her. Her patience and her various demonstrations of love brought healing to their relationship. But it was her quiet repentance and her determination to obey God that gave her the strength she needed to succeed.

Year After Year

I know a young man who has been trying to honor his parents for years. He still has more to learn—but he has come such a long way! In the bad old days, his father would get drunk and verbally abuse him and the rest of the family. The son would take it without much response, but inwardly he was building up enormous resentment against his dad. Meanwhile he was abused by his peers at school and generally felt safest in the company of his mother. He never found an appropriate outlet for his hostility, and he was still struggling with self-hatred and homosexual tendencies when he came to me for counsel. He has been helped over the years by pastors, counselors, and Christian ministries; my input was only part of a larger process of healing. Yet we both feel that honoring his father has been a key element in stabilizing his Christian life.

Having been impressed, over the years, with his persistent progress with his father, I asked my friend what practical steps he had taken to break down the barriers between them. I summarize his answer as follows:

- Face the truth: "I had to acknowledge that I was really angry at Dad."

- Respond to the truth as a Christian should: "I resolved to deal with my anger."

- Establish regular communication: "I decided to call Dad once a month. I would call him on his birthday and on holidays, and sometimes just because we hadn't talked in a while. In the beginning the calls lasted about fifteen seconds. When they started to last a couple of minutes, I would end each call by saying, 'I love you, Dad.'"

- Develop intimacy: "I decided to let Dad into my life, because he really didn't know anything about me. I confessed my anger toward him, and I asked his forgiveness. I began to share with him the good and bad times I was going through in life. Then, when Mom got sick and was hospitalized, Dad called me up and cried over the phone. He had never expressed deep feelings to any of his kids before. He even told me that he loved me."

- Be prepared: "I would think—'What's the worst thing that can happen if you tell your parent the truth?'—and I would prepare for the worst. Then I didn't worry as much about what would happen when I talked to Dad."

- Be firm when you have to: "On one trip to see my parents, I saved some time to be alone with Dad. He knew I was coming by that morning, just before I flew home, but he got drunk anyway. I told him, 'Dad, you always said that if I didn't like how you were acting, I should leave. Well, I don't like it, and I'm leaving.' I went home, and I didn't call or write him. Three weeks later, he called me, asked me to forget about what had happened, and started treating me with more respect."

- Learn to accept your parent as he is: "Dad still gets drunk sometimes. But now I can handle it better. I can't keep him from sinning, but I can keep myself from sinning in reaction to his sin."

It took a long time and a lot of success with Dad before this young man could face the fact that he really had a lot of sinful feelings toward his mother too. When we first spoke about her, he wasn't ready to deal with those feelings. Now he seems ready, and even though she has passed away, he expects to learn how to honor *both* his parents. I am confident that he will complete the good work he has carried on so long.

"I Was Hurting and I Was Ready."

If you think it must be harder to honor a deceased parent, consider the story of this woman in her forties. When she came to me for counsel, she recalls, "I was unable to see men as trustworthy or honorable. I would leave first in every relationship. All my intimacies were painful. When I talked to you, Phil, I was hurting and I was ready. I had nowhere to go." In other words, she was finally desperate enough to face her memories of her father.

Her father had been a lifelong alcoholic. He had raged at his kids and sometimes treated them roughly. She had seen little of him after her parents' separation (they had never been legally married) when she was less than ten years old. But her fear of and hatred toward her father had remained. "I couldn't be intimate with God. I had put all of Dad's attributes on Him," she remembers. She also had never married.

I tried to help her reinterpret some of her father's actions. She was angry that he used to take her into bars when she was little. I suggested that it showed how much he enjoyed her company. One day when she had taken home some tomato plants a neighbor had given her, Dad went into a rage and threatened to beat her if she went near the man again. She remained traumatized by that memory, even after finding out that the neighbor was a transvestite. I suggested that Dad had been trying to protect her, though his actions toward her had seemed so unloving at the time.

When we prayed, she sensed God pointing out her hardness of heart toward her father. She admitted, "The Holy Spirit showed me times when I had provoked Dad. I had remembered his rage, but I had forgotten what I had done to provoke him." She began to see that she was part of the problem, and she determined to take responsibility for it. She also came to believe, for the first time in her adult life, that her father had really loved her. Over time, that belief allowed her to form more positive views of her heavenly Father—and of men in general.

As this book went to press, I asked her to recount the steps that led to her healing. Here's my summary of them.

- She wrote her father a letter. It didn't matter that he was dead. She said everything she wanted to say, a very volatile letter, expressing lots of anger about abandonment and rejection.

- She learned to separate who God is from who her dad was. She listened to John Dawson's tape series *The Father Heart of God*, and she started telling herself the truth about God, standing on what He says in His Word.

- She took responsibility for what the Holy Spirit showed her was her part of the problem. It used to be all, "him, him him!"—all Dad's fault, not hers. She had to let go of the bitterness and forgive him.

- She began to search for the truth about her father. When a friend from her home state gave her an airline ticket she had purchased but could not use, my counselee could see the writing on the wall. She flew home and visited her father's brother. They spent a lot of time together. She saw where her father was born and grew up. She learned that her father's sins ran through the generations of his family and that he had been abused as a boy. From other relatives she found out that her father had been married previously and that his first wife had left him. So she reasoned that he may have had reasons why he refused to marry her mother. "Talking to my uncle helped me to see the good side of Dad. Now there are things about my father that I love. I cherish the mementos I have of him," she now says.

There is evidence that God is blessing her for keeping His commandment. Her peaceful, loving tone was very different from the way she spoke about her dad when I first met her. She can relate to authorities much better than before. She has lost twenty pounds, which she attributes to not needing a barrier to keep men away. She summed up the whole experience by saying, "It was painful to accept the humility, to see my own fault in the matter. But I wouldn't trade all the money in the world for the woman I am today. I don't contend with men anymore."

Her father's death has not hindered her repentance. She has developed a good working knowledge of the first commandment with promise, and it is well with her now. From her experience I would generalize that whether your parent is still living is not the crucial factor. Your readiness to accept conviction from the Lord—a readiness sometimes born of desperation—will determine the blessing that you'll receive from Him.

Fathers and Mothers

Most of the time I counsel people about their fathers. One reason for this is that I am simple-minded enough to take the words of our commandment in their literal order. Only occasionally do I suggest bypassing Dad to deal with Mom first. Those who have learned how to honor their fathers, I've discovered, will often make progress in dealing with their mothers too. Moreover, I find that some people, who have more conflict with their mothers and think Mom's the big hurdle, really have more serious problems with Dad. Thus, I encourage people to begin with their fathers, and I am no longer surprised to find their esteem for their mothers growing with little or no help from me.[6]

I really had to challenge one young man before he would speak the truth in love to his father. When he did, they experienced one of those dramatic turnarounds that make this ministry so rewarding. But it's the aftermath of his transformation that I want to bring to your attention. He went on to honor his mother, and his example helped his wife to honor her as well.

"The breakthrough with Dad helped to diffuse my anger," he recalls. "I had more inner peace after that, so I could approach Mom differently. I started visiting her with my family during our summer vacations. Each time was better than the last. We enjoyed getting to know her." He discovered that his mother had been neglected in her youth, which made it easier to forgive her neglect of him while he was growing up. Meanwhile, his attitude and actions made it clear that he repented of the anger he used to feel toward her.

His wife recounts how she was affected by the changes he was making. "He forgave his mom, and that freed me to do it too. I had been angry with her, because he had so many problems left over from his youth. But once he got straight with his Dad, he didn't try to impress his parents so much. Instead of grasping for their approval, he started paying more attention to me. That freed me up to love his mom, to get past my own bitterness and resentment of her." But there was another big change still to come.

Though this couple had four children of their own, the wife had always felt called to adopt others. Yet her husband had always been unwilling. "After he was healed toward his dad," she remembers, "he was finally willing to adopt. The funny thing is that his father and mother both look up to him now, because they see the good he has done, taking in the children of drug-addicted mothers. Now he has his parents' respect, which he always wanted, but could never obtain before."

You may think that you'll have to be awarded the Nobel prize, win the World Series, or make a million dollars before your parents will respect you. But it's likely that what you really need to do is repent of your sin, speak the truth in love, and follow the calling that you have from the Lord.

"O, No, Not Grandma!"

Our last story makes me smile, but it didn't start out as a laughing matter. A young man, shocked by his parents' divorce when he was a boy, had developed the habit of thinking the worst about them both. He had taken Dad's leaving home as a personal rejection, and he interpreted his mother's problems after the divorce to mean that she didn't care about him either. He rebelled in his teens and soon became acquainted with illegal drugs. Then he ran off and joined the army, where three big changes happened in his life. He gave His life to Christ; he got married; and he found himself thoroughly addicted to heroin.

The Lord delivered both him and his wife from their heroin dependencies, but plenty of other difficulties remained. Trying to live as a Christian should, he became more aware of his besetting sins, and that awareness led him to seek counsel from the Word. We had some significant sessions together. Since he has been helped by a number of people and ministries, I cannot determine precisely what effect my counseling had on him. But I can hold him up to you as an example of someone who took our commandment seriously, making it a part of his new life in Christ.

"There were many deep hurts left over from my childhood," he recalls. "There were many areas where I thought my parents had wronged me. But in counseling I discovered that it was my sins against my parents that I needed to attend to. I repented before the Lord, and then I went to my parents. I asked them to forgive me, without expecting them to reciprocate in any way. They freely forgave me, and a new life began for us. Over the last ten years I have enjoyed a restored, although not always easy, friendship with both my mom and dad, with varying degrees of depth of relationship.

"It was hard to accept them as they were at first; but as I began to accept them, the relationships opened up more and more. I started working for my parents on Saturdays, fixing up their houses. They paid me well, because they knew I was working to finance my kids' education. But I could do the work cheaper than professional handymen, so we all benefited. They started looking forward to seeing me on Saturdays, and that gave me a chance to talk to them and get to know them better.

"I had a major problem with my mom about discipline. I thought she was much too lenient with the kids. She thought I was much too strict. The funny thing is that we were both right. I was still an angry man, and I often took discipline too far or did the right thing in the wrong spirit. God wanted me to listen to my mother's voice of mercy. Over time, He showed me how to correct my kids without misusing my anger.

"At the same time He wanted her to learn from me about the biblical principles behind good discipline. About that time, she took in a teenage cousin of ours, who had recently been orphaned. In the process of helping him, she made a 180-degree turn in her ideas about discipline. We used to be very hesitant about letting her baby-sit the kids, because she was so lenient; but the kids were all for it. Now we don't have any problem; but sometimes the kids say, 'O, no, not Grandma again! She's too strict!'

"One thing I learned from all this," my friend reflected, "is that when you set out to honor your parents, God doesn't leave you out there on your own. His grace goes with you, making a way for you to succeed. You can't see how to make it work, but He can; if you step out in faith, He'll watch over you and bless you on the way.

"Another thing I learned is that our past sins can dramatically affect our present relationships. On many occasions, when people made insensitive jokes about our large family, I failed to stand up for my wife. I would tell her to ignore them, but she was really wounded sometimes. I was no help to her at all.

"Later the Lord reminded me that I had stood by and done nothing when my teenage friends used to insult my mom. I had been mad at her in those days because I thought she had rejected me; so, even though what the guys said to her really bothered me inside, I acted like it was okay. I never repented of that sin, and it was still blinding me to my wife's suffering. When I was finally ready to take responsibility for how I had failed my mom, things changed in a hurry. I've already had my first opportunity to stand up and defend my wife from someone's ridicule. Now that I've repented of my old ways, I can be the husband I want to be for her."[7]

CHAPTER 15

Making It Right

After we have repented before the Lord, we need to go to our parents. If your father or mother has passed away or cannot be located, go to the Lord, to your pastor or priest, to your spouse if you have one, and to any other people who were seriously affected by your sin. (Guidelines to determine which other persons, if any, to approach will be given later in this chapter.)[1]

Communicating repentance is more an art than a science; there is no set formula for how to go about it. The main ingredients are humility and regret. Flexibility and persistence may also come in handy.

Two things need to be accomplished. You must confess your sins (see Jas. 5:16; Luke 15:21)—without mentioning your parent's sins—and you must honor your parent with real communication. You have to clear the decks of what is past and begin building something better for the future. Whether this happens all at once or over time is not terribly important. Just begin the work that God has called you to, and leave the rest to Him.

Confessing Your Sins

Your parents may have trouble believing that your repentance is real. If you have dishonored them much, or if you have said you were sorry before (without proving it by your actions), parents are likely to be skeptical. Their doubts can be a blessing: They can help you see how real your repentance is. If you feel resentful of their doubts or fear that they will never believe you, your practical knowledge of our commandment is still incomplete. You may need to spend more time in prayer, or in Scripture, or with the Samuel in your life (see chap. 6).

You can lessen your parent's unbelief by getting specific about your sins. Don't say, "Would you forgive me for my sins against you?" Anybody can do that.[2] Show them that you have thought long and hard about the first commandment with promise. Recall specific events or particular attitudes when you acted, spoke, or felt dishonorably toward them. Tell them how it all seemed to you then, and how you see it now in the light of the Bible's teaching. But don't go heavy on the Bible, if your parents are not familiar with it. This is not the time to teach your parents about God's Word. This is the time to *show* them that the Word has brought you to repentance.

You don't have to make a long list of your sins. If you are able to resolve the worst of them, you will find there is little need to deal with all the others. If something still bothers you or your parent, you'll find time to talk about it later.

One of the Fine Arts

It's a fine art knowing how to bring up your own sins without dwelling on those of your parent. Let me explain why it's so important to master. If you stick to your own sins, you set a good example for your parent. You help your parent to do what you have done—to consider his or her sins against you and to express a heartfelt sorrow about them. Even if your parent says nothing—and you should expect nothing from your parent at such a time—he is likely to ponder his own sins in private.

On the other hand, if you focus on what your parent has done, if you speak with a demanding or a judgmental tone, you can short-circuit the whole process. Instead of helping your parent, you hinder his progress toward repentance. It is human nature to defend oneself when attacked, and parents can sense underlying hostility in their children. They may well resent our bringing up old incidents in which they disgraced themselves. Yet if we are careful to mention only our own failings at such times, we can probably prevent a defensive response.

Would some examples be helpful? If your parents are divorced, and you blamed Dad for the breakup of the family, don't say, "When you divorced Mom . . . ." or "When you shacked up with Sally . . . ."

No. Say something like this: "When you and Mom got divorced, I blamed you without ever getting your side of the story. Now I can see how wrong that was. . . . Would you please forgive me?"

If you had an argument with your parent that left you with injured feelings, don't refer to it as "that time you called me a brat and said you wished you had never had me." Say something like this: "Remember that terrible argument we had once, the one that started because I wouldn't take out the trash? I had some very hurt feelings afterwards that I never told you about. Now I can see how my silence and resentment ruined our relationship. . . ." If you do it right, your parent will probably respond, "What did I say that hurt you so much?" Then you can tell her, without putting her on the defensive. Never assume that your parent *ought to have known* how he or she hurt your feelings. I commonly find that even sensitive and concerned parents have no idea how adversely their words or their actions affected their children.

If you can't remember how your broken relationship with your parent began, don't say, "I always hated you because you were so mean." Say, "I can't remember a time when I trusted you and thought the best of you. It always seemed to me that you liked Johnny better than me [or that you only cared about yourself]. Now I can see that it was wrong to assume the worst about you, and I'm sorry that I did."

Planning Your Approach

Should you talk to your parents in person or call them on the phone or just write them a letter? That depends. I think it is best to speak to them in person. However, it would be better to call or write if you cannot visit your parent in the near future. If you are scared to death of your parent, you may want to have a third party present while you talk. But what would your parent want? If your parent would prefer a private phone call to a talk with a third party present, then speak to your parent on the phone.

I once counseled a young woman who rarely spoke to her father. Her mother nearly always answered the phone; she seemed to keep the daughter from having real talks with her father. Since she needed to clear things up with her dad, I advised a person-to-person phone call. She tried it—and had her longest talk ever with her father. It may be hard for you to say, "Mom, I really need to talk to Dad about something"; but when the operator says, "I have a long distance call for Mr. Smith," you can bet that your mom will get hold of Dad pronto.

In some cases, a two-step approach may be best. Another woman called her father and said, "I'm coming to visit you and Mother next week. Can you save some time for just the two of us to have a heart-to-heart talk?" When the time came, he was ready and willing. And I'll bet he was curious, too. There's nothing wrong with letting a parent know you have something significant to say—and waiting till the time is right to say it.

The main thing to understand is that your spirit, not your method of approach, is all-important. If you pick the wrong method but have the right spirit, you will probably succeed. But if you approach your parent with a resentful or blaming spirit, the best method in the world will do you little good. That's why this book is long on Scripture and short on the method of approach. Scripture, rightly understood, will improve your attitude toward your parents. No method in the world can do that.

Which Sins to Confess?

"Do I have to tell them *everything?*" you may ask. "I did a lot of bad stuff they know nothing about." Here again there is no pat answer for all situations. The key thing is your motivation. If fear or shame would hold you back from confessing a sin, it is probably better to tell it. If charity, affection, and concern for your parent give you pause about telling all, you may have reason to hold certain things back. I cannot decide this question for you. But I can give you my own rule of thumb: *It is better to err by telling parents too much than to fail them again by saying too little.*

There are some sins which you simply must confess. One of these is abortion. If you had an abortion or if you were a party to your girlfriend's or spouse's abortion, the fact must not be concealed. Of course, some parents may think getting an abortion was the right thing to do. No matter how they react, however, parents have a right to know. Do not deprive them of it. Do not decide for them what they can handle and what they can't. That can be very dishonoring.

In nearly all cases, I think promiscuity, drug usage, lying, and stealing should be made known to our parents. Whether the number or the details of these offenses should be related is another matter. Let your conscience and your sense of discretion be your guides. The point in confessing to our parents is not to wallow in our sins or to rub their noses in our sins. The point is to let them know who we really are, or have been, so that they may perform the roles of parents in our lives. If you tell a man to build you a brick house, but forbid him to use mortar between the bricks, whom should you blame when your dwelling falls down? Yet we commonly blame parents for not guiding us better when we held back what they needed to do the job well.

Underneath our obvious sins of the flesh, there is often a hidden violation of the first commandment with promise. If you tell your parents that you have used drugs or that you have stolen or lied, they may naturally inquire, "What caused you to do that?" If you know, tell them why. If you don't know, cooperate with them; allow them to help you figure things out. Even if nothing comes of it, at least you'll be working together.

I know a Christian man who could barely bring himself to confess his homosexual tendencies to his father. When he finally did, he was amazed by Dad's reply: "From the time you were in third grade, I knew that something was wrong." Instead of displaying the shock or anger or rejection which the young man had dreaded, his father showed unexpected knowledge of and compassion for his son.

When you hide your life from your parent, you put up a barrier that only you can destroy. A lot of repentant Christians find pleasant surprises waiting for them—when they finally decide to break down the walls.

Our Secret Transgressions

Most of the time, I have found, our sins of the flesh are rooted in hidden and subtle sins against our parents. That is, I believe, why the Lord placed the first commandment with promise before His prohibitions against killing, adultery, stealing, lying, and coveting. Many people who are struggling against some habitual sin are looking too far down the list of the Ten Commandments. They need to back up a little before they can hope to vanquish their sin.

I knew a young man who had a terrible problem with stealing from his employers. It got so bad that it landed him in jail. But he didn't shoplift or snatch purses—he only stole from his employers. And, yes, they tended to be men about his father's age who trusted the young man and were genuinely concerned about him. And, no, he wasn't taking food to feed his family or money to pay the bills; he wasn't stealing out of any obvious need. To me it looked like a pretty clear pattern. So I asked him about his father—and hit a flowing spring of bitterness and resentment. After hearing him out, I said,

"Until you mend your broken relationship with your dad, you'll never be able to stop stealing." He didn't like what I told him; he didn't believe it could be true. When finally he was willing to take my advice, he didn't implement it perfectly; but he did meet with his father and talk about what was wrong between them. And when he got out of jail, he went more than a year without any charges for stealing. After that we lost touch.

You may have disgraced your family by your actions; you may have cursed your parents or laughed them to scorn. But the sins that are keeping you from God's blessing are likely to be hidden sins of the heart, sins that are not apparent, and, yes, sins against the first commandment with promise.

If at First You Don't Succeed . . .

Sometimes persistence saves the day. Years ago I counseled a woman who thought that her father didn't love her. (I wish she were the only one whose life was blighted by this error!) When she was six years old, her younger sister had been very ill. She saw her father holding his sick little child, and somehow she decided then and there that her sister was beloved, but that she was "fat and ugly." She never said a word to her father about all this, and she still believed it was true when I counseled her some thirty years later.

I attempted to show her the sinfulness of her unilateral decision, which had assumed the worst about her father. Eventually she worked up the courage to call him and talk about whether he loved her or not. As per my instructions, she told him what she had felt when she was six and her little sister was in his arms. His response was only laughter. She felt devastated—and that was the end of the discussion.

When I saw her afterward she was certain that her father had mocked her. I tried to show her that other, more honoring, interpretations were possible. It took time to convince her that on her next visit she should ask him why he laughed. A few months later she saw him, and she was brave enough to try it. "I laughed," he responded, "because what you said was so far-fetched. The idea that I loved her more than you seemed so silly—I had to laugh!" Then they talked, and she began to realize how wrong she had been about him.

A couple of years later, the woman's older brother died. She went with her father and her siblings to the funeral. When she came back from it she told me, "Now I know that my father loves all his children." Do you know that about your father? If not, are you willing to search for the truth?

We can learn several things from this woman's experience. The chief one is not to give up when things don't go well at first. The second is to try to think the best of a parent whose reaction disappoints you. And the third is to be patient. If it takes two or three years to accomplish this work, it's still very much worth doing.

Dealing with Third Parties

If you have involved other people in your sins against your parents, you may need to speak to some of them. You don't have to go to every fool you once hung around with—for some of us that would be an endless work. But there are two kinds of people with whom you may need to talk.

The first group consists of persons who knew your parents and were influenced by your negative view of them. Your siblings will probably head the list. Your parents' friends, relatives, employees, or neighbors may also belong on it. It's good to go to them, as the Lord leads, and tell them how your view of your parents has changed. Be selective. Few of us need to speak to many people in this way, but we all ought to be open to the Holy Spirit's guidance.

If your actions brought disgrace to your parents, it might be good to express your repentance to the persons you offended. Did you steal from your father's boss? Did you wreck the neighbors' property, or seduce one of their children? Did you cause your parents great embarrassment in their church? Perhaps you should go to that boss or neighbor or church, apologize for your actions, and express regret for the disgrace you brought upon your parents.

The second group would be people whom you influenced to think the worst of *their* parents. When we are busy breaking the first commandment with promise, we can easily lead others astray. There might be someone in your life who could be helped by you now, as he or she was hurt by your influence in the past. If the Lord brings such a person to mind, don't be afraid to look him up and tell him what you've learned.

Building a Right Relationship

Some people I've counseled have repented deeply, confessed their sins, and asked their parents' forgiveness, all in the best possible way. They have mended the broken relationship with a parent and, for the first time in years, started to enjoy being with that parent again. Then they have run into a problem.

I remember when the light dawned on one young man. "This isn't a one-time thing," he told me. "You're asking me to have an on-going relationship with my dad." "Precisely," I replied. But for him it was scary. After twenty years of sweeping everything, including abusive situations, under the rug, it was a shock to think of being honest with Dad on a regular basis. "Once I can handle," he said, "but time after time?" He proved to be equal to the challenge.

A middle-aged woman had another reason for not being real with her father. "After all these years, we finally have a good relationship. I'd hate to do anything that might ruin it." In other words, her father's love, so recently discovered, was too precious to put at risk. What if being real caused a conflict? Now she had too much to lose.

We cannot honor our parents if we treat them like china dolls. We have to be willing to take risks. The more we believe that they love us, the more easily we will venture to speak the truth in love. That this can be scary at the beginning, I freely admit. But you'll never get past the beginning, if you're afraid to take a chance.

What do I mean by "speaking the truth in love" (Eph. 4:15)? I don't mean that we must always be examining our relationship with our parents and talking to them about it.

There are lots of ways to honor our fathers and mothers. One way is simply to spend time with them, preferably doing something that they really enjoy. What if you love computers, but your father likes to fish? What if you want to be out saving the lost, but your mother likes to bake cookies? When the first commandment with promise is worked into you, you may learn to enjoy fishing or baking, simply because of the joy that it brings to your parent.

You say, "Well, my dad would never take me fishing. Or if he did he would just tell me I'm no good at it." You may be surprised to find what a difference a change in your attitude can make. You don't have to know much about fishing to have a good trip, *if* you know a lot about honoring your father.

When we spend time with our parents, troubles are sure to arise. How do we handle them? It is important to separate our troubles into those we can digest and those we cannot. We can pass over many a hurtful remark or thoughtless action once we view our parent with charity and compassion. Whether it stems from old age, irritation, or even selfishness, we need not respond to every distress a parent causes us. But for those troubles we cannot digest, those that continue to clank in our souls, like an old can in the belly of a goat, we must learn to speak the truth in love.

It may take a little while to discern whether you need to speak to your parents about something that has bothered you. When you recognize that you cannot digest the item in question, bring it back up for discussion. Try to do it at an appropriate time, when there is sufficient leisure to talk and an absence of other tribulations. Try to say, "I felt hurt," instead of, "You hurt me"; "I didn't understand," rather than, "How could you do such a thing?" Try to listen and understand, rather than to assume that you have full knowledge of the situation.

I found that when I came to my parents or in-laws with a good attitude, I could count on a gracious response. If graciousness is not your parent's strong suit, you still need to persevere in this good work. Over time, you and your parent will learn how to communicate, to deal with problems in the present, rather than twenty years later, or not at all.

Some parents, and some children, are not very adept at verbalizing their feelings. You need to figure out what works best for you. Instead of a long drawn-out discussion, perhaps it would be better to say, "Dad, would you be willing to give me another try on a fishing trip? I'm sorry we had so much trouble, and it's important to me that we learn to get along." If God has commanded you to honor your parents, there must be a way for you to do it. But if you still have a broken relationship with your earthly father, you may not have much confidence in the benevolence of your heavenly Father's commands.

It's a wonderful thing to know that you can count on your parent—not to be perfect, of course, but to deal honestly with his or her imperfections, and with their consequences in your life. It's wonderful to be heading into a discussion of some difficulty, and to be able to think the best of your parent, to trust that together the two of you can work this thing out. It took me years to arrive at such a blessed assurance. May God bring it quickly to you!

CHAPTER 16

Blessed Are the Peacemakers

King David said of the commandments:

> More to be desired are they than gold, yea, than much fine gold: sweeter also than honey and the honeycomb. Moreover by them is thy servant warned: and in keeping of them there is great reward. (Ps. 19:10–11)

Thinking the best of you, as I ought to do, I believe you have taken the teaching of this book to heart, and you are making a real effort to honor your parents. If you continue patiently in this good work, what kind of "great reward" should you look forward to?

Let me begin with a disclaimer. Keeping the first commandment with promise won't solve all your problems. Though it may enable you to overcome the sins that have plagued you till now, God will surely leave you with some reminders of your frailty. Either some of your past sins will remain, like the Canaanites in the land, to test your true reliance on the Lord; or, though you have won a great victory over your previous sins, God will make you aware of others in your life, ones that you never took seriously before. Like a New England farmer who has cleared his land well, you will find new boulders rising to the surface of your life. This latter condition is really a sign of spiritual progress. We ought to rejoice when God reveals our sins to us, when He trusts us to take on new spiritual labors. Clear your fields as best you can; build your stone walls and stone houses. If you truly believe that your works will glorify God, that some of them will remain on the last day, you shall not grow weary in well doing.

What keeping our commandment *will* do is make a healthy Christian life possible. It will enable you to build on a good foundation. The structures you erect won't be perfect, but they'll be useful and long-lasting. You won't enjoy all the blessings I enumerate at once, you may never possess them all at the same time, but you will find them increasing in your life. And you'll more quickly discern what else may be hindering your spiritual development, when you're no longer deceived about the first commandment with promise.

Our Father . . .

The greatest blessing that comes from honoring our earthly parents is that we get to know our heavenly Father better.

When my father was in the hospital, about two months before he died, we had one of those tender moments that compensate affliction. As I was saying good night to him, he told me, "You're a good son." It's the only time I remember him using those words. I replied that he was a good father. Then I added, "I've learned a lot about God from you." Since he was a nonbeliever, he looked at me quizzically. "How is that?" "Because you love your children," I replied, "and you're generous to them." I don't remember what else we said that night, but I walked out of his room feeling wonderful.

The point is that nearly every parent reflects the character of God in some way. If we can focus on their good points and overlook, but not deny, their sins, we will find God's love for His children vividly illustrated in our parents' love for us. You may think this is possible only in model families, but I assure you that it can happen to you, though your parents' sins are as red as scarlet, or though you come from a broken home. If you honor your father and mother as David honored his parents and Saul, you will see gleams of heavenly love in the earthly love of your parents. The gleams of celestial treasure have a value of their own.

I can't prove it to you directly from Scripture; I can't give you evidence from scientific studies; I can only tell you what I and many others have experienced: When you honor your parents, you see God in a new light. And some verses in the Bible do support what I am saying.

> If a man say, I love God, and hateth his brother, he is a liar:
> for he that loveth not his brother whom he hath seen, how
> can he love God whom he hath not seen? (1 John 4:20)

If we do not honor and esteem our parents, whom we have seen, how shall we honor and esteem our Father in heaven?

Many Christians violate the first commandment with promise and still have a real relationship with God. But it's not the same relationship they would have with Him if they were honoring their parents. Sins against our parents impair our fellowship with God. Repentance breaks down that barrier. As we get to know our parents better, as we view them with compassion, we discover facets of the love of God we never saw before.

God designed part of His revelation of Himself to come to us through our parents. You can read the Bible forever, you can fast and pray, but until you honor your parents you'll still be missing a particular element of God's personal revelation to you. It's like electricity: We don't know how it works, we just know that it does.

It's a wonderful thing to find that your relationship with your parents and your relationship with the Lord are working together for good. The one reinforces the other. I was formerly so negative to my parents that I needed a strong dose of God's discipline and love before I could keep the first commandment with promise. But once I began, I learned more about *His* love and forgiveness—from the love and forgiveness shown to me by my unbelieving parents.

What God shows you about Himself through your parents will be different from what He has shown me through mine. But it will, I trust, be equally fulfilling. And no one on earth will ever know what it is, until the day you discover it for yourself.

A Basis for Love

You may remember from chapter 1 that this book began with an improvement in my marriage. If you are married or if you hope to marry, you and your spouse will both be blessed by your honoring your parents. If you are divorced or widowed, you can still benefit from understanding how your or your spouse's dishonoring sins may have hindered your marital joy.

Marriage in our culture is difficult enough without adding the burdens imposed by breaking our commandment. It's hard enough to be a good spouse when you think the best of your mate. How much harder then—when you view him or her through the disfiguring lens of a parent you still think the worst of?[1]

The first commandment with promise is a good foundation for marriage. You can build a marriage on it that will last. As you learn to believe the best about your parents, you will tend to believe the best about your spouse. By doing so you will deprive Satan of his favorite stronghold in marriage. You may also notice that your in-laws begin to look less like enemies and more like reinforcements.

How many Christian marriages are plagued with in-law problems! How few of these problems are all the in-laws' fault! What a blessing it is to feel that parents and in-laws are on your side, that they want your marriage to succeed! And they almost surely will, once you subtract your sins from the problem. The chief one, of course, is having gotten married without their blessing—and their blessing is more than their grudging permission. But whatever the sin, and whatever the path to healing, a blessing comes to the husband and wife who learn how to honor their parents. First, they are able to love each other with relative wholeness. Second, they are likely to find more support from their parents. And, most important, God will smile upon them as they model in their marriage the love of Jesus and His Bride.

There is a Latin saying, *caveat emptor,* "let the buyer beware." Usually when someone honors his or her parent of the opposite sex, an improvement in the child's marriage results. But there are exceptions. I have experienced only one of them, and I think you ought to know about it.

The woman involved, a mature Christian, came to me because of trouble in her marriage. When I inquired about her father, she assured me that he didn't love her. I challenged that assertion, and she was willing to hear me out. A few months later, she had developed a warm and loving relationship with her father; it was a joy to behold. Better still, their new relationship has lasted long. When I called her just before this book went to press, she told me, "My father has become a better friend to me than I could have ever dreamed." She found a great blessing through keeping our commandment. But soon after things got better with her dad, her marriage took a turn for the worse. She and her husband got a legal separation. They had had troubles for years but never anything that involved the courts. I couldn't shake the feeling that the wife's changed relationship with her father had somehow precipitated the separation.

My thinking is that when a married person is reconciled to the parent of the opposite sex, it changes the dynamic of the marriage, usually for the better. But that depends on the reaction of the spouse. If the spouse feels threatened by his mate's improved capacity for intimacy and trust, he may react negatively to the prospect of a more loving relationship. Yet I can't say for sure. Thus you see both the limitations of your author and the uncertain consequences of keeping the first commandment with promise.

Those in Authority

One of the most common results of honoring parents is greater ability to relate well to those in authority. The process is simple and the same as with marriage. Your parents were the first man and woman in your life; all subsequent love relationships will be affected, for better or for worse, by the initial ones. Your parents were also the first authorities in your life; you will tend to approach subsequent authorities in the light (or the darkness) of your experience with your parents.

We are likely to transfer to employers, pastors, teachers, and police the attitudes and behavior patterns we developed at home. 'Tis no easy thing for them to absorb the mostly unconscious slings and arrows that estranged or abused children shower on those in authority. When we keep the first commandment with promise, we bring blessings to our workplaces, our churches, and our schools. What a help we are to our employers when we are loyal and think the best of them! What a blessing to our pastors when we honor them with double honor (1 Tim. 5:17)! We cannot really obey the apostolic injunctions about employers and elders unless we know how to honor our parents.

We should not assume that every hard-working employee, diligent student, or loyal church member has mastered our commandment. Far from it! But we will tend to be among them as we esteem our parents—and our loyalty and diligence will spring from godly motivation. Others may labor in a good cause from compulsion, ambition, or the need for attention. These driven souls may outperform us at times, but I doubt that in the long run they will prove more valuable to those in authority.

When the first commandment with promise becomes second nature to us, we tend to esteem authorities without even thinking about it. When our family moved from California, I was surprised by our senior pastor's telling the congregation that my support of and reluctance to criticize the pastors had been a blessing to them. It was all the more telling because he knew that I had differed from them on significant points without making our differences public. I had never really thought about it that way. From my point of view, it just sort of happened. But now I see being a help to the pastors as a fringe benefit of honoring my parents.

And lest you think I'm just naturally submissive, my first pastor could tell you that it was not always so. I could not follow Paul's advice—"Do not rebuke an elder man, but exhort [him] as a father" (1 Tim. 5:1–2, MKJV)—until I learned to keep the first commandment with promise.

And to Your Children

Many a parent of a rebellious adolescent unknowingly contributes to his child's delinquency. The sins of the fathers are visited on the children (Ex. 20:5), especially the sin of dishonoring one's parents. If you have a broken relationship with your parent, chances are your children will have trouble honoring you. If you keep the first commandment with promise, it's likely that your children will too.

Seeing how our sin affects our children can motivate us to honor our parents. Though you have lacked the courage to examine your own life or to bring up difficult topics with your parents, your love for your son or daughter may inspire you to face your fear. As you do, your child will be freed from the shadow of your sin, from the burden of your bad example. The amazing thing is that even if he or she knows nothing of your repentance toward your parents, you will probably observe a change in your child's behavior—a change that brings sweet relief to your soul.

Many parents work so hard to provide a good neighborhood and a good school for their children. And they ought to do so. But how can their children be properly brought up and educated when they live with a parent who is daily breaking a chief commandment of God? Conversely, though your neighborhood or school is not the best, if you are a good example to your children, you are likely to rejoice someday in the fruits of their education.

I cannot emphasize too strongly that you don't have to get it all together before you can be a blessing to your children. All you have to do is take a step or two toward fulfilling our commandment and be willing to try again, as the Lord directs. A little repentance goes a long way in a family that has been under a curse. After all, you're not the only sinner perched within your family tree. It's a wonderful thing to be a pioneer in bringing your family back to the blessings of God. It's a wonderful thing to see your children really growing in the Lord.

And Give You Peace . . .

No doubt there are other fringe benefits to keeping our commandment. But I pass over the rest of them to concentrate on the sum of the parts:

> On this wise ye shall bless the children of Israel, saying unto them, The Lord bless thee, and keep thee: The Lord make his face shine upon thee, and be gracious unto thee: The Lord lift up his countenance upon thee, and give thee peace. (Num. 6:23–26)

Peace is a great blessing. In the world we shall have tribulation, but we can have peace in the midst of it. Rest in the soul, like a good night's sleep, is the precious gift of God to His beloved. Those who love Him and keep His commandments are likely to receive it.

Conclusion:
"You Shall Believe and Live"

Who are the wicked? Just the men who say
That God is dead or that He is not good?
The Great Deceiver has a better way
T'express his hatred—little understood
By those who build manhood or womanhood
Upon the rubble of their parents' name.
Esteeming gold to be but rotten wood,
The source of all their riches they disclaim
By misering their praise and lavishing their blame.

Of all good gifts the gift of life is first.
Our parents place the precious cornerstone
We build our lives on. Be they best or worst,
Kind or unkind to us, known or unknown,
The edifice we build will be our own.
Yet he who treats his parents with respect
And honors them in word and deed and tone—
Ages to come shall find his work erect,
As though he had the plans of some great architect.

The day our Lord rebuked the Pharisees
He could have named a hundred sins of theirs,
But singled out a custom made to please
Men more than God. His written word declares
That God delights to bless the man who cares
For aged parents, making it his creed
To leave his church or personal affairs
To aid them at the time they are in need.
Thus men show whom they worship, whether God or
    greed.

Why did Christ choose that Fifth Commandment sin?
Though it seem little midst the hundreds of
The laws of Moses, it has ever been
Essential as a cornerstone of love.
Or as the keystone hanging high above
Some great cathedral crossing may seem small
Among the thousands which the workmen move—
And yet without it all the work must fall—
The keeping of this law is key to keeping all.

When a man says he loves God, and yet he hates
His brother—God calls his love a lie.
Then what of him who never hesitates
To blame his parents (though he did deny
Them access to his heart)? He wonders why
It is not well with him, and soon concludes
That it must be their fault. From God on high
He asks deliverance from his gloomy moods—
And prides himself upon his Christian attitudes.

"My sanctity is much in evidence,"
He thinks within himself. "For it is rare
To find a man forgiving such offense
As I received while in my parents' care.
The mighty works of Hercules declare
That he had strength from Heaven. Am I not one
Destined by God to have the lion's share
Of grace? For I forgive all they have done.
A victor in the spirit, I have fought and won.

"His cleansing of the stables—what is that
Compared to my disposing of the mess
Left in my mind by them? Their sin begat
Lions of rage, hydras of guiltiness,
Man-eating mares of fear. Could it be less
Than Herculean (knowing they're to blame
For all my woe) t'accept their poor redress?
It is my glory to forgive their shame.
Let other Christians see, and seek to do the same."

But He who sits on high shall laugh at him
Like a father laughing at his willful child,
Lest he should grieve and grief should make him grim.
The Lord will discipline a man beguiled
To justify his sin. What he has styled
His parents' fault, rather than face his own
(As if the tamer makes the lion wild!),
To his own face the Lord will make it known,
To help him to repent—or reap what he has sown.

The Lord would have us always think the best
(Compatible with truth) that can be thought
Of those who gave us life. A simple test
Of whether we have done this as we ought
Is, How do we respond when we are caught
In the nets of slander and the half-truth lies
The world springs all around us? Have we sought
To think our parents good and pure and wise?
Or are they, when accused, found guilty in our eyes?

Men think it hard, making bricks without straw,
Or growing healthy crops in time of drought.
But harder than Pharoah's whim or Nature's law
Are grown-up children who are still without
Compassion for their parents. How they pout
About parental ignorance and sin!
But did they really share their hearts about
Their feelings and their fears? Did they begin
To speak the inmost truth, or hold it fast within?

One might as well grow wheat upon the sand
Or seek to gather straw for Pharoah's kiln,
For it is an impossible demand
To think that any person can or will
Be an effective parent, knowing nil
About the yearnings of his own child's heart.
Speaking the truth in love—that is God's will.
Concealing truth is more the devil's part;
And all his children are well-practised in that art.

"Yes," you may say, "Impossible is right!
You ask what is impossible to do:
To face the fear, the paralyzing fright
Of telling all . . . Oh! if you only knew
How I grew up: the names, the things he threw,
The way she nagged me! Daniel in the den
You say I should have been. I wish that you
Could walk in my shoes, be where I have been.
If you did that, I'm sure, you'd stop your preaching then!"

Your argument is not with me, but God.
(I never said 'twas easy to be good.)
St. Peter taught us not to think it odd
When fiery trials come. He understood
That simply doing what God says we should
Requires courage great enough for war.
Where Jesus walked, surely no coward would.
O, follow not, as Peter, from afar;
For where the Spirit leads, the true disciples are.

But do not think your struggle is with men:
The foe is not your father but your fear.
If you withheld your heart from parents when
You might have told them all—did they appear
Implacable, unloving, or unclear?
It takes a leap of faith to think the best,
To trust a parent rather than a peer;
But he, who with his parents does invest
The treasure of his heart, shall heartily be blest.

A wise investor, when he takes a risk,
Has a reason for it. Can we calculate
A reason here, one Satan cannot whisk
Away by pandering to fear and hate?
Our God is love. 'Twas He who did create
The special love within the parent's soul.
And though that love seem in a dormant state,
Under the ash of sin it is a coal,
And he who digs for it will find it hot and whole.

The rediscovery of parents' love
Is like sweet water in a desert land:
It brings forth blessings. And the greatest of
Them all is this: Soon as we understand
That, like a treasure buried in the sand,
The love we wished for so was always there
(Sufficient to supply all our demand)—
Our eyes are opened to our Father's care,
As we behold the love He did for us prepare.

Whatever sin our parents did commit,
Incest, brutality, or what you will,
It is not possible to prove by it
They did not love their children. If we fill
A water-glass with gravel there is still
Much water (though not lucid) left inside.
The water which the stones displace and spill
Might be recovered, if we only tried.
Though it has been displaced, love must not be denied.

"I see," you say, "But how do I begin?
How can I ask a parent to forget
The height, the depth, the length of all my sin?"
If you will pray, if you will humbly let
The Spirit lead, a few words can beget
More healing than you dream: "Would you forgive . . . ?"
Sincerely said, before the sun has set
They can bring forth more good than you believe—
But by the grace of God, you shall believe and live.

Endnotes

Introduction

1. When the Ten Commandments are taken from Deuteronomy 5, as they have been by some Catholic writers, the Ninth Commandment is, "Neither shalt thou desire thy neighbor's wife," and the tenth, "Neither shalt thou covet thy neighbor's house" (Deut. 5:21).

Chapter 1

1. Had I been older and wiser, I might have remembered that the Bible puts it a little differently: "Charity . . . beareth all things. Charity never faileth" (1 Cor. 13:7–8).

2. Most of the other commandments linked to those precious words are general—"Walk ye in all the ways that I have commanded you, that it may be well unto you" (Jer. 7:23). (See also Deut. 4:40; 6:3, etc.; 2 Kings 25:24; Jer. 38:20.) In the category of general promises I include Psalm 128:1–2: "Blessed is every one that feareth the Lord; that walketh in his ways. For thou shalt eat the labor of thine hands: happy shalt thou be, and it shall be well with thee." The second sentence simply lists the blessings that come to those who fear the Lord.

There are a few specific Old Testament commands with our promise attached to them: "If a bird's nest chance to be before thee in the way, . . . thou shalt not take the dam with the young. But thou shalt in any wise let the dam go, and take the young with thee, and *that thou mayest prolong thy days*" (Deut. 22:6–7, emphasis added). Notice that even here, our welfare is connected with treating the mother gently. (See also Deut. 12:25; 19:13.) These commandments, properly understood, have relevance for us today, although they seem less than memorable to many modern readers.

3. With special permission, Satan can do plenty, as he did with Job. But that's another story.

Chapter 3

1. Some commentators count "Honor thy father and thy mother" as one of the Commandments relating to piety and love of God. Whether we place it on the first or second table, it precedes all other commandments relating to our duty to others.

2. In the Septuagint text "that it may be well with you" also appears in Exodus 20:12.

3. Most commentators apply the promised blessing to the individual believer: Keep this law and you will be blessed physically, financially, and spiritually, blessed in this world and in the world to come. Yet even they admit that God deals differently with each of His children and that not every believer will live to old age. Some scholars think the promise is meant to apply to whole cultures as part of a general covenant, particularly in Exodus. They say the blessing is a general promise to societies that keep God's laws. While some who keep the Law may not live to old age or may not experience prosperity in this world, most of the families in an obedient culture will be blessed with long life, prosperity, and peace. It is not the purpose of this book to take sides among good interpreters of Scripture or to delve unnecessarily into the subtleties and symbolism of the commandment. Therefore, I will apply the promise as broadly as possible, emphasizing the blessings to the individual, but not ignoring the wider benefits that are promised to society as a whole.

4. See, for example, Exodus 21:17; Leviticus 20:9; Proverbs 20:20; 30:17.

5. Leviticus 20:9; Deuteronomy 27:16; Proverbs 20:20; 30:11–12, 17; Matthew 15:4; Mark 7:10.

6. A passage related to Exodus 21:15 is 1 Timothy 1:9–10. Notice that the first specific offense mentioned is the murder of father or mother. Another related passage is 2 Chronicles 24:20–25, where King Joash murders his foster father's righteous son. The Lord's vengeance for his crime was not slow in coming.

7. If so, Absalom was an exception to this rule (2 Sam. 17:1–4).

8. I do not mean to extenuate Jeremiah's sin, which the commentators severely condemn. (Calvin calls it "a state of despair," "sacrilegious madness," "something monstrous.") The point is that when he had seemingly lost all control of himself, Jeremiah still refrained from cursing his parents. His respect for them was, so to speak, built-in or automatic.

Chapter 4

1. "Blessed Lord, which hast caused all Holy Scriptures to be written for our learning: Grant us that we may . . . hear them, read, mark, learn, and inwardly digest them" (From the Collect for the Second Sunday of Advent, *Book of Common Prayer* [Anglican, 1559]).

2. Or, "Truth is what sells." This ironic observation on the "pecuniary phi-

losophy" of our culture was made by anthropologist Jules Henry in *Culture Against Man* (New York: Random House, 1963), 50.

3. Do you feel pursued by this subject and anxious to escape it? You could be running from Francis Thompson's "Hound of Heaven":

> From those strong Feet that followed, followed after.
> But with unhurrying chase,
> And unperturbèd pace,
> Deliberate speed, majestic instancy,
> They beat—and a Voice beat
> More instant than the Feet—
> "All things betray thee, who betrayest Me."

But notice these verses from the ending of that magnificent poem:

> "All which I took from thee I did but take,
> Not for thy harms,
> But just that thou might'st seek it in My arms.
> All which thy child's mistake
> Fancies as lost, I have stored for thee at home:
> Rise, clasp My hand, and come!"

4. Matthew Henry, *Commentary* (McLean, Va.: MacDonald, n.d.), 3:793.

5. See Psalm 111:10; Proverbs 9:10. Again the context is instructive: "The fear of the Lord is the beginning of wisdom: and the knowledge of the holy is understanding. For by me thy days shall be multiplied, and years of thy life shall be increased" (Prov. 9:10–11). Here the specific promise of our commandment is attached to "the beginning of wisdom." Do you see how inseparable biblical wisdom and respect for parents are?

6. For this reason I think it is appropriate to keep motivated students home from school or from their home school studies when they have failed to show their parents elementary respect and obedience. In other words, let's show our children that we put first things first. When the child gets a passing grade in obedience, so to speak, then he or she is ready to pursue academics. Of course this strategy will not be effective with kids who hate school anyway, or where no parent can stay home with the child. But if we treat disobedience or rebellion as a lighter thing than measles or mumps, I wonder what message we are really sending our children.

7. Of course our ultimate rule should be the revealed will of God. If, for example, our parents urge us to marry a nonbeliever or to sue another Christian in court, we should obey God rather than man. But in the vast majority of cases, I find that the Ten Commandments do very well as a quick reference point for obeying our parents.

8. Dr. John Gill, *Commentary* (London: William Hill, 1852–54, and Grand Rapids: Baker, 1980), 3:458 (on Prov. 6:23).

9. Victims of incest have my sympathy and my prayers for their healing.

10. *King Lear* 1.iv.294–95 (Yale Edition).

Chapter 5

1. Genesis 20:7 and 20:17. Not everyone agrees that Abraham's deception

of Abimelech was sinful, however.

2. There are many promises of blessing to the children of the righteous in Scripture (e.g. Prov. 11:21 and 20:7), and many promises of evil to the children of the wicked; how shall these be reconciled with the principle illustrated here? I take it that these are general promises which are true for society as a whole. Otherwise, how shall we explain the Scriptural examples of good fathers with wicked children, and of wicked fathers with good children? Hezekiah, for example, was a good king sandwiched between a bad father and a worse son. (See 2 Chron. 28:1–3; 28:27—29:2; and 32:33—33:2.)

Whether the parent is good or bad, the child is likely to resemble the parent, for the sins of the fathers shall be visited on their children (Ex. 20:5). Though the children can determine how long those "visitors" remain on their premises, it is probable that they will react to them as their fathers did. Therefore, a son is likely to resemble his father, inheriting the same blessings or curses which his father experienced.

Yet every individual stands before God, and each of us may break the pattern established in our families, whether for good or for evil. Therefore the individual child's reaction to his parent determines whether or not it will be well with him, just as it happened to Shem, Ham, and Japheth.

3. But consider this explanation: "It is a common social custom among many primitive people to attribute the greatness of a son to the father, who then receives the honor for having raised such a worthy child. . . . A man in blessing his own son was in fact blessing himself. This was true when Noah blessed Shem and Japheth. By the same token, however, if he had cursed Ham, the real offender, he would at the same time have been cursing himself. Quite logically, he could only pass judgment upon Ham by cursing Ham's own son, which is what he therefore did." Arthur C. Custance, *Noah's Three Sons* (Grand Rapids: Zondervan, 1975), 26.

4. Cush, Mizraim, and Put (Gen. 10:6) were neither blessed nor cursed by Noah. They and their descendants (including the Egyptians and the Philistines) are simply omitted from his prophecy.

5. See Genesis 25:23. C'mon now! Can you imagine *anyone* keeping secret for decades, even from her spouse, such a word from the Lord? I can't. Consider also that the prophecy favored Jacob. What motive, then, had Rebekah to keep it hidden? Isaac had reason, in his love for Esau, not to heed what Rebekah said, but she had no reason not to tell him.

6. Most commentators have said that Jacob sinned, some of them clearly underemphasizing the sin of Isaac and the temptations to which Jacob was subjected in the crisis of the moment. Some scholars have exonerated Jacob on the grounds that he was doing the will of God. See *The Dominion Covenant* by Dr. Gary North (Tyler, Tex.: Institute for Christian Economics, 1982), 184–97. Dr. North, a Christian economist, sees Jacob's economic success as proof that his deception was not sinful. As a Christian counselor, I lay more emphasis on Jacob's disastrous family life, and come to a different conclusion.

James Jordan, in *Primeval Saints* (58–60, 64, available from Biblical Horizons, P. O. Box 1096, Niceville, FL 32588), presents another defense of Jacob. His strongest point, I think, is that the Hebrew word describing Jacob as a "plain/ simple/ mild/ or complete" man in Genesis 25:27 is the same word used to describe Job as "perfect" or "blameless" in Job 1:1. Yet Bible translators do not call Jacob "perfect" or "blameless," and one must still account for Jacob's being deceived by Laban exactly as he himself deceived his father.

I like the summary provided by Keil and Delitzsch:

> Jacob remained blessed . . . but the deceit by which his mother prompted him to secure the blessing was never approved. On the contrary, the sin was followed by immediate punishment. Rebekah was obliged to send her pet son into a foreign land, away from his father's house, and in an utterly destitute condition. She did not see him for twenty years, even if she lived till his return, and possibly never saw [him] again. Jacob had to atone for his sin against both brother and father by a long and painful exile, in the midst of privation, anxiety, fraud, and want. Isaac was punished for retaining his preference for Esau, in opposition to the revealed will of Jehovah, by the success of Jacob's stratagem; and Esau for his contempt of the birthright, by the loss of the blessing of the first–born. In this way a higher hand prevailed above the acts of sinful men, bringing the counsel and will of Jehovah to eventual triumph, in opposition to human thought and will.

C. F. Keil and F. Delitzsch, *Commentary on the Old Testament, in Ten Volumes* (Grand Rapids: Eerdmans, 1973), 1:279–80 (on Gen. 27).

7. If our parents really are abusive we may be unable to avoid a fleshly fear of their wrath. But let us seek to retain, in those difficult cases, a holy fear of displeasing them through our sinful or negligent behavior.

8. Compare Elijah's reaction when he thought he was the Lord's only remaining servant in a land completely devoted to idol worship (1 Kings 19:4, 10, 14, 18).

9. "Question: Who are meant by father and mother in the fifth commandment?

Answer: By father and mother, in the fifth commandment, are meant, not only natural parents, but all superiors in age and gifts; and especially such as, by God's ordinance, are over us in place of authority, whether in family, church, or commonwealth."—*Westminster Larger Catechism,* Question 124 (A.D. 1648).

10. Some commentators are quite critical of Naomi's advice and Ruth's obedience to it. They think it was all wrong for Ruth to approach Boaz alone and at night. Others, making allowance for a unique provision of the Law (Deut. 25:5–10) and the customs of the time, are inclined to defend the women. But they quickly point out that we must not use Ruth's example as a precedent in such matters! Either way, since Ruth did not know the manners of the Jews, those charitably inclined may find reason to excuse her.

11. When Boaz invokes the blessing of the Lord as the due reward of Ruth's piety (2:12), he begins to illustrate a principle well known to experienced Christians. When you pray, remember that God may use *you* to bring about the answer to your own prayers.

12. See also endnote 3 of chapter 11 for more on young people's callings.

Chapter 6

1. See 1 Samuel 18:11; 19:10, 12, 18; 20:1, 42; 21:1, 10; 22:1, 5; 23:13–15, 26; 24:22; 27:1–2, 7.

2. David's subjects did try to overthrown him, but God had made it clear

beforehand that Absalom's rebellion would be the result of his sin with Bathsheba (2 Sam. 12:9–11).

3. David is not the only biblical character to model this inquiring and submissive approach to an abusive authority figure:

> And when the ass saw the angel of the Lord, she fell down under Balaam: and Balaam's anger was kindled, and he smote the ass with a staff.
>
> And the Lord opened the mouth of the ass, and she said unto Balaam, *What have I done unto thee, that thou hast smitten me these three times?*
>
> And Balaam said unto the ass, Because thou hast mocked me: I would there were a sword in mine hand, for now would I kill thee.
>
> And the ass said unto Balaam, *Am not I thine ass, upon which thou hast ridden, ever since I was thine unto this day? was I ever wont to do so unto thee?* And he said, Nay.
>
> Then the Lord opened the eyes of Balaam, and he saw the angel of the Lord standing in the way, and his sword drawn in his hand: and he bowed down his head, and fell flat on his face. (Num. 22:27–31, emphasis added)

When the Lord enables us to speak as graciously as Balaam's donkey, we may fully expect that He will open the eyes of those in authority over us. It's easy for God to get Balaam to see the things of the Spirit. Nobody talks about that. Getting the ass to speak well—*that's* the miracle of this story!

4. This incident with Abishai (1 Sam. 26:6–9) gives us cause for reflection. David asked two of his friends to go with him. One of them seemed to lack the necessary boldness; the other had too much of it. One would not take the inevitable risks involved in communicating with abusive authority; the other would, but only to communicate with his spear. If you can find a friend to help you with this risky business, one who believes that your parent can still be reasoned with, you have found a rare person. Don't take that friend for granted.

5. Even after Saul's death, David honored his wicked father-in-law: "Saul and Jonathan were lovely and pleasant in their lives, and in their death they were not divided; they were swifter than eagles, they were stronger than lions. Ye daughters of Israel, weep over Saul, who clothed you in scarlet, with other delights; who put ornaments of gold upon your apparel" (2 Sam. 1:23–24).

6. See 1 Samuel 14:44; 18:11; 19:1; 20:32–33.

7. See 1 Samuel 14:2, which tells us, "Saul tarried in the uttermost part of Gibeah under a pomegranate tree." While Jonathan took the offensive, Saul was *sitting* in a safe place.

8. See *Student Map Manual: Historical Geography of the Bible Lands* (Grand Rapids: Zondervan, 1979), section 1–13.

9. "Yesterday" to Josephus might mean nothing more than that the sun had set, for the Jewish day begins at sunset.

10. *Antiquities,* 6: vi, 5 [in *The Life and Works of Flavius Josephus,* translated by William Whiston (New York: Holt, Rinehart and Winston, n. d.), 182].

11. Matthew Henry, *Commentary* (McLean, Va.: MacDonald Publishing,

n. d.), 2:356 (on 1 Sam. 14:43).

12. Obadiah, the righteous servant of wicked Ahab, submitted to his master in all things, except murdering the prophets of the Lord (1 Kings 18:3–16).

13. Matthew Henry, *Commentary,* 2:389 (on 1 Sam. 20:2).

14. Adapted from John Milton, Sonnet 12 ("I did but prompt . . ."), lines 13–14.

15. Specific advice on communicating with parents may be found in chapters 14 and 15. The basics, however, are these:

> 1. Let your parent know how you really feel about things. If you cannot speak the truth in love, as you ought to do, it is usually better to tell the truth than to remain silent. At least your parent will have some idea what's going on inside you.

> 2. Take an interest in your parent. Try to find out what your parent is really like, and how he or she got to be that way. If your parent is deceased, you may be able to find out more than you think from surviving friends and relatives.

16. Dr. Gill thinks we should read 1 Samuel 20:34 thus: "for he was grieved for David, [and] because his father had treated him shamefully"— meaning, Jonathan was grieved because David's life was in danger, because he must be separated from his friend, and because Saul had treated him [Jonathan] shamefully (which he surely had). Dr. John Gill, *An Exposition of the Old Testament* (London: William Hill, 1854, and Grand Rapids: Baker Book House, 1980), 2:195 (on 1 Sam. 20:34).

17. William Gurnall (1617–1679), *The Christian in Complete Armour* (Edinburgh: Banner of Truth, [1864] 1979), 1:12.

18. I am not speaking of natural courage. When Jonathan went into battle, his trust was in the Lord (1 Sam. 14:6). The Spirit that strengthened Peter, who had cowered before a servant girl (Matt. 26:69–70), can surely strengthen us. Remember that "the cowardly" lead the list of sinners who are headed for destruction (Rev. 21:8).

19. If you are unwilling to make the same concession, Jonathan's (supposed) falsehood would fall, I think, in the category of lifesaving lies, such as Rahab's (Josh. 2:3–6), Hushai's (2 Sam. 16:16–19) or the Hebrew midwives' (Ex. 1:17–19). Good Christian commentators have long been divided about whether such statements are truly sinful. I think they are not.

Some commentators are sure that David did *not* go to Bethlehem, meaning that Jonathan lied to his father. Among them are Keil and Delitzsch: "We see from these words that David did not look upon prevarication as a sin" (C. F. Keil and F. Delitzsch, *Biblical Commentary on the Books of Samuel* [Edinburgh: T. and T. Clark, 1866], 208, [on 1 Sam. 20:6]). The authors of Lange's commentary concur: "As David, according to v. 5, is to hide in the *field till* the evening of the third day, his excuse for absence can be regarded only as a pretext, or a 'lie of necessity'" (John Peter Lange, *Commentary on the Holy Scriptures* [New York: Charles Scribner's Sons, 1877], 5:261 [on 1 Sam. 20:6]).

20. The only greater example of grace under pressure, I think, is Job's miraculous reply to his wife: "You speak as one of the foolish ones speak" (Job 2:10, MKJV).

Chapter 7

1. Matthew Henry, *Commentary,* (McLean, Va.: MacDonald Publishing, n. d.), 5:1003, (emphasis added).

2. Please don't go looking for this particular kind of trouble. If your ways are pleasing to the Lord, He will bring it to you soon enough. All I'm saying is that, when this form of persecution comes to you in the way of duty, it is "the honor that cometh from God only" (John 5:44; compare Acts 5:41).

3. Because our parents are people, not gods, this kind of thinking can be carried too far. We must not idolize our parents, but we should speak of them in the same reverential tone that Christ expressed toward His Father. In our culture which do you think is the greater problem—idolizing authority or failing to honor it? If you're in doubt, look at a few political cartoons depicting our president.

4. Matthew Henry, Commentary, 2:28 (on Josh. 5:13–15).

5. "And the Jews marveled, saying, How does this Man know letters, not being taught?" (John 7:15, MKJV). Would they have asked this question, if His father were an educated man?

6. Needless to say, I see the same virtue in Mary: "Then Mary said, Behold the servant of the Lord! Let it be to me according to your word" (Luke 1:38, MKJV).

7. Dr. John Gill, *An Exposition of the New Testament* (London: William Hill, 1854, and Grand Rapids: Baker Book House, 1980), 1:432 (on Luke 2:43).

8. Dr. Gill comments, "[Mary] began to chide, or rather to expostulate with him after this manner: *Son, why hast thou thus dealt with us?* which was said with great tenderness of affection, and in much mildness; and may be a pattern to parents, who should not provoke their children to anger, but deal gently and tenderly with them." Gill, *New Testament*, 1:433 (on Luke 2:48).

9. A Roman Catholic commentator is quick to explain: "These words do not imply any reproof on the part of Mary. They simply express the sorrow and anxiety which filled the mother's and Joseph's hearts. Neither do these words of our Lord contain a rebuke to His mother. Our Lord was simply calling her attention to the fact that the Father's business, which He had come on earth to perform, was His most important duty." Rev. Charles J. Callan, O. P., *The Four Gospels* (New York: Joseph F. Wagner, 1918), 288–89.

On the other hand, John Calvin comments: "The holy virgin would a thousand times rather have died, than deliberately preferred herself to God: but, in the indulgence of a mother's grief, she falls into it through inadvertency. . . .

"Our Lord justly blames his mother, though he does it in a gentle and indirect manner. The amount of what he says is, that the duty which he owes to God his Father, ought to be immeasurably preferred to all human duties; and that, consequently, earthly parents do wrong in taking it amiss, that they have been neglected in comparison of God." Calvin's *Commentary* (Grand Rapids: Baker, 1979), vol. 16 (part 1), 170–71.

Arthur Pink, a learned Protestant, says: "The answer that Jesus returned to her inquiry, when rightly understood, also reveals the honor in which He held His mother. We quite agree with Dr. Campbell Morgan that Christ does not here *rebuke* her. It is largely a matter of finding the right emphasis—'Wist *ye* not?' As the aforementioned expositor well says, 'It was as though He had said: "Mother, surely *you* knew me well enough to know that nothing could detain Me but the affairs of the Father."'" Arthur W. Pink, *The Seven Sayings of the Saviour on the Cross* (Swengel, Pa.: I. C. Herendeen, 1951), 53.

I cannot withhold this additional nugget from Calvin: "Mary *kept in her heart* those things which she did not fully understand. Let us learn from this, to receive with reverence, and *to lay up* in our minds, (like the seed, which is allowed to remain for some time underground,) those mysteries of God which exceed our capacity."

10. Matthew Henry, *Commentary*, 5:609 (on Luke 2:51).

11. Jesus spoke to His mother on the cross, but she did not reply (John 19:26). Once His ministry begins, we hear nothing from Mary. It is interesting to note that John never refers to Christ's mother as Mary, but always as "the mother of Jesus" or "His mother."

12. Reverend Charles J. Callan, O. P., attributes this quotation to Justin Martyr, a saint of the second century, but gives no reference for it. (Charles Callan, *The Four Gospels* [New York: Joseph F. Wagner, 1918], 421.) My cursory search of Justin Martyr's genuine works failed to turn up this quote or anything like it. Possibly it occurs in one of his disputed or spurious works.

13. If she learned the lesson Christ taught her in the temple (Luke 2:49), and I trust she did, she'd have restrained her maternal concern for her Son.

14. See Mark 2:13; 3:7; 5:21.

15. See Mark 4:1; 6:2; 6:34; 8:31.

16. Those who think we should approach Christ through prayer to His mother rarely mention the sequel to this passage. See 1 Kings 2:19–24. Would Adonijah have done worse to have asked the king himself?

17. See John 19:28, 30. Compare Matthew 27:46 with Psalm 22:1. Compare Luke 23:34 with Isaiah 53:12.

18. Jesus did not have a wife and kids to worry about, but He did have a fiancée—the church. While no doubt John was a help to Mary in her later years, we should not underestimate what a blessing the church received through John's daily life with the Messiah's mother. Of all the disciples, John knew Jesus best; but no one knew Him as Mary did. Her living with the apostle was a mutually beneficial relationship, of benefit to every soul who ever read John's writings.

Chapter 8

1. "Pharisees," in *The New Westminster Dictionary of the Bible*, ed. Henry Snyder Gehman (Philadelphia: Westminster, 1976), 742.

2. Rev. James B. Jordan, in his *The Law of the Covenant* (Tyler, Texas: Institute for Christian Economics, 1984), 105–9, takes an extended look at Christ's treatment of Exodus 21:17 ("He that curseth his father, or his mother, shall surely be put to death."). Some of Rev. Jordan's conclusions are as follows: "Jesus applies the death penalty for dishonoring parents directly to those who refuse to care for them in their old age. . . . Notice that [in Mark 7:9–13] Jesus sets Exodus 21:17 right next to the fifth commandment in binding force. . . . This passage shows us that *in the practical legal sense, refusing to care for parents in their old age is a capital offense. . . .*

"A few comments may be helpful. When a son marries, he sets up a new household, according to Genesis 2:24. If parents come to live with their married children, they must adjust to the rules of their son's or son-in-law's house. Honoring parents does not mean permitting them to destroy one's home. . . ." (See endnote 15, chap. 12, for further quotation from this portion of Rev. Jordan's book.)

3. Paul expressed this principle so forcefully that I shall say nothing more

about it: "But if any provide not for his own, and specially for those of his own house, he hath denied the faith, and is worse than an infidel" (1 Tim. 5:8).

4. Alexander Jones, *The Gospel According to Matthew* (New York: Sheed & Ward, 1965), 219 (emphasis added). Dr. Gill, that great source of obscure information about the Hebrew Scripture, offers little on this point: "[This] inversion of order is of no consequence: so the *seventh* commandment is put before the *sixth*, and the *fifth* omitted, in Romans 13:9, and with the Jews it is a common saying, *there's neither first nor last in the law*; that is, it is of no consequence which commandment is recited first, or which last." Dr. John Gill, *Gill's Commentary* (Grand Rapids: Baker, 1980), 5:176 (on Matt. 19:19).

5. "The word *hate*, here, means simply to *love less*. See the meaning of the verse in Matt. 10:37. It may be thus expressed: 'He that comes after me, and does not love his father *less* than he loves me, etc., cannot be my disciple.' We are not at liberty literally to *hate* our parents. This would be expressly contrary to the fifth commandment." Albert Barnes, *Barnes' Notes on the New Testament* (Grand Rapids: Kregel, 1986), 227 (on Luke 14:26).

6. Alfred Edersheim, *The Life and Times of Jesus the Messiah*, 2d ed. (New York: Anson D. F. Randolph & Co., 1884), 2, 133.

7. John Trapp, *A Commentary on the New Testament* (Grand Rapids: Baker [1656] 1981), 321 (on Luke 9:62). I'd love to ask that old tantalizer just what he meant by this comment, but as he nearly always tells me much more or much less than I want to know on a given passage, so it is here.

8. Following Christ meant full time discipleship and training for ministry. There were many true believers in Christ's day who did not follow Him in this sense; they were not called as the seventy disciples were.

9. I speak of the saints in general. Let us consider, however, that "External gifts of grace, or such gifts of the Spirit, which qualify men for ministerial work, for public service in the church . . . these may be taken away, as the *parable* of the *talents* shows." Gill, *Commentary*, 6:104 (on Rom. 11:29).

10. I cannot prove that the would-be disciple was not called. It is possible to argue from the context that Jesus had also said to him, "Follow me." If so, he was still guilty of presumption. Hadn't he just heard Christ tell the other disciple not to return home, not even to bury his father, and possibly to comfort his grieving relatives? Was it reasonable then to expect permission for an extended good-bye?

Chapter 9

1. Though there is much to be gleaned from the other apostles' writings (e.g., when Peter exhorts the believers "as obedient children" [1 Pet. 1:14]), I do not find in their epistles new teaching on the first commandment with promise.

2. Dr. John Gill, *Gill's Commentary* (Grand Rapids: Baker, 1980), 6:455 (on Eph. 6:1). I consider the rest of Dr. Gill's comment on this verse too precious to omit:

> The persons whose duty this is, *children*, are such of every sex, male and female, and of every age, and of every state and condition; and though the true legitimate, and immediate offspring of men may be

chiefly respected, yet not exclusive of spurious children, and adopted ones, and of children–in–law; and the persons to whom obedience from them is due, are not only real and immediate parents, both father and mother, but such who are in the room of parents, as step–fathers, step–mothers, guardians, nurses, etc., and all who are in the ascending line, as grandfathers, grandmothers, etc.; to these, children should be subject and obedient in all things lawful, just, and good; in every thing that is not sinful and unlawful, by the word of God: and in things indifferent, as much as in them lies, and even in things which are difficult to perform: and this obedience should be hearty and sincere, and not merely verbal, and in show and appearance, nor mercenary; and should be joined with gratitude and thankfulness for past favours . . . *for this is right;* it appears to be right by the light of nature, by which the very heathens have taught it; and it is equitable from reason that so it should be; and it is just by the law of God, which commands nothing but what is holy, just, and good. (Ibid., 454–55)

3. See the parallel passage, 1 Thessalonians 2:11: "You know how we exhorted, and comforted, and [implored] every one of you, as a father does his own children."

4. I suppose some readers will dislike my applying to children a passage addressed to slaves. But Peter's words sum up the attitude of Jonathan and David toward Saul, who while he was to them father and father-in-law, was also employer and king. Jesus accepted the centurion's analogy drawn from one kind of authority to another (Matt. 8:8–10). Is my comparison more far-fetched than his? And consider Paul's teaching: "Now I say, that the heir, as long as he is a child, differeth nothing from a servant, though he be lord of all" (Gal. 4:1).

5. Exodus 21:26–27 recompences the slave with freedom when seriously abused by his master. Should a child be required to endure abuse which would free a slave forever?

6. William F. Arndt and F. Wilbur Gingrich, *A Greek-English Lexicon of the New Testament* 2d ed. (Chicago: University of Chicago, 1979), 269.

7. Ibid., 617.

8. Gill, 6, 611 (on 1 Tim. 5:1). Dr. Gill later limits his statements with, "This must be understood of lesser crimes, and not of atrocious and flagitious ones, obstinately continued in." Ibid.

9. Sir Thomas Browne, *Religio Medici* (A.D. 1643), part 2, section 5. (Everyman edition, 72, 74.)

10. See Luke 15:11–32. Bear in mind that the prodigal son is a parable about sin and salvation, about the Gentiles and the Jews. It is only indirect teaching on the first commandment with promise.

11. Jean Daillé (1594–1670), *An Exposition of Philippians* (Florida: Tyndale Bible Society, n. d.), 154 (from Sermon XV, on Phil. 2:19–24).

12. See 2 Corinthians 6:3–13; 7:2, 12; 10:7—13:10. See also Galatians 1:6—3:4; 4:8–20; 6:17.

13. Paul was not the only apostle to encounter such ingratitude. See 3 John 4, 9–12. "I wrote unto the church: but Diotrephes, who loveth to have the preeminence among them, receiveth us not" (v. 9).

14. John Calvin, *Calvin's Commentaries* (Grand Rapids: Baker, 1979),

20:ii, 255 (on 2 Cor. 6:11–12).

15. Dr. John Gill, *Gill's Commentary* (Grand Rapids: Baker, 1980), 6:314.

16. Albert Barnes, *Notes on the New Testament* (Grand Rapids: Kregel, 1962 [19th century]), 864.

17. Charles J. Callan, O. P., *The Epistles of St. Paul* (New York: Joseph F. Wagner, 1922), 1:509.

Chapter 10

1. See Matthew 7:9–11. ("If you then, being evil, know how to give good gifts to your children") I am not attempting to subvert the doctrine of complete depravity, which is an article of faith for some Christians. If I were addressing ardent Calvinists only, I would say rather that parental love is a prime ingredient of God's "common grace" to fallen man.

John Calvin himself, commenting on this passage, remarks, "Our Lord contrasts the malice of men with the boundless goodness of God. Self-love renders us malicious: for every man is too much devoted to himself, and neglects and disregards others. But this vice yields to the stronger feelings of a father's love, so that men forget themselves, and give to their children with overflowing liberality. Whence comes this, but because God, *of whom the whole family in heaven and earth is named* (Eph. 3:15), drops into their hearts a portion of his goodness?" *Calvin's Commentaries* (Grand Rapids: Baker, 1979), 16:i, 353.

2. Some people have no such memory of their parent's love in childhood. The broken relationship is all they can remember. For them the path of healing is the same—recognizing and repenting of their sinful attitudes and actions. It is good to go back to the origin of the broken relationship, when its origin can be established. But where it cannot be determined, the blessing of God to those who repent is in no way diminished.

I am firmly convinced, from my counseling experience, that God will bring into our minds all that we need to be healed. Lack of memory is rarely the problem. When it is, through prayer, reflection, and speaking with older relatives, we can recover enough information and/or memories to honor our parents and repent of our sins.

3. I have heard this attributed to Erasmus, but I am unsure of its origin.

4. Quiz Evaluation: Each "A" answer indicates an area of deficiency in honoring your parent. The "B" and "C" answers are all acceptable; a mix of the two is probably healthiest. A string of "B" answers might indicate a tendency toward idolizing your parent. A string of "C" answers could reveal a lack of emotional involvement with your parent.

Chapter 11

1. Walter Bagehot (nineteenth-century economist and essayist), "Shakespeare—The Man," in *The Works of Walter Bagehot* (Hartford: Travelers Insurance Co., 1891), 1:265.

2. A relative, an old family friend, or a school your parent attended may be able to provide a current address. If not, try a combination of prayer, patience, and systematic searching. It can yield surprising results.

3. Every believer has a general calling as a Christian and one or more specific callings to a particular kind of work (or situation in life, or disability, etc.). As Christians we are called to grow in the Lord, to develop into spiritually mature adults. This requires a more-or-less gradual process of learning to take our orders directly from our Maker instead of indirectly from our parents. There is no simple formula for determining how this transition should be managed in individual cases.

To unmarried young adults I recommend paying close attention to the wishes and the advice of one's father and mother. Turning eighteen or twenty-one (or any other age) does not automatically release us from obedience to parents. Neither does moving out of the home necessarily establish our independence. On the other hand, spiritual maturity requires a capacity for independence. We cannot follow an all-knowing God if we are always doing the will of fallible parents. Even if you have no clear specific calling from the Lord, your general calling as a Christian may require you to disobey your parents. My only advice is to do so sparingly, to fight only the most necessary battles.

4. See Ephesians 5:22–24; Colossians 3:18; 1 Peter 3:1.

5. See Romans 13:1; 1 Corinthians 11:3; John 13:13–17; Hebrews 13:17.

6. If other answers to this question should arise in your heart, all I ask is that you think the best of your parent. Do you have real evidence, such as a personal confession from your parent, that *proves* his or her motivation in restricting you was not benevolent? Until you have certain knowledge, you should hold your parent guiltless. By the way, a parent whose motivation *was* sinful may readily express remorse for that sin, if only the child approaches him or her in a spirit of love and forgiveness.

7. At such times, church leaders might have helped us resolve disagreements with our parents. When parents sense that we intend to obey them, they are often willing to consult a pastor or Christian counselor.

8. I could write a chapter full of comments about the biblical love stories and their relevance to our theme. Instead, I shall comment briefly on Isaac, Leah, Moses, Samson, and Michal.

Isaac was not present when his father's servant recognized Rebekah as the bride God had chosen for him (Gen. 24). But it is reasonable to assume that he fully consented to his father's plan. Had he not trusted his father, even when he bound him on the altar to slay him? Isaac's trust in Abraham is the chief Old Testament foreshadowing of Christ's trusting His Father, even at the cross. As I see it, father and son both consented to the choice of Rebekah, and the issue was a happy one. "[He] took Rebekah and she became his wife; and he loved her" (Gen. 24:67). A marriage that culminates in love is better than a love that ends in marriage.

Leah consented to her father's deception of Jacob: A word from her would have ended the whole charade. However unjust their deception was (and however much Jacob may have deserved it), father and daughter were united in desiring her union with Jacob. In the end, I believe, it proved a good marriage. Though Jacob hated her at the start, I believe he grew to love her, to see the hand of God behind the trickery of Laban. There is a great deal implied in his simple statement, "There they buried Abraham and Sarah his wife; there they buried Isaac and Rebekah his wife; and there I buried Leah" (Gen. 49:31). Had he hated her still, would he have given her this place of honor in the tomb of the patriarchs, where he himself was soon to be buried?

"And Moses was content to dwell with the man: and he gave Moses Zipporah his daughter" (Ex. 2:21). Clearly Moses was willing to receive Zipporah as his wife. Since she had six sisters who might have taken her place, and since in the desert of Midian Moses was nothing short of the prince in a fairytale, I cannot imagine that she was unwilling to have him.

Some good commentators see Samson's desire for his Philistine wife (Judg. 14) as a worthy symbol of Christ's love for the Gentiles. In any event, it's clear that God had a hand in the whole business (14:4). Though Samson's parents objected to the match at first, evidently they became reconciled to it before the wedding took place. As the story shows, however, events proved the wisdom of their original reservations.

Michal and Saul both consented to her marriage with David (1 Sam. 18:20–21), but while the bride's motivation was genuine, her father's was sinful. The marriage ended unhappily, perhaps in part because Saul's blessing was feigned. (See 1 Sam. 25:44; 2 Sam. 3:13–16; 6:20–23.)

Thus, we should amend our definition of the biblical model to read: *parents and children must both consent to the marriage* and *be motivated by godly principles.* The child should not be marrying to impress others, to escape his or her parents, or to avoid some other difficulty of family life. The parents must guard against pressuring the child to marry into money or prestige, or into marrying without the hope of love. If you think such things happen only in novels, you have little exposure to the secret life of families.

9. Denying parents their rightful role in choosing spouses for their children is hardly the sole cause of the ills of our culture. But among those causes, it is far from the least.

10. Herschel Rosenbaum and Ida Goldwasser, my grandparents, were married near the end of the nineteenth century, in a Jewish community in Poland (which at that time was ruled by the Czar of Russia).

11. Keith Green, a gifted evangelist, used to say, "If you're not called to stay, you're called to go [to the mission field]." Am I wrong in thinking that we are called to serve needy parents until God directs otherwise?

Chapter 12

1. It is interesting to observe that Luther and More both treated the Pope as they did their own fathers. Luther refused to accept the Pope's authority, while More became one of the chief defenders of papal doctrines. [I recognize that some devout Catholics think that Luther's father was right—that Luther *should* have become a lawyer.]

2. I do not deny that a young person may have a valid calling from God, but as David and Jesus remained subject to their parents in their youth, so should we. See endnote 3, chapter 11.

3. Rahab lied to wicked soldiers to save her family from destruction (Josh. 2:4–6, 11–13), and I would do the same. But with the exception of saving innocent lives, I cannot see how Christians can justify deceit.

4. I do not assume that smoking is automatically a sin, and I beg the pardon of those who are sure that it is one. But in many cases, due to one's health, one's finances, or one's example to others, I would consider it sinful behavior.

5. One answer would be that the man's leaving father and mother sym-

bolizes Christ's leaving His heavenly family to unite with His bride (Eph. 5:30–32).

6. If a husband is defending his marriage from hostile in–laws, he may be right to tell his wife not to see her parents. But is this likely to occur when the young couple have sought and obtained parental blessings before entering into marriage?

7. I do not deny that some older people *seem* to live for nothing but tormenting their children. However, an open and loving approach will work wonders with many of them. As we seek to know our parents, to understand their misery (especially our own contributions to their misery!), and the hidden desires of their heart for something better than we see, then we may be able to help ourselves and them. But where we see only a selfish, uncaring person, one with no possibility of improvement, we can only hinder our families; we can only make things worse.

If a parent is really beyond reach—and Saul's example shows us that very few parents are beyond hope of at least temporary improvement—we can still help the situation by dealing lovingly with that parent. If we must be firm, we can be firm in love. "If you can keep your head when all about you/ Are losing theirs, and blaming it on you" (Kipling), you can be a big help to your family in dealing with miserable parents.

8. This is a perfectly legitimate question, when asked in a loving spirit. Is your intent to test the depth of their teaching or to reproach your parents with past failures?

9. I am assuming that the parents are not hindered by a broken relationship with or an unfairly distrustful attitude toward the grandparent.

10. From the examples in Scripture, I gather that a child should be under parental authority until he or she marries or discovers a calling from God. Either way, assuming God approves of our marriage, it is He who delivers us from parental authority. ("It is he that hath made us, and not we ourselves" Ps. 100:3). Woe to the man or woman who refuses to wait on the Lord! (See endnote 3, chapter 11 for more on the call of God and how it limits our obedience to parents.)

11. The model here is the same as for marriage: It is best if neither party acts unilaterally. The child should not be forced to use his money in a particular way, and he should refrain from disposing of it without parental consent. As the child matures or exhibits a gift for giving or investing, a wise parent will allow the child to make more decisions on his own. But where the parent stubbornly refuses to do so, I believe God will bless the child who chooses to obey his parent (even when it means losing some money).

12. If you refuse to support your mother because she lost the job you got her with a piano mover, your interpretation of this Scripture may need some adjustment.

13. The apostle John, I trust, thought differently when he took our Lord's mother into his home.

14. While scholars may debate just how the Greek for *at home* (literally, *house*) should be interpreted, one Greek lexicon defines the usage in this passage as "the inmates of a house, all the persons forming one family, a household." Joseph Thayer, *The New Thayer's Greek-English Lexicon of the New Testament* (Lafayette, Ind.: Associated Publishers & Authors, [1889] 1979), 441.

15. "When a son marries, he sets up a new household, according to Genesis 2:24. If parents come to live with their married children, they must adjust

to the rules of their son's or son–in–law's house. Honoring parents does not mean permitting them to destroy one's home. If grandparents undermine the discipline of the children, or if the mother–in–law constantly badgers and harasses her daughter–in–law, something will have to give. Parents do not have an absolute claim to honor. . . . [Yet] this is not to say that we should not put up with senility in aged parents." Rev. James B. Jordan, *The Law of the Covenant* (Tyler, Tex.: Institute for Christian Economics, 1984), 107–8.

16. See previous note.

17. See Deuteronomy 17:2–5 (compare 13:6–11).

18. Compare Matthew 22:36–38 and Ephesians 6:1–3.

19. Some commentators condemn Naaman the Syrian for saying to Elisha, "for thy servant will henceforth offer neither burnt offering nor sacrifice unto other gods, but unto the Lord. In this thing the Lord pardon thy servant, that when my master goeth into the house of Rimmon to worship there, and he leaneth on my hand, and I bow myself in the house of Rimmon: when I bow down myself in the house of Rimmon, the Lord pardon thy servant in this thing" (2 Kings 5:17–18). Because Elisha replied to him only, "Go in peace," I take a more lenient view of Naaman's request. Your conscience and Scripture (see 1 Cor. 10:20–33) must guide you in deciding what religious customs you cannot participate in, even for the sake of your parents.

20. On the grounds that neglecting the Lord's worship is a form of having other gods before Him.

21. This brings up the question, What is a Christian church? If other recognized Christian churches accept your parents' church as Christian, rather than cultic, as capable of leading some of its members to salvation, rather than all of them to perdition, that should be enough for you. If the vast majority of Christians utterly repudiate your parents' church, my remarks in this section would not apply to it.

22. I can't see how I would have ever written this book, if I had not followed the Lord's call to California.

23. See 1 Samuel 17:32–37. I am being charitable to Eliab, for even Saul's servant knew that David was "a mighty valiant man, and a man of war" (1 Sam. 16:18).

24. See Jeremiah 28:1, 15–17. Compare also Jeremiah 1:1–3, 25:1–3, and the related chronologies in the last chapters of 2 Kings and 2 Chronicles.

Chapter 13

1. The most famous of the *Sonnets from the Portuguese* begins, "How do I love thee? Let me count the ways" (Sonnet 43).

2. Rudolf Besier, *The Barretts of Wimpole Street: A Comedy in Five Acts* (Boston: Little, Brown, 1930), 13. Of Besier's depiction of Mr. Barrett, a competent scholar has well said, "Biographically it was libelous nonsense" (Elvan Kintner, ed., *The Letters of Robert Browning and Elizabeth Barrett Barrett, 1845–1846* [Cambridge, Mass.: Belknap Press, 1969], xxxviii.)

3. This is how the Brownings' correspondence began:

> "I love your verses with all my heart, dear Miss Barrett,—and this is no off-hand complimentary letter that I shall write,—whatever else, no prompt matter-of-course recognition of your genius, and there a

graceful and natural end of the thing: since the day last week when I
first read your poems, I quite laugh to remember how I have been
turning and turning again in my mind what I should be able to tell
you of their effect upon me—for in the first flush of delight I thought
I would this once get out of my habit of purely passive enjoyment,
when I do really enjoy, and thoroughly justify my admiration—perhaps even, as a loyal fellow–craftsman should, try and find fault and
do you some little good to be proud of hereafter!—but nothing
comes of it all—so into me has it gone, and part of me has it become,
this great living poetry of yours, not a flower of which but took root
and grew. . . . I do, as I say, love these books with all my heart—and
I love you too."

Elvan Kintner, ed., *The Letters of Robert Browning and Elizabeth Barrett
Barrett, 1845–1846* (Cambridge, Mass.: Belknap Press, 1969), 3.

4. When the Brownings first rented an apartment in Pisa, "Dinner was at
two, and since neither they nor Wilson [the maid from Wimpole Street] had
the remotest idea of how to cook, they had their meal sent in from a trattoria."
Margaret Forster, *Elizabeth Barrett Browning: The Life and Loves of a Poet*
(New York: St. Martin's Press, 1988), 196.

5. *The Encyclopedia Americana* (Danbury, Conn.: Grolier, Inc., 1991),
4:637.

6. *The World Book Encyclopedia* (Chicago: World Book, Inc., 1989), 2:656.

7. Gardner B. Taplin, *The Life of Elizabeth Barrett Browning* (New Haven:
Yale University Press, 1957), 350.

8. "Edward Moulton Barrett's determination to have his own way, to dom-
inate his family, has become legend, a legend unfairly distorted: that he was
essentially a fine character there is no doubt. He was upright, scrupulous, and
kind. His children loved and respected him. As a man and as a father he must
not be judged by the standards of today. . . . So far as can be gathered from
incomplete evidence, Edward Barrett was a man to be pitied rather than
wholly blamed. . . . His sons' letters from school to their "Puppy" are not con-
strained: to them their father was far from being an ogre. Through years of
arbitrary treatment they loved and respected him. The few letters too I have
seen from him to his children are friendly, affectionate—even playful. When
conveying his wishes he is firm but not dictatorial, often leaving it to them to
make their own decisions. There is no doubt that his anger was sometimes
capricious and to be feared, but there is no hint of the physical punishment
usual in those days." [Dorothy Hewlett, *Elizabeth Barrett Browning: A Life*
(New York: Alfred A. Knopf, 1952), 4–5, 8].

"The death of Elizabeth's mother put Edward Moulton Barrett in supreme
and direct charge of his family. Posterity was to depict him as the tyrant of the
sick-room and the bane of his children's lives. While there was ample justification for this view, it was less than the whole truth" [Donald Thomas, *Robert
Browning: A Life within Life* (New York: Viking, 1982), 105].

9. Margaret Forster, *Elizabeth Barrett Browning: The Life and Loves of a
Poet* (New York: St. Martin's Press, 1988), xv.

10. Shakespeare, *Merchant of Venice*, 2:86–88.

11. When he died, Mr. Barrett's other son-in-law besides Browning "was
amazed to see all the Barrett sons openly weeping at the graveside. Far from
there being any grim satisfaction that a tyrant was dead and they were free, it

was evident how much they had loved him" (Forster, 321).

12. Note Forster's comment on Mr. Barrett in his youth: "With Edward, pride was all" (Forster, 7).

13. Ibid., 43.

14. Ibid., 65.

15. Jeannette Marks, *The Family of the Barrett* (New York: Macmillan, 1938), 311.

16. Ibid., 602.

17. EBB, letter to Browning, August 20, 1845. Elvan Kintner, ed., *The Letters of Robert Browning and Elizabeth Barrett Barrett, 1845–1846* (Cambridge, Mass.: Belknap Press, 1969), 170.

18. Ibid., 169.

19. Forster, 162.

20. Ibid., 98–99.

21. Ibid., 157.

22. All quotations from *The Letters of Robert Browning and Elizabeth Barrett Browning, 1845–1846,* edited by Elvan Kintner, (Cambridge, Mass.: Belknap Press, 1969). [Three dots indicates an omission from the text; two dots are Miss Barrett's way of indicating transition. I have underlined the last sentence for emphasis; the italics are hers.])

23. EBB to Mrs. Martin, October, 1846, in *The Letters of Elizabeth Barrett Browning,* edited by F. G. Kenyon (New York: Macmillan, 1899), 290–91.

24. Forster, 158–59.

25. Daniel Karlin, *The Courtship of Robert Browning and Elizabeth Barrett* (Oxford: Clarendon Press, 1985), 16–17. ("No . . . economic obstacles" because Elizabeth had enough inherited income to support the couple in modest circumstances.)

26. "[The Barrett brothers' hostility] seems to have arisen more from their embarrassment at the clandestine form of the marriage than from solidarity with their father's [presumed] opposition to it taking place at all. The blare of gossip cannot have been pleasant, especially when it accompanied an aria of paternal fury; Browning and Elizabeth Barrett, insulated by distance and intimacy at Pisa, had left them to face the music" (Karlin, 17–18).

27. Jeannette Marks, *The Family of the Barrett* (New York: Macmillan, 1938), 531–32.

28. "My desire is that you . . . may accept from me the inscription of these volumes, the exponents of a few years of an existence which has been sustained and comforted by you as well as given. Somewhat more faint-hearted than I used to be, it is my fancy thus to seem to return to a visible personal dependence on you, as if indeed I were a child again" (Charlotte Porter and Helen A. Clarke, eds., *The Complete Works of Elizabeth Barrett Browning* [New York: Thomas Y. Crowell & Co., 1900]) 2:142. The quotation is taken from Elizabeth's "Dedication: TO MY FATHER" in her *Poems* of 1844. This dedication was written only two years before her marriage to Browning, and only one year before she began deceiving her father about her relationship with the poet.

29. EBB to RB, July 16, 1846. Elvan Kintner, ed., *The Letters of Robert Browning and Elizabeth Barrett Barrett, 1845–1846* (Cambridge, Mass.: Belknap Press, 1969), 881.

30. Forster, 209–10.

31. Her sister Henrietta did act in the light. When her suitor's request was

rejected, she married him publicly in London. Her brothers, wishing not to antagonize Mr. Barrett, did not attend the ceremony, but they made it clear that they thought the couple had acted honorably (Forster, 241).

Mr. Barrett, after Elizabeth's deception, was hardly the same man he was before. Thus, we cannot be certain how he would have reacted if Elizabeth had taken the path that Henrietta took later.

32. "'The griefs that are incurable,' wrote Elizabeth Barrett Browning [the year her father died], 'are those which have our own sins festering in them.'" Betty Miller, "Elizabeth Barrett and her Brother," *The Cornhill Magazine* (Spring 1952): 228.

33. EBB to her sister Henrietta, May 15, 1857. Quoted in "Mrs. Browning and Her Father's Forgiveness," by Leonard Huxley, *The Cornhill Magazine*, LXXIV, new series, (March, 1933) 335. (I believe this is the only place where the full text of this letter has yet been published.)

34. Dr. Peter Dally, *Elizabeth Barrett Browning: A Psychological Potrait* (London: MacMillan, 1989), 4, 9, 11.

35. His father forsook his wife and young children, took money that belonged to his sons, and fathered children by several other women.

36. Some good points Mr. Barrett might have found in his father are listed by the chief biographer of the Barrett clan: "Charles Moulton's good nature . . . was apparently endless, and there is no suggestion that he resented anything. Nor to be questioned either was his generosity to those for whom he had any responsibility (and they were apparently many), or his quaint and affectionate dependence on his Barrett sons Edward and Samuel, [who had taken the name Moulton-Barrett when they inherited their maternal grandfather's fortune.] Charles Moulton did what many whose lives have been more favorably reflected from the mirrored surface of their family group do not do: he provided for those he had made happily or unhappily dependent on him." Jeannette Marks, *The Family of the Barrett* (New York: Macmillan, 1938), 312.

37. Ibid., 602.

Chapter 14

1. For most of us, this kind of repentance is an acquired taste, a delight we must learn to enjoy. But once the taste is acquired, it is a joy forever.

2. C. F. Keil and F. Delitzsch, *Commentary on the Old Testament, in Ten Volumes* (Grand Rapids: Eerdmans, 1973), 2:388 (on 2 Sam. 12).

3. In some families with both parents present, the mother is more the authority figure than the father. In broken homes, on the other hand, a child's dishonoring attitude toward his absent father, rather than his actual conflicts with his mother, may be the true root of continual clashes with authority figures.

4. Of course some people who come for counseling are unable to accept my conclusions about what is really the source of their problems. Of these, some come round to my point of view at a later date, but others never do.

5. Other things being equal, of course, you are better off with a pastor, elder, or therapist who is experienced in family counseling.

6. I recognize that this may not be the whole story. I understood my father better, and was closer to him, than I was to my mother. If I am a better guide to others in the areas I have traveled most myself, that would hardly be

surprising. Yet I am not conscious of any difficulty in helping people to honor their mothers.

7. When I read to my friend what I had written about him, he commented, "It's okay, except that it makes me sound like I've got it all together." He knows, as I do, that we all have plenty to work on while God keeps us in this world.

Chapter 15

1. You can still make a good use of this chapter by thinking of what you would say to your parent if he or she were still living or could be located at last. Such thinking can help you to solidify your repentance and the blessings that come with it.

2. The prodigal son did not get specific about his sins: "Father, I have sinned against heaven, and in thy sight, and am no more worthy to be called thy son" (Luke 15:21). We need to remember that this parable is not primarily a teaching about honoring earthly parents. Yet if your repentance is as hearty as the son's, and your parent is compassionate as his father, you may safely ignore my advice on "making it right" with your parents.

Chapter 16

1. Men who believe that their mothers don't love them can hardly be certain that their wives will. Women who feel unsure of their father's love will not easily rest secure in the love of their husbands.

In those very rare cases where even I might agree that a living parent is beyond the reach of a child's love, God will supply the grace required for a good marriage. I say this as a concession. I have not personally witnessed a single parent who was clearly beyond the reach of a child's best effort to love and honor him or her. I have, of course, witnessed situations where the child retained some anger or bitterness toward the parent, and the results of biblical counseling were disappointing to all involved.

The Lord will not supply His grace to a presumptuous child who wrongly imagines that his parent is totally selfish or incapable of love.